Dancing
in the
Bamboo Forest

a
travel
memoir

Djahariah Mitra

FOREWORD BY SWAMI RAMANANDA

DANCING TREE BOOKS

Printed on recycled paper using soy based inks.

Dancing Tree Books
111 E14th Street #169
New York, NY 10003
www.dancingtreebooks.com

Library of Congress Control Number: 2014908459
ISBN: 978-0-9960876-0-5

The following were reprinted with permission:

From Satchidananda, Swami, The Yoga Sutras of Patanjali. Copyright © 2013 by Integral Yoga Publications. Reprinted by permission of Integral Yoga Publications/Satchidananda Ashram-Yogaville, Inc.

The All Faiths Logo is a registered trademark/service mark of Satchidananda Ashram - Yogaville Inc. Used with permission. © 1986 Satchidananda Ashram - Yogaville Inc.

Passages from the "Sunlit Path" and "On Women" by the Mother reproduced with permission of Sri Aurobindo Ashram Trust.

From The Katha Upanishad translated by Swami Ambikananda Saraswati, published by Frances Lincoln Ltd © 2001. Reproduced by permission of Frances Lincoln Ltd.

Names have been changed to protect the privacy of individuals.

Cover and Interior Design: Lindsey Andrews
Content Editor: Sarah McGowan
Copy Editor: Amy Lucas

For my mother

CONTENTS

Foreword

"the illusion of normal"
By Swami Ramananda

here again–
the daily miracle
right before the eyes
the immense sphere of earth turns
revealing sun and moon,
the clouds parade while
sea waves infinite offerings
on countless shores

every cell breathes in endless ebb and flow,
every leaf and stem
an art,
a world itself

under what ancient spell,
some veil descent,
we look as if it's all the same
the illusion of normal reigns

with all our quicksand plans
and if-only dreams,
what do we really see?
what if the world was witness–
looked at the mind and laughed
at petty charms and anxious faces,
lines of longing etched into stony hearts
weighing on the soul

by what gravity do we not fly
to see a mountain lake,
wake with wonder
when a sacred guiding star rises
from the inner sky,
an ocean of unspoken sound
names the secret
passage home

Swami Ramananda

Senior Teacher, Integral Yoga

Where it began, where it ended

I run my fingertips gently across the gray stone body
of a temple dancer.
Frozen in her dance.
Engaging me with her steady gaze from the laughing
wall where she lives.
Her body full with joy and movement.
Our vibrations resonate and she begins to move,
already three dimensional, stepping gracefully from
the wall to the earth, into my world.
Vibrant color returning with each flickering eye
movement, fingers curling into *mudras*, invoking
energy, the body fluid and powerful.
She dances around me; her anklets softly chime as she
pounds the ground with rooted feet.
I breathe her in and she dances in me, through me,
as me.

India lived in me as a dance. A dance that resonated with movements
from a deep-rooted connection; a dance that swayed my hidden dreams
to the surface, reminding me of how I used to see myself; a dance that
moved a healing energy through my body. I woke up.

I stayed in India longer than anticipated for reasons that are difficult to explain. I wasn't on some spiritual journey or in crisis or seeking eastern wisdom or deep answers like many travelers I encountered along the way. I couldn't initially identify with these intentions but I respected their seeking, focus, and energy, and wondered–why had I come to India?

It began with yoga. While I had heard of yoga in college, I had shied away from it–as a dancer I found the movements stilted and inorganic. At that point I had only been exposed to the physical aspects of the practice. Soon after moving to New York City in 1998 I found myself at the Integral Yoga Institute. I remember the incredible feeling of peace that flooded my being at every class after the breathing exercises and meditation. A peace I thirsted for in the marathon of life in the city that never sleeps.

Years later, I became a yoga teacher, broadening my experience of this profound spiritual path, and committing myself to life as a perpetual student. Spiritual practice is a constant work in progress; it is a journey toward growth, which is infinite. Teaching aids in staying focused on the path of learning, it creates a discipline in your own practice as you share the practice with others.

Yoga was an integral part of my experience in India. Attending a teacher training program was the initial impetus and then as I struck out on my own traveling, learning, meeting new experiences and people with open eyes, it became an unbroken thread that lead me along from an inner place through the turmoil of the outer world. I tried to encounter life through a yogic lens.

I intended to travel through India for two months but stayed for nearly eleven, unable to release myself from the vivacity, the pulse, the energy that had been missing from my life for far too long. An inner dance I had allowed to lie dormant began to stir.

There was nowhere else I would rather have been; I didn't miss "home," I belonged to the world and I belonged in that moment–wherever that moment was. My time in India didn't feel like a journey, a vacation, a departure–I experienced it as a continuation of my everyday life, a life that has led me along a path of travel, discovery, and constant curiosity.

I've always felt transitory, migratory, removed. I have roamed far and wide, lived place to place, and discovered that this energy of movement feeds me. This is how I feel at home. I feel settled in the eye of the storm, comforted by the frenetic life whirling around me, witnessing the beauty of what it is to be human wherever it is in the world I am standing.

Physical travel and the spiritual journey are undeniably parallel. I wonder, "where are we going?" and "where are we coming from?" When we contemplate deeply, we may come across answers that reveal an understanding of our perception of the self: the self we have created, the self we have become, the self we see in the world, and the self the world sees in us. If we go even deeper, we touch upon an understanding of our greater Self, the unchanging core of our being that is a part of the Divine.

From which place in our lives, from which self, do we wish to depart so that we may arrive at another place, another self? Is travel a necessary component on a spiritual journey? If we go to a "spiritual destination"–a location we think exudes a deepness we can't find anywhere else–will we find guidance? *Guidance.*

Outward change can provide a blueprint for internal change or space to concentrate more fully. Forced out of our comfort zone, we have the opportunity to evaluate the self in reaction to new stimuli. These reactions are indicators of the steadiness of one's spiritual path.

Is compassion retained when pushed to the brink?
Does honesty remain when fear and uncertainty seep in?
Does generosity still exist when resources are exhausted?
When lost, is God still there?

The Dalai Lama says, "In fact, the techniques themselves do not lead to enlightenment or a compassionate and open heart. That is up to you, and the effort and motivation you bring to your spiritual practice."[1] Any religious or spiritual practice is a reflection of our intention. It is a path to help us encounter and focus on our true Self. If done superficially, its meaning is superficial. If done without intention, it is a way to get lost.

These practices offer guidance, but we also have to be present to truly receive this guidance: to live it, to practice it, to lose our way, to find it again, to be compassionate toward ourselves throughout the journey, and to continue to practice.

Yoga has been a journey for me, inwardly and outwardly, it has brought me to new places within myself and to new places out in the world. It led me to the readiness to live life fully. Yoga was my path to life.

1

The big orange bus, misty vistas, Raj memories

We were too many bodies stuffed inside a small van wading through a tangled sea of loud horns, hot dust, and exhaust. The American contingent of the yoga group I was a part of were wide eyed at the reality of Indian traffic, the masses of people, and thick air. We arrived with relief at a local Shiva temple and were given thick garlands of marigolds to offer to "the Auspicious One." The happy orange color and sweet smell brightened our energy as we walked barefoot onto the cool stone inside the temple. We crawled into a tiny room and sat cross-legged against the smooth walls. We hardly knew each other as we sat body to body feeling our inner selves vulnerable in this spiritual place.

A group of strangers experiencing each other through the inner without much knowledge of who we were on the outer, in the world. I was a northern California hippy chick yoga teacher whose life had become still. I was searching for movement. I was a traveler who had gotten lost in a stagnant life. I was in a place of emptiness. *Empty.*

After the dark sanctum of the temple, flickering candles, incense, and burning ghee, we visited the bright, airy, and open early home of Sri Swami Satchidananda. It had been converted into a museum with inspirational quotes, stories, and photographs from his life. Swami Satchidananda founded Integral Yoga and initially was known in the west as the spiritual leader who opened Woodstock with his invocation of peace, making peace within ourselves and sending that peace out into the world.

We sat for awhile in the open courtyard or next to a little pool in the middle of the home talking in hushed tones or just absorbing the energy. I felt Swami Satchidananda there, I felt him laughing. I felt him telling me to smile and laugh and not to take on any responsibilities, but just to go along for the ride and enjoy. Great advice.

We squeezed back into the minivan and practiced patience through more traffic. Gridlock reminded me of the ups and downs of the spiritual path. One moment you feel a flow, an energy, some guidance and peace, and the next you feel blocked. Forward movement seems impossible and you struggle through the present challenge. This is natural. The challenges are where we learn what practice truly is.

Back at the Integral Yoga Institute, my fellow non-Indian yoga teachers, new travelers who had arrived to join the tour, and I packed up our things and chaotically jumbled into a big orange bus to begin our tour of South India. We joked about the color of the bus, which matched the color of the robes swamis wear–"It's the swamimobile!" Swami Krishnananda, our fearless leader–an American monk who had run the Institute in India for over 10 years–pasted a photograph of Swami Satchidananda to the small television screen at the front of the bus. We prayed for safety with the *tryambakam mantra*, and set off.

This chant helps to release the fear of death and bring a calmness, courage, and happiness to the chanter. It is also chanted when someone is ill or in danger. It is considered especially powerful, even life saving.

Om tryambakam yajamahe
Sugandhim pustivardhanam
Urvarukamiva bandhanan
Mrityormuksiya mamrtat

Om shanti, shanti, shanti

We worship the All-Seeing One
Fragrant, you nourish bounteously
From fear of death may you cut us free
To realize immortality

Om peace, peace, peace[2]

We settled into a hotel nestled in the trees at the foot of a mountain. I felt ready. Excited. Alive. I laid in bed with eyes wide open listening to the thick quiet, save for bat wings beating the air and the distant calls of monkeys.

We awoke before dawn, stumbling with flashlights through the hotel gardens, down a dirt road, through a dark lobby, up some stairs, and finally to our yoga class and meditation. We sat together in a room lit with candlelight and the early softness of the sun before it has fully risen. After stretching our bodies and minds we smiled in anticipation for the day.

In the early morning chill of January, bundled in multiple layers, we staggered out, high from meditation, to our orange bus that would take us to the little blue train that would take us all the way up the Nilgiri Hills to the famous hill station of Ooty in the state of Tamil Nadu. Hill stations were vacation destinations developed by the British to provide a respite from the sweltering summer heat. The train station was small and hectic, a little platform attached to a small building for ticketing. We were surrounded by smiling vacationers. The Nilgiri Blue Mountain Train is an old-fashioned steam train built at the turn of the last century. Swiss engineers designed the rail line to accommodate the steep climb and high altitude.

The narrow blue metal train sat awaiting us at the station. Our little yoga group of about 15, led by two women swamis, sat 4 across with a little aisle in between, each row with a large glassless window, just a gaping hole, to take in the crisp air and verdant lushness of the mountain. We soon met our neighbors, many of whom were honeymooning couples, and ate breakfast together–the South Indian staple of *idly* and *sambar*, a steamed fermented rice spongy bread and lentil, potato, and onion stew out of metal tiffins. We chatted excitedly as we passed through rich green forests in the just waking day.

In the distance giant rocks formed spirit shapes, and slowly, very slowly, we climbed the mountain. A tunnel of variegated stone cliffs flanked our little train. Stubborn, delicate flowers growing from the rocky crags smiled at us, just inches away.

When we broke free from the narrow walls around us we felt the earth drop away below, as if we were suspended in mid-air. We leaned out the windows, peering down below us to see tumbling waterfalls erupting from tall glittering trees, the cascading water crashing over soft, round stone. We climbed higher, reaching toward the magestic eagles floating above us. Exquisite views of misty mountainsides opened before us. Monkeys looked on with curiosity from their steady boulders.

We rushed back and forth to each side of the train, sticking our heads out the open windows, knowing our photos wouldn't do justice to the experience of this journey, knowing the beauty was indescribable. At times it was literally breathtaking and I had to remind myself to breathe.

Three times the train unexpectedly seemed to stop working. The first time, as we rounded a bend, I stuck my head out the window and looked back at billows of black smoke wafting behind us. The train eventually came to a halt and then started slipping backwards. This was a bit concerning as we were balanced precariously on a tiny track over a cliff with water violently smashing huge boulders under us. Somehow the train managed to move forward again to the first station, which was nothing more than a single building and a small road leading into the wilderness. Rumor spread that the train crew had put out a fire in the engine and then, without any explanation, the engine detached and chugged back down the hill leaving us stranded.

Delayed for over an hour, more rumors circulated that the engine had run out of water, overheated, and had gone all the way back down to the base to refill. Most of the passengers got off the stalled train, walked around, stretched, and checked out the views.

We cheered as the engine reappeared, reattached, and resumed our journey up the mountain. We arrived at another station where we again halted and disembarked while the crew attempted to refill the engine with water. This took some time, as the water seemed to turn to vapor as soon as it touched the hot metal of the engine.

Some passengers walked around to stretch their legs; our group played around with a few yoga poses. A few of us hiked down a narrow dirt trail to a village, and found a place to have tea. The dark, cool structure was actually someone's house with a few little tables in the front room and a wood burning stove. There was much gesturing and smiling, as even Raudra our guide, a yoga teacher and writer from Tamil Nadu, could not communicate with the owner in a common language. Everyone in the village wanted to meet us and take photos, including the local policeman. We brought back little plastic cups of tea and coffee to those in the group who had remained on the train.

We set off again passing steep hillsides covered in tea plants where workers dotted the green lushness harvesting the leaves. The sweet air kept us in good spirits. I sat next to Swami Arthyananda, an American woman who had become a yogic monk over thirty years ago. She had gray bangs and smiling blue eyes–a waif of a woman imparting deep lessons learned through a life of simplicity. She shared some personal encounters with Swami Satchidananda and my eyes glistened as she told me her experience around his death. He told her it was his time. He knew and returned to India to move on. I thought how beautiful she looked glowing with his memory. I tried not to cry.

I gave her my soft yellow sweatshirt as she wasn't prepared for the crisp mountain air; she loved it. I wondered if she would be able to wear it back home at the ashram in the US since it wasn't the approved peach color of a swami.

Swamis wear a uniform–clothing in some version of peach or orange. Their attire is comfortable and plain. The color is not meant to flatter or impress; it represents the burning of desires and renunciation of worldly things. I heard that at the ashram in Yogaville they are quite strict.

More delays ensued but we were enjoying the journey so much that it was as good as the arriving. We climbed higher and higher, still surrounded by beauty. At the next breakdown our intrepid leader, Swami Krishnananda, decided it was more important to make our lunch appointment at a historical hotel in the hill station Coonoor than continue on the never-ending train ride. She pulled out her mobile phone and called the bus driver who was meeting us at the top.

Somehow we found a trail down the mountain that took us to the road where he would pick us up. I was bewildered as to how this was possible considering we didn't know where we were or where this half-hidden trail may lead. We hiked through farms and villages and forest, over creeks and down cliff sides. We spilled out onto the side of the road and walked up a little way to a border crossing. We sat in the sun, ate some snacks, and waited for our driver. We rejoiced almost in disbelief as he finally appeared around a corner. We drove the rest of the way along hairpin turns to The Royal Taj Garden Retreat, an old British colonial club, now a public restaurant and hotel that offered unimpeded vistas of the mountains below. In this surreal British lodge, with its manicured lawn and garden, I felt I could have easily been in England.

After a delicious Indian lunch of various vegetarian dishes, rice, sweet desserts, and tea, we lounged on the impeccable lawn. Swami Arthyananda and I laughed as we swung on an ancient set of tandem swings until, like children reluctant to stop playing, we were pulled away by the already jeopardized schedule.

We visited Sim's Park, a botanical garden, where we wandered soft hillsides of diverse trees with big floppy green leaves or spiny needles, cones and flowers from both South Asia and Europe. The grass and canopies of green created a hush. We stopped to smell the flowers. At the center of the gardens was a small lake. The Swamis turned into giggling girls as they shared a paddleboat, pedaling through the water, past ducks and swans and lily pads.

We never did make it to Ooty, the pinnacle of the mountain. Back on the bus for several more hours, we made our way down the other side of the mountain, along more winding twists and turns bordered with low stone walls lined with families of monkeys looking on at us disinterestedly.

We finally arrived at Mudumalai National Park and Wildlife Sanctuary, which sat at the base of the mountain. I was enthralled at the promise of elephant rides and encounters with tigers. Tigers! We stayed among the trees in rustic cabins built on stilts. We practiced Hatha yoga on a small grass clearing under dancing trees that swayed like wise old ladies, laughing at our poses. After dinner we sat around a bonfire talking and absorbing the day. One body would disappear from the firelight, then another, until finally the fire was left alone as we all collapsed for the night, exhausted.

We arose before dawn, excited to go on our safari. It was below freezing outside so I bundled on all of my clothing. I wore three pairs of pants, two long tops, a sweater, two scarves, socks, and sneakers. I don't think there was much left in my suitcase. Raudra leant me something called a monkey cap, fuzzy and warm, it transformed my head into the shape of a monkey. I wondered if they were laughing at me as we saw them jumping between trees, competing with each other to see who could jump the farthest, the branches swinging and rebounding like rubber bands from the ground up twenty feet into the air and higher, catapulting a laughing monkey who then deftly landed on the branch of the next tree over. We were hoping for wild elephants and leopards.

"Do you see it?"

"See what?"

"Is that something over there?"

"Over where?"

"I don't see anything now."

"Wait!"

"Never mind, it's a bush."

We headed back to our cabins, disappointed, bumping along on the hard seats in the back of the jeep.

We packed up the bus and headed out. The temperature rapidly increased the farther down the mountain we traveled. We started at freezing and ended up in the 90s stripping off layer after layer as we descended.

Our next stop was Mysore. A metropolis within what was once the vastly powerful Mysore Kingdom, this Kingdom ruled a large area of South India for hundreds of years, became a Princely State under the British, and finally joined the Union of India after Indian Independence.

The one lane road grew into a highway. Traffic began to swarm around us, traffic lights appeared, buildings grew and clumped together, until suddenly we were in the heart of a major city. Tall modern office buildings and hotels mingled with older storefronts and ancient markets. White marble monuments stood at attention over open spaces and in the middle of roundabouts. Traffic had a flow, the city appeared mapped and structured, planned.

We settled into our rooms at a basic hotel and ate lunch ravenously. An excursion to a famous market was organized to buy Mysore Silks. A few of us weren't too interested in shopping at this massive tourist bazaar, so we took off on our own to walk around the city and taste some of its flavor. Two young men befriended us as we walked along exploring the streets. Initially wary of their attention we lied about where we were from and whom we were with, not wanting to open ourselves up to being taken advantage of, not wanting to admit to being American and the connotations that holds for women. We soon realized their genuine interest and generosity and I felt ashamed. Generally I am an honest person, but these slips reminded me of the importance of vigilance in the yogic practice of *satya*–non-lying. However small or insignificant a lie may seem it carries with it a growing darkness that not only pollutes the self, but also negatively manifests in unpredictable ways.

With our new friends' guidance we found a locals' market and ducked inside to meander through the dark, stone passageways lined with stalls. Older women in *saris* combed through fresh produce, children ran through a labyrinth of adult legs, religious paraphernalia and statues of gods oversaw the activity. Quiet men sat behind their pyramids of ground spices, a rainbow of browns, reds, greens, and gold, waiting for customers. Flowers filled the air with soft, sweet scents. We made friends with some children who followed us curiously. They wanted photos with us.

We window shopped as we made our way back to the hotel. We found a scent shop and smelled all the various oils and incense. The owner told us what each scent represented and how or when it should be used. We wondered at unfamiliar musical instruments stacked in a window, at the vibrant colors of fabrics in a clothing store, at the number of gold jewelry stores filled with hanging chains and cases of diamonds encased in rings and earrings. We arrived at the hotel, sated.

The next morning we rose early to watch Pattabhi Jois teach a yoga class at his world famous center, the K Pattabhi Jois Ashtanga Yoga Institute. He teaches a style of yoga called Mysore Ashtanga, which is comprised of six series–specific postures done in a specific order with a progressive purpose of internal cleansing. The mostly foreign students were packed into a large classroom, mat to mat, sweaty and dedicated. Required to know all of the series before they come to the center, the students are then able to concentrate on breathing and pushing themselves to perfect the postures.

Pattabhi Jois counted the breathing pattern out loud for each *asa-na* pose as his son assisted the students with physical adjustments. The students moved from one *asana* to the next according to the counted breath. *Asana* is physical movement done with intention and delibera-tion. When perfected this deliberation melts away into harmony and surrender. Focusing on the body is a way to cease focusing on the mind. Following the breath brings you into awareness of the pranic body. Hatha practice is finding the balance between *ha* and *tha*, inhale and exhale, sun and moon, active and passive, and bringing them to-gether into harmony.

While there is more to the Mysore Ashtanga expression of yoga than the physical postures alone, watching this particular class, I only noticed the focus on the physical and felt the students' desires to push the body to some kind of perfection that seemed to have little to do with inner peace.

After class we were given an audience with Pattabhi Jois where I had hoped to hear more on his deeper perspective and intention, to glean some wisdom from his lifetime of experience. We had each pre-pared a question in advance, but in the end didn't have an opportunity to ask any of them, as our allotted time was monopolized by a few at the expense of the many. So I came away with little true understanding of this style.

We then bustled over to the magnificent Mysore Palace for a whirl-wind tour. Kalyana Mantapa–the peacock room–an octagonal hall with a mosaic floor and stained glass ceiling celebrating this sacred bird, ac-cented with chandeliers and iron pillars, captivated me. In the elephant courtyard, I could imagine the king mounting his enormous regal el-ephant from his balcony several stories above the ground. We stood in a room that appeared to have been dipped completely in blue. We looked at our own reflections in a giant hall of mirrors that opened out onto an expansive courtyard far below where we imagined the royal party ad-dressing tens of thousands of gathered people looking up in awe.

Swami Krishnananda had hired an informative guide who we followed around like ducklings as he explained each room and the expansive history of Mysore, but as soon as he started to speak, at his first "hello, my name is Pradeep and I will be your guide," his lilting accent struck me so deeply I could hear nothing else–the way he shaped his words, the intonation, the soft and loud. He had my grandfather's accent, his voice.

Something in me started to vibrate. I was thrown by feeling a sense of "home" so far from home from a total stranger. I felt a sudden deep connection to this land, to my ancestors.

Born and raised in India, my grandparents on my mother's side were part of the British Raj. My grandmother, an Anglo-Indian, spent most of my life denying her Indian background. I remember feeling bewildered at the assortment of non-Indian blood we were associated with–Armenian, Scottish, German, French, Russian, English. My grandfather, however, remained true to his heritage of mixed English and Indian. He had an Indian accent, an accent I thought particular to him, he cooked Indian food, and continued to speak, Urdu, Hindi, and several other Indian languages.

Hearing my grandfather's voice in India surprised me and reminded me of how little I know about my grandparents' pasts, their lives in India, their parents' lives in India. They were so young. In their early thirties, already married for over 10 years and with three children, they emigrated to England.

I thought about my own life in my early thirties and how quickly the generations had changed. I thought about no longer being able to ask my grandfather about his life. I thought about how much I missed him.

My mother spent her childhood in Pakistan, amidst the culture of the

Raj. She had a bit of what we liked to call a "Raj complex." In my family we teased her about her slightly upturned nose. My mother always
had to have the best.

Sitting on the manicured green lawn of the Royal Taj Hotel would
have been heaven to her–so civilized with tea and white washed walls,
leisure and space, attentive service. On top of the mountain, looking
down at the terraces of tea and mist below, I thought about coming
back with her. I asked my mother if my grandfather had ever spent time
in Mysore.

According to my mother, my maternal great-great-great grandfather was a Russian aristocrat who fell into political disfavor, fled Russia
and went into hiding in the French countryside. He married a farmer's
daughter and took her name. His son, born in France, went to India
to find his fortune and eventually became the Economic Minister for
the Maharaja of Gwalior. He married an Indian woman of high caste.
Then there was a violent uprising against the Maharajas for collaborat-
ing with the British and his son, my great grandfather Ivo, was sent to a
Catholic boarding school in South India for protection. My great-great
grandfather was assassinated. Family legend has it that he was covered
in honey, buried up to his shoulders, and eaten to death by red ants.

My great grandfather Ivo grew up under the care of nuns and as
a young man was hired to be a troubleshooter by the British Indian
Railway. He explored the jungles of South and North India for appropriate routes and served as the overseer for the building of the tracks
and stations along the way.

While working within the many independent kingdoms throughout India, Ivo was wined and dined by Maharajas and other leading
aristocratic Indian figures. He impressed them particularly with his skill
as a tiger hunter. It seemed that he was quite famous on this score and
would often be called from his work to hunt down a marauding or
rabid tiger ravaging local villages.

My grandmother grew up on a train; the carriages that were their home were filled with tiger skins. My mother remembers, "Even in our house growing up there were tiger skins used as rugs on the floor. I used to play with the skins, with my arms around the tiger head, pretending I was riding the tiger."

She fondly describes her grandparents, "Ivo was 6'5; Aideen, 5'3. They were very funny together. When Grandpa wanted to hug her he'd pick her up off her feet and hug her. Sitting outside on the veranda in the evening heat, he'd sit her on his lap. He called her Girlu because she was so tiny. Grandpa Ivo died one morning after a bowl of cornflakes. He was just gone, sitting at the table. Girlu discovered him and pretty much went to bed after that and never got up again. A few months later, I sat with her after coming home from school and asked her why she wasn't getting better. She said to me, 'I can't live without my Ivo. He's waiting for me and I've got to go.' I knew then that I was going to lose my beloved Girlu, but I was also happy that she would be in Grandpa Ivo's loving arms again. Her hands were on her prayer book, wrapped in her rosary, and the next day she was dead."

My mother was born three years after partition in Lahore, Pakistan. "The first place I remember I guess was Rawalpindi. Our beautiful large rambling home with servants and servant's quarters and parties every weekend–Mum and Dad had a huge community of friends–it was the Raj community. British club every Friday night, a swimming pool, orchestra, dancing, parties. The Catholic Club. I loved going to the American embassy to watch cowboy movies and eat American ice cream, which was different from Indian ice cream. I saw this one movie and I just knew I was going to go to America, marry an American, and live in America, I knew that was where my true home was." (And she was right.)

The Pakistan she grew up in felt no different from the India it had just been. "Dad was a Major in the army. When the British left, the British Army became the Pakistan National Army. Immediately after Partition, the whole family knew they were 'going back' to England.

Everyone believed in an idealized notion of England as home. The reality is India was home. It was an untenable situation... going back to the 'home country'... Anglo-Indians were caught in a difficult choice. If you stayed you would accept blending into the culture, marrying lower caste Indians, or living as an outsider. Either would be difficult and possibly dangerous amidst the violence of the times. Mum and Dad didn't envision that. It was a family decision."

"Going back to England" felt like an odd concept considering none of the family, for generations on my grandfather's side and never on my grandmother's side, had ever lived there. But as part of the British Raj, that was the "home" country.

After Partition, the elders were sent to England first then the children went over in waves. My Grandpa Ted took on the role of Patriarch and worked, saved, and bought ocean liner tickets for the family, sending the oldest brothers and sister and their families first and then the younger families. My mother's family was the last to leave.

My mother was transplanted to suburban England as a young woman. She recalls, "No one talked about where we were from. We were really trying hard to not be Indian in England. Mum said, 'we are going to be English and speak like proper upper class Englishmen.' I took elocution at school. I was brown; it was difficult. We suffered racial prejudice."

I have no reference to draw upon to understand my mother's experience. I wasn't born in a colony among the colonialists. As someone who views the negative repercussions of colonialism all over the world and sympathizes with those who are oppressed, enslaved, and culturally attacked, I grew up not wanting to understand my mother's perspective or life experience. I made fun of her, jovially of course–but she owned her upbringing. She would fake the posh English accent that she had lost years ago when she transformed into an American hippy academic. We would fake it together over milkshakes and laugh.

I never talked to my grandfather about his life in India; he died before I knew I wanted to know. Grandpa Ted had a stiff upper lip; he was understated, reserved, and generous with a love that poured quietly from his heart. You could taste it in the food he cooked. You could feel it when he became Father Christmas, passing out gifts from his big red bag. You could see it when he laughed at us children when we naively thought he could really read the playing card he had stuck to his forehead in his wondrous magic trick. I loved his laugh. He only laughed when he truly could not help it. It came from deep inside. It was sincere.

I grew up in a very different world. Only now am I really confronting my own heritage, awakening roots I didn't realize were there. I experienced small things in India from a place of surprised recognition, I connected with reminders or odd familiarities that weren't about modern India. I personally associated more with something older.

Is this why I had come to India?

2

Withdrawal of the senses, time, flight

Why India? A month earlier, hanging out on the cliffs in Santa Cruz, California overlooking Steamer Lane, watching surfers crash through wild waves, exhilarated and alive, I decided to just do it. I wasn't seeking any desperate spiritual answers. I wasn't intrigued with consuming the "exotic." I wasn't running from anything or concerned with the cultural expectation of following a path called "settling down." I wasn't rooted to be uprooted or trapped seeking freedom. I wasn't bound to be untied. I was unattached in a personal and material way. I wasn't leaving home or looking for a home.

I may have been lost but that wasn't anything new. I may have felt like I wasn't doing anything with my life, that I was stagnating–but that wasn't anything new either.

Negative reinforcement has always been a personal crutch. I've spent most of my life criticizing myself, accusing myself of commitment phobia, of a lack of initiative and drive. I then reinforce my self-hate by characterizing all those traits as negative and the cause of my pointless life. Focusing on what I decide is negative rather than acknowledging any accomplishments or positive aspects about myself, I only see the future pointlessness of my existence and my lack of worth. I only value what I feel I can't achieve. I feel incapable of accomplishment, and if I don't contribute to the world in a particular way, then what is the meaning of my existence?

Recognizing my thought patterns was a step forward. The next step was understanding I needed to do something major to break my patterns. I needed to wake myself up, my real self (whoever that was). It is a long path retracing my mental formations and healing them one by one.

I bought my ticket to India, got my visa and immunizations. I had two weeks to get excited, pack, and talk down any fears. I was afraid of male harassment and my own health issues. I saw my doctor to check the size of my recurring ovarian cysts and stocked up on my supplements to keep my endometriosis at bay.

I watched myself from above, a bird coasting on a breeze, observing myself making my preparations.

> Floating through a blur
> Grasping at reality
> In a waking dream

We live in many layers of existence and awareness. Bodily/sensorial awareness, energetic/pranic awareness, mental awareness, emotional, spiritual, inner, outer, lower, higher, material, ethereal. There seem to be countless ways to think about existence, to separate and define and experience. While there exist separate layers, they are all interdependent and coexistent. It's helpful to bring our awareness to the differences in order to more fully understand ourselves and understand what is going on within us in the present moment.

Body awareness includes the five senses: seeing, hearing, tasting, smelling, and touching. It is an awareness of our physical reality and our interaction with our environment. It is our body's reaction to outside stimulus, from tasting a sweet fruit to developing painful growths in our organs in response to toxins. Isolating our awareness of each sense heightens our awareness even further. Swami Satchidananda explains:

> The senses are like a mirror. Turned outward, they

reflect the outside; turned inward, they reflect the
pure light. By themselves the senses are innocent, but
when allowed to turn outside they attract everything
and transfer those messages to the mind, making it
restless. Turned inward, they find peace by taking the
form of the mind itself.[3]

One yogic practice to isolate and understand the senses is *pratyahara*, the withdrawal of the senses. By focusing on one sense we withdraw from all others and can more fully understand the effects of the
one. Eventually we are unaware and unaffected by any of the senses,
totally withdrawn, the mind is left deeply available to meditation and
beyond. While that experience of mindlessness is still unavailable to us,
we can focus on how we are affected, manipulated, distracted by our
interactions with the world through our senses and the physical body.

The energetic body is the pranic body and *prana* is moved by
the breath. *Prana* is the life force; it is an intangible energy. *Prana*
exists in and around us forming a subtle body around our physical
body. Awareness of our subtle body shows us what is happening in our
physical body. Maybe it is also related to the sixth sense of intuition, a
way to feel and understand through energetic connection rather than
a sensorial awareness. We affect the energetic body through control of
the breath in the yogic practice of *pranayama*.

Mental awareness is the ability to step outside the mind and observe its machinations. It is the ability to act as an outside observer of
the mind, to see how it is occupied, how it functions, and how it inter-
acts with other levels of awareness. Observation of the mind reveals the
ego and the creation of a self defined from the outside. We see who we
think we are. We see all the effects of life experience, culture, upbringing, education, and gender, on this character we call our self.

Who do we think we are? Who do we walk through the world as?
The yogic practice of meditation is an effective tool to focus on the
workings of the mind and to separate the self from the mind, cultivat-

ing the ability to let go of the mind and experience what exists beyond.

Emotional awareness is connected to mental awareness, as emotions are mostly tied to mental reactions. Emotional fluctuations are tied to mental understanding. For example, sadness, joy, jealousy, fear all result from mental disturbances, misunderstandings, and defied expectations. Exploring an emotional response is a good way to understand the mental creation of the self.

The *yamas* and *niyamas*, yogic principles on how to live peacefully, teach us how to understand our behavior and our reactions. We move into a true understanding of who we are, a kind of wisdom. A clear perception of reality begins to dawn. Once reality is seen as bright as the sun, bliss is experienced.

Well, that's one way to describe where the yogic path leads. For most of us it is a never-ending journey.

Inner, outer, lower, higher, material, ethereal are all ways to distinguish life experiences in our need to categorize and understand, while in reality everything exists simultaneously. We simply are what we are. Life is what it is.

It is our inability to know all that we are simultaneously that leads us to strive for the path to that realization. In that realization we may find that all of who we are only exists on a material level and is unimportant in the bigger divine picture. Our ego is challenged; our entire sense of self is called into question. Reconciling our experience of our ego self and our true divine Self is a scary process. Completely letting go is the goal.

But is it for all of us? We are human. We are here in a body, on this earth, with this mind and heart. It appears to be a natural separation. Is it?

Most religions separate the kingdom of Earth from the kingdom of God. In other words we can only truly understand the Divine after leaving this earthly body. But what is that divine level? Why can't the Divine exist within everything at all times? Us included. Why is it considered a separate level? Why does experiencing it within us mean devaluing our humanness? Would I want to live in a cave alone with no concern for my human body, mind, and heart in exchange for constant blissful communion with the Divine?

In some semblance of an awareness of reality, not present in my body, I watched as it moved from place to place, from movement to movement. I watched myself pack a suitcase and print my boarding pass. I watched my mind think and react as I marked time. I saw my eyes seeing but didn't see through them. I heard my voice speaking as if it were someone else's. I taught my final yoga class. I heard myself say my goodbyes. I disconnected from relationships.

I drove to the path overlooking the Pacific Ocean and stood in the rain. The earth smelled sweet, the plants sang, the waves beat the rocks. I watched the world in its tumultous rhythm, its wild conversation, while I felt nothing but the cold of the drops of water against my numb skin.

I floated. Time was only on a clock and important only for getting my body to arrive in my seat on an airplane at the right time to arrive somewhere else on the planet.

I managed to get some sleep on the flight to Hong Kong. The first leg of the trip wasn't too bad, although in the beginning I wrestled with some claustrophobia issues because the seats were so narrow and close together. It was the craziest feeling landing in Hong Kong and knowing I was halfway around the world. Airplanes still truly amaze me. I walked around the airport and stared out the giant glass walls at the island. Ships and boats of all sizes and purposes floated along the water in front of me, silhouetted against the setting sun. The view was serene and still like a painting, an odd trick when reality was a bustling motion of constant activity.

Getting back on the plane after those 15 hours (with only an hour break) knowing I still had many hours ahead of me was not easy. Finally, there was sun out the window–between cloud layers as we gained altitude, the sun shot out in millions of light pink beams, which were filtered through the clouds down to the sparkling water below like diamonds on the waves.

We landed in Singapore and after over 20 hours of travel, I had to get out of the airport. The airport offered a free shuttle to downtown, a map, a ride back to the airport, and a complimentary shower at the airport spa. I took them up on all of it.

I stepped out of the cool airport into a great hot, sticky, sweaty climate. Unfortunately, I had to carry my yoga mat and a backpack full of books, wearing sweatpants and heavy sneakers. Singapore is quite a bustling city with interesting European colonial architecture mixed with Chinese architecture. A metropolis, it is the definition of cosmopolitan.

I decided to eat my way through Singapore. I walked to Chinatown and sampled tea smoked crispy chicken and rice. At a Dim Sum house, I tried yam dumplings, surprisingly savory and filled with pork, shrimp and banana dragon dumplings, strange, but an interesting flavor combination, and steamed scallops with seaweed. I tried some vegetable *samosas* from a street vendor and to cap off my extended meal in Singapore–of all the things to run into–the Coffee Bean & Tea Leaf Co and my old addiction–an Ice-Blended Mocha!

Walking on a major boulevard in the heart of Singapore, I came across old, cracked stone steps that led up into a shroud of trees. I followed. The shady path led me farther and farther until I reached the top of a small hill. I had stumbled upon Fort Canning Park. As I wandered around old stone buildings, I was drawn to the spaces between and the trees that inhabited them. I stood in awe under these amazing ancient, royal trees that held the secrets of the past. The most magnificent was the Rain Tree, named so because its leaves curl up when it's going to rain. A giant palm frond covered the entire side of a small greenhouse; I imagined living in a house with walls made of leaves. It was cooler in the park and quieter. I was alone.

Stone carvings served as a memorial to the history of Singapore and to this hill that used to be an ancient castle in the 1300s. There were ancient relics strewn around, such as the recreation of the original botanical garden, which paid homage to eras past. Spices that have survived through centuries of turmoil provided an enticing aroma; large floppy leaves canopied above provided shade, creating a serene respite from the hustle of city life. I believe the English destroyed the original buildings on this hill in the 1600s but they couldn't destroy those ancient trees.

I reluctantly left the park to return to the airport bus pick-up point. I took the scenic route back in order to see as much of the city as possible during my short stay. I crossed through various sections of the city and walked along the Singapore River that winds through the city. The water was so alive, green, and awake. I stood on one of many bridges that connect the different neighborhoods, divided by an emerald snake making its way to the sea, and wondered at all the history, the travelers, the longing looks of dreamers that snake had seen.

I walked for three hours and sweated liters; I felt exhilarated, like at the sight of the rising sun after staying up all night. My calves were swollen and weirdly numb. I stopped often to stretch and massage. They just needed to be elevated, all the sitting and walking was taking its toll. I realized I hadn't been horizontal since I slept Saturday night and now it was Tuesday–sort of. Time seemed subjective at this point with the time spent in the air, the time difference, and my altered state of being.

Singapore reminded me how much I love to travel and experience the vastness and interconnectedness of the world. To breathe in an air filled with the breath of different people. To see the same smiles broaden around the world. To hear the bustle of life in other languages. To smell and taste plants and animals growing from a unique soil and sea.

I felt so free in a new land far from everyone I knew, far from my life, far from who and what reinforced a perception of me that didn't feel true. The blur was replaced with clarity, the dream suddenly faded into sharp reality. The thread of my life had not been broken; it continued in its interweaving trajectory creating the web of my existence, a creation seemingly tangled but that I know in its entirety is beautiful.

I got back to the modern, gleaming Singapore airport, took my free shower in the airport spa, used the complimentary Internet, and updated friends on my progress. Refreshed and tired, I boarded the plane for the final flight to Chennai, South India.

3

Tapas, tigers, laughing and letting go

Chennai airport was a drastic shock compared to the modern, gleaming, and organized Hong Kong and Singapore airports. Dark and dirty, a dingy greeting, everything was closed. I was shuttled back and forth four times to different counters and given a different story each time as to why it wasn't possible to exchange my money. Luckily, I had arranged for my hotel to send a car to pick me up, and I was able to pay at the hotel with a credit card.

I did not sleep well. I woke up early, happy to leave my dark room filled with mosquitoes, and spend a few hours exploring. The early morning was peaceful and calm, the streets nearly empty. I crept along the dusty sidewalks, unsure and out of place, until I found a temple. Inside, a garden welcomed me and I sat for a while in peace.

Realizing the time, I scurried back to my hotel, grabbed my bags, and made my way back to the airport for the final portion of my journey to Coimbatore.

After a short flight aboard a brand new plane on India's newest domestic airline, I arrived at Coimbatore airport in the state of Tamil Nadu, South India. The airport was small but clean, bright, and open aired. Expecting the clambering rush of taxi drivers to accost me, I strode outside with a false air of confidence, with determination, looking for my prearranged ride. The shouting taxi drivers left me alone. My ride did not appear.

I calmly walked back into the airport, my mind a whir of anxious-
ness, and called the Integral Yoga Institute. I finally spoke with Swami
Krishnananda who apologized for being unable to pick me up and instead gave me explicit driving directions. I went back outside to pick a
taxi driver from the crowd but was surprised to find the place deserted.
All the other passengers had already left. I searched for a taxi and eventually asked a security guard for help. He went around the corner and
found a few drivers sitting on a curb smoking.

My driver pulled up in his white 1950s style Ambassador taxi. I
told him the address and without question, we began our journey.

The Institute was farther than I had expected and the driver periodically leaned out his window and asked someone on the street for
directions. As the city appeared to be a giant maze to me, I assumed
this was a normal practice. Coimbatore was a considerable metropolis
of over a million people spread out in different sections and neighborhoods. We wound our way through the city until we made a quick unexpected turn down a small, residential street and stopped in front of
a white three-story building with the symbol of the Institute in bright
colors over the entrance.

An ashram is a place dedicated to a spiritual path. Generally, a resident spiritual guide runs the ashram and classes are offered for those who
would like to explore the spiritual path. Ashrams vary greatly in size and
offerings. Usually they have guest rooms for practitioners to stay and
experience immersion in the way of life laid out in the spiritual teachings.

At the Integral Yoga Institute immersion entailed classes in yoga,
meditation, and philosophy, vegetarian meals and simple living quarters. Swami Krishnananda was the resident spiritual guide during my
time there and exemplar of the yogic path. She was an American woman who had dedicated herself to this path as a practicing monk for over
30 years. She had long gray hair pulled tightly back in a bun at the
crown of her tall frame. She spoke soft words over a hidden strength;
she was somewhat intimidating.

I dragged my exhausted body out of the comfortable taxi and unloaded my little rolling carry-on bag, purple yoga mat, and backpack. At the Institute's entrance, I was told to leave my shoes outside on the marble steps. I turned back around, took off my heavy sneakers, happy to feel my toes, returned barefoot, and was finally greeted at my destination. I was met with a smile, no introduction was necessary, and was led to my room, the first at the top of the stairs, to finally rest and refresh.

My body swam in a floating reality. I lay on the hard single mattress, absorbing the serenity as my head spun. More than 48 hours had passed since I had taken off from San Francisco, since I had really slept, since I had been motionless and could relax.

The room was simple with two twin beds, a wardrobe, a little bedside table with a lamp, and mosquito netting on the windows. It had an attached bathroom with a western toilet and a hot water shower. Crisp clean sheets and a towel were neatly folded at the bottom of the bed. Every part of me was excited except my body. My body wouldn't move.

My mind drank in the quiet, the stillness, the peaceful color of the walls, the soft light filtering through the window, the coolness of the hard floor. My eyes wandered the room until they too could no longer move and eventually closed.

The rooms at the Institute had little nametags hanging on the center of each door, each one named after a different *yama* or *niyama*. The *yamas* and *niyamas* comprise the first two limbs on the eight-limbed path of yoga, or Ashtanga yoga, as laid out in Patanjali's *Yoga Sutras* in Book 2 Sutra 29. Patanjali was an ancient sage who wrote down the teachings of yoga in *sutras*, or threads of thought. These are teachings that had been passed down orally through the centuries until they were finally compiled in written form. Over the years, countless yogis have elaborated on the *sutras*, explaining their meaning and the essence of the teachings.

The first two limbs on this path focus on guidelines to walk in this world in a way that develops peace within ourselves and with others. They are spiritual vows, virtues to aspire to. The first limb outlines *yamas*–the restraints, and the second, *niyamas*–the observances. Restraints focus on what to avoid and observances focus on behaviors to practice.

The *yamas* (restraints) are:

o *Ahimsa* (non-violence) – Non-violence, or non-harming, refers both to physical and mental harming of others as well as of our selves. *Ahimsa* means not only refraining from hurting another living thing, like killing a bug or a cow, but also from cultivating hurtful thoughts and feelings, such as through spreading rumors about others or generating anger towards ourselves.

o *Satya* (non-lying) – Truthfulness in deed and thought cleans the mind and heart. *Satya* is the practice of being honest and living honestly.

o *Asteya* (non-stealing) – Non-stealing of material objects as well as other's time or anything of value. Practicing *asteya* is showing respect to others and cultivating a freedom from desires.

o *Brahmacharya* (abstinence) – Abstinence refers to refraining from sexual activity as well as other activities that distract from the spiritual path. *Brahmacharya* is the practice of the discipline needed to stay focused on the path.

o *Aparigraha* (non-greed) – Avoiding greed is a practice in non-attachment. Practicing *aparigraha* leads to no longer desiring more than we need, to no longer being driven by desire.

The *niyamas* (observances) are:

o *Saucha* (purity) – Purity is a cleanliness of mind, body, and spirit.

o *Santosha* (contentment) – Cultivating contentment brings peace in accepting the ups and downs of life with a lack of passion, re-

placing vacillation with steadiness. *Santosha* is the practice of being
ok with whatever happens.

o *Tapas* (self-discipline) – Self-discipline is accepting suffering while
at the same time not causing others to suffer.

o *Svadhyaya* (self-reflection or the study of spiritual texts) – To stay
focused, inspired, and actively engaged in our own spiritual path
by reading spiritual texts, studying with teachers, and studying
ourselves. Writing this book is my own practice of this observance.

o *Isvarapranidhana* (surrender to the Divine) – Finally, surrender
must be practiced. This is possibly the most important, most direct, and fastest way to experience the Divine.

While this is an extremely limited reading of the *yamas* and *niyamas*,
it may still be apparent that these are common principles within most
religions and spiritual paths. Practicing the principles of these first two
limbs prepares the mind and heart to be receptive to the ultimate goal
of yoga–union with the Divine.

At the Institute I was placed in the room called "*Tapas*." Fitting
since *tapas* is the one concept I find most difficult to fully comprehend
and practice. It entails the acceptance of suffering and difficulties as fuel
for burning up the impurities within us. In practicing *tapas* we are supposed to accept suffering in our lives with joy, as suffering increases the
speed with which we become pure and karmically lighter. Suffering can
be felt as a result of acts inflicted upon us by others, as well as by our
own actions and thought patterns. Self-discipline also produces hardships and suffering which lead to joyful rewards. I guess it is a concept
I find hard to believe. It takes great mental self-discipline to find the joy
in suffering–maybe that is where my disconnection lies.

I see the extremities of self-discipline in asceticism, austerity, and
inflicting more suffering upon oneself beyond the suffering life already
offers. I find this path goes against my sense of fun and joy in living.
There is plenty of suffering in each of us and around us. Why aban-

don fun and beauty? Why abandon being human and the beauty of humanity and human expression? If the Divine permeates all, why deny one's self? As a dancer, the concept of *tapas*, as I was attempting to understand it, flew in the face of my joy in movement and my indulgence in beauty.

I danced around my little room in rebellion. I watched my fingers feather out, spreading like wings, twisting into the movement of air, swooping around, opening, closing, rotating, swinging, flexing, holding, letting go. Shapes metamorphosed into thoughts and feelings and into a sensory experience of inexplicable, thoughtless beauty.

Austerity's compatibility with art has remained elusive to me. There are those who embrace suffering in order to portray this suffering in their art as the reality of human existence. Is it necessary? And if so, do we need to fuel the suffering, to go to extremes, to increase the pain to be authentic in art? If we burn up all our impurities, what is there left to express that others can relate to? Then art becomes worship for the Divine, not created for human consumption. It is taken back to the original motivation behind the creation of beauty, as a reflection of the Divine.

The renowned yogi BKS Iyengar explored yoga as art:

> Art uses nature's beauty and transcends it. It is a communication of the feelings of the artist, an expression of inner awakenings and experiences. Its development depends on the need it fulfils and on the vision of the artist. Its purpose is to be aesthetic, uplifting, beautiful, outstanding, educative and clear. Its ultimate goal is divinity, which the artist seeks to transmit to each individual and to society.[4]

Should all art be spiritual in essence then? Or is there no separation from art reflecting the human experience and the divine experience? If we are human and made in the image of the Divine then isn't everything we do and think and feel a reflection of the Divine?

Beauty Is
God, peace
color, warmth, touch
flowers, sunshine, smiles
equality, tranquility, self-esteem
movement, integrity, flexibility, dance
heart rhythm, inner strength, control, calm
balance, clarity, even thinking, openness
Oneness with others and the earth
compassion, health, presence
looking deeply and truly
living Truth.

I braved the thought of attending my first Hatha yoga class at the Institute the evening of my arrival. I dragged my stiff joints and tingly calves down the hallway, through the dining room and through the back door that led to a little patio outside. I clambered up the tight, winding spiral fire escape stairs to the roof, arriving a little befuddled with my black foam mat, ready for yoga class.

There were only two other women; classes tended to be primarily male attended and taught. The Indian women wore full *salwar kamise* (a long tunic over pants) with the ends of their *dupatas* (shawls) either tied around their waists or left draped over their shoulders and constantly adjusted throughout class. The men wore western style sweat pants or slacks, and t-shirts. I was the only westerner. The other teacher trainees would arrive in a few days. Half the class would be foreign, half Indian. This yoga class followed the same routine I had known for years in the US. It was a bit of familiar amidst the unfamiliar. It was comforting.

The warm air and crisp view of the surrounding mountains relaxed my joints and muscles, abused from days of travel. Breathing in the sunset enlivened my heart. Watching the moon watching me in *savasana* (corpse pose) balanced my energy, my sense of being, my place on this little planet.

Lying on my back on the roof at dusk, looking up at the moon and just awakening stars, I felt my body rotating with the Earth, glued to its surface as it hurtled through space–a tiny living being staring into space on the opposite side of the planet than usual.

In the dining room the next day, I met two foreign women who had already been staying at the ashram for a while. Jan and Madalena were returning from their mountain travels and partying in Ooty. Jan was tall and blonde, a centered Swiss woman full of adventure, traveling by herself through India. Madalena was a small, 17-year-old Mexican girl, with almond colored skin and big green eyes.

"Hey did you just arrive?" Madalena bounced up to me.

"Yeah. Did I miss lunch? Can we use the kitchen? I'm still figuring things out." I slowly drawled.

"Sure. I don't know. We ate out. I'll show you where the tea is."

She was moving too fast for me, a vibrating orb of energy.

"Thanks. How about you? How long have you been here?" I asked.

"I've been here for like, a month. I had to get out of here though." She exchanged a knowing glance with Jan. "We just went to Ooty for the weekend. It was so much fun! You have to go."

Madalena skipped subjects like a stone on a pond, "I totally know what you're talking about. It took me a while to adjust. I still don't sleep at the right time. What are you doing here?"

"I'm here for ITT," I replied.

"Me too! Did you do your beginner training in Yogaville?"

"No."

"Oh, I did. When I was 16, I did their summer program. It was so much fun. I love Yogaville!"

We realized we knew some people in common from the ashram in Virginia, shared stories and laughed.

"You just have to get out there and not be afraid. I'll take you out later. Just come find me."

I smiled at this young girl telling me to not be afraid. At 30, I had traveled extensively, lived in many countries, and lived adventurously. Sometimes teachers arrive in our lives in unexpected packages.

Madalena became, not exactly my guide, but a trajectory for me. She was taking a year break to travel and explore her passion for yoga before going to college. She chose India for her year off while her friends went to Europe to travel in luxury and party before university. Her priority was to continue her yoga studies and spiritual journey. She had recently dyed her hair. Its coarse nature and golden hue transformed her into a lion with a wild mane.

Madalena felt a profound connection to Swami Satchidananda during her time at Yogaville, his ashram in Virginia. She felt his presence and received his teachings on a deep inner level. She knew she was on the right path, her path. She knew he was her guru. I wondered how that felt.

How do we know who our guru is? Guru simply means teacher, but in a profound sense on a spiritual level. A guru is someone who has experienced higher levels of consciousness and spends his or her time guiding others along their own path.

I felt Swami Satchidananda's presence for the first time in Mexico at a teacher training program the previous year. His shining eyes smiled out at me from the altar and warmed me. I began to read more of his teachings and I heard his voice through Swami Ramananda, his disciple and our teacher during the program. I welcomed his presence but didn't accept him as more than that. I have never been attracted to having a guru. I've never felt a need. I have God, the divine presence in my life.

Sanjay, a teacher at the Institute in Coimbatore, went through a

rough spiritual period and for a while was convinced that he was literally going to die. He heard Swami Satchidananda speaking on television
about death and suddenly knew he had found his guru. What Swami
Satchidananda taught was comforting and resonated with Sanjay's own
beliefs and feelings. Sanjay found his path. Sanjay was fortunate to have
met Swami Satchidananda in person, which further inspired him on
the path.

I felt Swami Satchidananda in India. His presence would appear
within me here and there, a wordless voice offering guidance. I felt him
laughing–guiding us all to laugh. Life isn't so serious, so heavy, so dire,
so permanent. That was his guidance for me. We are beings of energy,
not stone. Life is movement and change. Let go and be moved. *Let go.*

Laughing is love.
Life isn't so serious.

Madalena began her tutelage of me with cultural cliff notes from her
experiences in India and a reassurance that however I am will be fine,
so long as I follow a few basic rules like always wearing a *dupata*, even
with jeans. Swami Krishnananda instructed that women must wear
three layers covering any sensitive body parts at all times: Your underclothing, pants, and tunic over the bottom, underclothing, tunic, and
dupata over the top. Three layers of defense. It's funny until you have
to dress in that custom every day without respite to protect yourself
from men's inability to control themselves and society's lack of expectation for them to do so, if tempted.

Madalena advised, "You just have to ignore them or confront
them. I was walking down this street once and this guy kept following
me on a bicycle saying awful things to me. He was circling me and then
I'd think he had left but he'd come back. I finally yelled 'Rape!' really
loudly and people came running to see who was doing this. He turned
bright red and ran away with everyone staring at him. You just have to

shame them. Oh, here is the department store. Come on. They have super cute earrings for really cheap."

We went into a six-story shiny emporium of jewelry and clothing. Madalena bought some earrings. I bought a *kamise* that helped me feel a little more comfortable, to blend in ever so slightly. "They even tailor here; it just takes a couple of days." We went to lunch and Madalena assured me I would feel more confident soon, I just needed to be me and not worry about it when people gave judging looks.

I felt out of place and not free to explore. Every little thing was so different. I am a believer in maps and felt lost with no visual guide; I could never get a good sense of where I was, the streets looked so similar. Indian directions were hopeless.

The Institute's yoga teachers were friendly and open to meeting people from different walks of life. I spent the afternoon in engaging political and cultural discussions. The first question I came to find was always, "Why are you here? Why would you want to come to India?"

At first I would answer, "Why not?" That wasn't much of an answer and I knew it. I had no answer. Why do people come to India? I asked, "Don't you want to go to the US?"

"No. Why would I want to leave my beautiful country?"

"To see other cultures, to see the world."

"But we have everything here. And anyway, all you westerners come to us. We are the source for your yoga."

"Do you think yoga is different here?"

"I don't know, but the ashrams are all more expensive now. I wanted to go to the Ashtanga center in Mysore but they don't even have Indian prices anymore."

"Indian prices?"

"They charge westerners western prices and Indians Indian prices."

"But what about the yoga?"

"I don't know. I don't know what yoga is like in America."

"So come to the US and find out!"

"No thanks. You can tell me."

We easily shared and opened ourselves to each other. We sat on the front stairs, or in the dining area, or on the little back patio in different groups learning unexpected things from each other.

During a quiet afternoon break, I swayed slowly on the bench swing on the balcony overlooking a school across the street. I watched the schoolgirls stream home in their blue and white pinafores and shiny thick braids. The adherence to tradition felt at times like a time warp. Some girls peddled home on old-fashioned bicycles adorned with a little bell on the wide handlebars. The rest walked in little groups laughing, carrying their books secured with a leather strap. I could imagine my mother dressed exactly the same 50 years ago. I vaguely remember a photograph of her with two looped braids in a school uniform. Or is that image only in my imagination?

I felt settled in the Institute. It had a peaceful, calm, and clean energy. It was easy to feel at home there. I focused inward. I thought about inner and outer and what true freedom is–feeling free inside while the world outside may cause you to feel or be imprisoned in some way.

In morning meditation, I saw an image of a tigress rolling onto her back in front of me, wanting me to rub her belly. I did and she became my devotee, rubbing against me like a small cat, standing or sitting beside me everywhere. Following me, accompanying me. Something about me felt safe and loving to her. I had no fear of her nature, her ferocity, her wildness. She was no less a tiger, no less wild, but with me she was gentle and loving.

I walked with a tiger beside me as my companion. The feeling was powerful.

4

Training, *prana*, cultural lessons, naked detoxification

Preity was a part of the training program. She had traveled from Udaipur in the North with her husband. Married late by Indian standards, she was my age and a newlywed. She waited for love and found it, along with an extremely controlling and jealous husband. He told her what to wear, how to talk, what to do, and was with her at every moment. They loved each other but the conflict behind her eyes was apparent. He treated her as a daughter; she was ready to be a woman. When she was alone with Madalena and me, she became that woman. When she was with him, she shrank into a little girl.

Preity was new to yoga and insecure about teaching but I saw a clear power in her that had little opportunity to shine.

Though her husband mostly kept her from being alone with any-one, we found our opportunities and had wonderful talks about meditation and the spiritual life. She was an avid practitioner of meditation. Talking with her and Madalena on the back porch of the Institute, thick green plants around us, our legs curled up on plastic chairs, we all went into a deeper place. The air hung thick with inspiration.

One day I went exploring some of the main shopping streets in our area with Preity, her husband, Madalena, and a few others. Across the street, I spied a familiar face.

"Look its Andy Roddick!" I exclaimed. His faded poster hung in a store window reminding me of this small world we inhabit where sports stars of all nationalities are part of a universal popular culture.

"Who's that?" someone asked flatly.

Maybe he wasn't as widely known as I had thought.

We continued on past a camera shop, sweet shops, clothing stores, jewelry stores, a shoe shop, all lining the large avenue. In the center of major intersections, a little stone platform elevated a uniformed policeman who directed traffic with hand gestures and a whistle.

"I've eaten there; they have really good North Indian food. We should go sometime." Madalena pointed to a restaurant and invited Preity for some more familiar food. Preity smiled demurely.

"We eat at the ashram, no need to go outside," Preity's husband answered.

A wrapper of some sort stuck to the bottom of my shoe. I stopped and balanced on one foot looking at the culprit, deciding how to remove it without actually touching it.

Preity exclaimed, "So that's what yoga is for! So you can balance on one foot so easily and clean your shoes." We all laughed.

"You need to study more Preity, you have to catch up. We are going back." Preity's husband abruptly ended our merriment. They left.

I was filled with sadness for her. I wanted to help her and understand her; I wanted to know what to do.

I realized I had thrown myself into a vastly different world with an endless supply of cultural lessons. I listened. I observed. This opportunity to learn was challenging and exactly what I needed for my new focus in life–to engage. I wanted to befriend everyone, to hear about his or her life, to understand the human experience. I drank in their stories, their life experiences, their way of being in the world that was so different from mine.

There was a reason I found the name Mitra. Thich Nhat Hanh translates *maitri* as love or loving kindness with roots in the word *mitra*–"a friend to all." "In Buddhism, the primary meaning of love is friendship."[5] Changing my name was a beginning in my journey to love: to loving myself. I chose a name that was, in itself, an affirmation. Hearing a reference to friendship and love every time someone called my name quietly penetrated my being.

I had been searching for a way to shift away from the negative life patterns I had fallen into over the previous years. The tool for that shift came in the form of a new name. I came across the name Mitra and wrote it down on a list among many others, but they quickly faded. Mitra was my new name and inspiration to emulate this god of the rising and setting sun, and of *prana*.

I had become so focused on my body, in reaction to the disease endometriosis, and so in my head from depression, that I needed to focus on something else, I needed to let go of where the physical and mental pain was coming from. I needed to heal what was in between, the connection that had been disrupted, the balance that had been broken. *Prana* was what was in between.

The incredible power and properties of *prana* are explored in the book *Science of Breath* from a scientific and non-scientific outlook, uniting the rational with the irrational, the quantifiable with the un-quantifiable.

> Fortunately in the East, and in particular among the practitioners of meditation, the relationship between body and mind has been thoroughly explored and found to constitute an intermediate link relating the body and the mind. It has its own properties and its own topography. Moreover, it is explicitly taught that this intermediate level has to do primarily with energy.[6]

Prana is that energy–it is the life force within us, and around us that connects all aspects of our being. When those aspects are out of balance, manipulating *prana* is a way to re-find those connections.

I was at a point in my life where I was focusing on my holistic self, finding the links between body and mind, between heart and soul. The pranic body is that connection, the divine energy resonating without boundaries. The name Mitra called to me. It came to me. It insisted. It was my guide to befriending myself, to healing myself.

At a fire ceremony, on a sacred site in the woods of a California mountain, surrounded by the powerful women of my life, I officially changed my name, burning away the past, burning away the heaviness that had been pressing me down. A new self arose from the flames. I released aspects of my previous form. I chose items that represented those aspects and ceremonially burned them in the flames. I chose a name of energy and allowed that energy to fill my life.

The name molded my life; it led me to immersion in yoga and to become a teacher. It took on that energy itself without my awareness. I didn't make a calculated, reasoned decision to become a yoga teacher. I didn't follow my heart. It just became as if there was no question I was to do anything else.

While browsing through a website, I clicked on a beautiful photograph and was taken to information about a yoga teacher training program. I said to myself, "I need to be there." During my first teacher training, Swami Ramananda offered to give Sanskrit names to anyone who would like a spiritual name. I had already been given mine. It guided me there.

The first day of the yoga teacher training course began at 6am. The course was comprised of half international students, mostly American, and half Indian students, all of whom were active teachers at the Institute. We meditated on small cushions in a big hall under slowly whirring fans. I began by focusing on being surrounded by an orb of blue energy. It turned into a ring of blue flames, my energy swirling around–in protection. I was then awash in blue sky and my body lifted up and back.

The sun arrived while our eyes were closed. We put away the cushions and arranged yoga mats along the hall to begin the morning *asa-na* class, after which we would have a break for breakfast and then the lectures would begin.

The course consisted of a more advanced level of the study of anatomy and physiology, *asanas* (postures), *pranayama* (breath control), meditation techniques, adjusting students, yoga philosophy and science, Ayurveda, and understanding *chakras* and other energetic levels in the structure of our being. The training covered many yoga styles including influences from Iyengar, Vinyasa, and Ashtanga styles, but still retained the elements of the Integral Yoga Hatha practice.

An Integral Yoga class consists of chanting, *asanas, yoga nidra, pranayama*, and meditation. It follows the structure of the eight-limbed path. The first two limbs, *yamas* and *niyamas*, outline practices that nurture a peaceful way of living. The third limb of Ashtanga yoga is *asana*, the physical postures. These movements bring the body, internally and externally, into a state of health and balance, preparing the body to comfortably sit in meditation with no remaining awareness of itself. Fourth is *pranayama*, the practice of controlling the breath and *prana*, or life energy. The breathing practices not only cleanse the body, but they also create a link between the body and the mind, allowing awareness of the body to float away. Fifth is *pratyahara*, where the senses withdraw from outside influences taking one deeper into the self. Controlling the breath and the senses allows one to understand and disassociate from the influences of the body and mind.

The final three limbs are concerned with meditation and reaching *samadhi*, the ultimate realization of the Divine. Enlightenment. Bliss.

The body is purified through *asana* and *pranayama*, the mind through philosophy and meditation, the heart through *bhakti* (devotion) yoga and *karma* (selfless giving) yoga. The eight limbs are not necessarily progressive. One can focus in any order, or on only one intensely, and theoretically reach *samadhi*. Ashtanga yoga is a map for not only reaching *samadhi*, but for living a peaceful and deep life connected with the Divine in everything we do. It is a holistic approach to the health of the mind, body, and soul.

Throughout the training, we learned from each other as teachers in different cultural contexts. One lively discussion erupted around the practice of physically adjusting students in the postures.

In India, it is generally inappropriate for a man to touch a woman. Even married couples do not touch in public. The buses have separate sections so women don't have to be harassed by men close enough to break the rules. In a yoga class, a male teacher would not adjust a female student, and a female teacher would not adjust a male student. Some of the Indian teachers said they would in very non-intimate ways, like moving an arm or hand, with someone they knew well enough. The Indian women were completely uncomfortable with the idea and we discussed at length how to make verbal adjustments.

The other sensitive area is the feet. According to Indian custom you should never touch someone else with your foot; it is an insult, polluting. If you touch their foot with your hand, they become uncomfortable, thinking that you are showing them deference, which is confusing when you are the teacher and they feel they should be touching your feet to show respect. The student bows, "I'm sorry" touching the teacher's feet, apologizing. The teacher protests, "no really, please," not letting the student touch their feet. Confusion ensues.

It was an interesting lesson in body dynamics and interpretations of intimacy. Even expressions of intimacy are a cultural construct.

Inhibitions, body language, areas of the body that are considered polluted, gender dynamics, expressions of friendship–all are constructed and learned behavior. At home not embracing a friend would imply some problem in the friendship. Embracing someone of the opposite sex here would not be a signal of friendship, but of something entirely inappropriate. Seeing this as all a construct throws a light on the decisions we make based on these outer constructions that may not reflect the truth we feel inside.

What is truth? Wars are fought over these cultural constructions. People die, torture, oppress, enslave, revere, segregate, and rejoice in what is decided upon as truth. Structure is necessary in society but deciding on the parameters of that structure inherently leads to conflict, inclusion, and exclusion.

In order to clarify my perceived intentions, I studied how Indian women behaved to minimize being misinterpreted and treated in a disrespectful way. For example, I did not follow the American custom of shaking hands with a man when introduced. I refrained from any physical contact. I also only wore long pants to avoid baring my legs and followed Swami Krishnananda's three-layer rule.

More comfortable now, I explored Coimbatore attracting less attention and able to move more seemlessly through the streets. Taking a break between classes, I went for a walk, rambling randomly until I was suddenly walking through a flower market. The myriad scents masked the piles of garbage and billows of exhaust that surrounded me. I managed to find a coffee shop with café lattes and Indian MTV to write in my journal and feel a little bit of home. In some inexplicable way it felt so normal to be in India.

Swami Arthyananda joined us from the ashram in the US for this training, as well as to stay on to lead the Beginner Teacher Training course that was scheduled for the next month. She was a whisper of a woman in body, with lively eyes, a constant smile, and a love for chatting. Although her hair was gray, she exuded youth.

Many of the Indian teachers and the two Swamis personally knew Swami Satchidananda. I found myself enraptured by stories of their experiences with him. I never missed him before; I never *felt* him before. At the Institute in New York, I had shied away from any seemingly religious aspect to the practice, including following a guru. But in India his presence was palpable and sweet. His eyes smiled inspiration. His presence lives through the words of those who knew him in body.

I felt some kind of emptiness, an apparent loss, engulfing Swami Krishnananda and Swami Arthyananda, a lost look behind their vows. They chose this life immersed in the glow of Swami Satchidananda's love, and have continued to walk this path for four decades. Swami Arthyananda lived closely to Swami Satchidananda for years, acting as his translator when he traveled. Living in such close proximity was, I'm sure, at times very difficult. I sensed a great void in Swami Arthyananda's heart.

Swami Arthyananda told me a story about washing dishes. Swami Satchidananda came in and criticized her. She wasn't washing them properly. He made her do them over and over. She eventually realized, after some exasperation, he was waiting for her to wash them with total awareness, being totally present, to wash the dishes as a practice in meditation. He was teaching her to make every mundane, daily moment a meditation, to find a way to worship in everything we do.

Swami Satchidananda passed on in 2002.

Swami Krishnananda appeared to me as if she had created a sort of cocoon around herself. The only time I saw her open and spread her wings was at Swami Satchidananda's youth home. Her love–like a daughter's love–poured forth there.

These two women monks have lived for decades dedicated to the path of service, observing strict rules with joy. If the final state of *samadhi* has not been reached, full living liberation, in his presence, will it ever?

There must be some doubt that creeps in after so many decades of practice. Once your source of inspiration is no longer there to hold your hand, does the devotion weaken? Do you begin to question some of the choices that are made for you? How to dress–does that really lead to enlightenment? How to eat, how to talk, how to sit, how to love, how to live? When the lessons have been learned, the meaning of each practice mastered, are those practices still necessary? Or are they never mastered? And is mastery really that important?

I accept learning discipline in order to truly find oneself on the deeper level, the level of understanding the separation of ego and the true Self. Learning to let go of all the distractions is important. When we have mastery over our desires, needs, bodies, and minds nothing can influence or obstruct the way within. When the body is healthy we are free from it, we are free to focus inward. When we have cleaned the mirror of the mind, only our pure Self is reflected back at us. When our hearts are pure, only God's love radiates forth. But we can never remove ourselves from being human, imperfectly human. *Imperfect.*

Does true mastery mean mastery over human nature and the natural weaknesses that entails? If overcoming our humanness is impossible, should that be an obstacle to enlightenment? Is *samadhi* only possible with perfection?

If you have dedicated this life to following the path, with patience and diligence, laid out for you by a trusted guru, and enlightenment (or the ultimate *samadhi*) is not attained, then what happens in the next life? What if your next incarnation has no propensity toward a spiritual life? Was it all a waste? Was it all a joy? Is how we live our lives really that important in the end? Is there an end?

At the Institute, I was given the task of keeping the ceremonial flames burning, little vessels on every altar throughout the Institute that should always be alight. This job entailed pinching off the burnt, blackened end of the cotton wicks, filling the little vessels with ghee, and relighting them. I also helped clean the guest rooms and bathrooms for the newly arriving participants. I enjoyed feeling useful. In joy.

I decided to visit the doctor who was giving us lectures on Ayurveda, an ancient Indian medical system. He sat me in his small, sparse office on a hard chair next to his desk, held my wrist, felt my pulse, and asked me many personal questions. He looked in my eyes and at my tongue. He covered every area of my health, and I discussed my particular issues. He instructed me to eat raw fruits and vegetables once a day and to reduce eating meat, as it was making my body work too hard and took away from my body's own ability to heal itself.

He then gave instructions to his mother for the herbal mixture to be added to the massage oil and the particular way she should massage me.

She led me into a square concrete room with a large wooden table at the center and instructed me to undress while she warmed the oil. I stood naked holding my clothes in a bundle in my arms. She gestured for me to put them on a chair and lay on the table. She generously slathered me with the warm herbal oil. The excess oil drained off into deep grooves around the edge of the table but left an exceedingly slippery surface.

As she worked, she moved me around and helped me flip over making sure I didn't slide off the table. Her touch was vigorous, strong, and somewhat painful as she meticulously followed the energetic paths of my body, penetrating all points of blockage, tension, or dysfunction with her strong fingers. These areas were tender and deep. I felt bruised. She worked through every system of the body through the pattern of her movements: lymphatic, digestive, circulatory.

Then she led me to a little bathroom and scrubbed the oil off my body with coarse salt until I was raw. She left me with a bar of soap and a bucket of hot water to clean off. I felt warm and smooth. She brought me a towel and I was led back to my clothes to dress. She smiled caringly as I walked out the door and back into the dusty heat of the street.

So many toxins were released that I felt ill for days as I healed. I had been suffering from shooting pains from my root up into my lower back and along my spine whenever I sat down. I was also fatigued and ended up sleeping through early morning meditation off and on to keep from collapsing. Behind my eyes felt tired. I began sleeping more heavily. I had hoped my visit to the doctor would help.

In meditation the following evening we were asked to visualize the

Divine–I saw the sun. We were then asked to create an imaginary *puja* (ceremonial offering) to that divine image. I tried offering flowers to the sun but they would get burnt. So I offered a mirror in the form of bodies of water–the Earth is covered in water for the sun to look at itself in. The water honors the sun's beauty.

Our days were full of classes, lectures, and practice teaching sessions. Meditation and all of our lectures were held in the large, high-ceilinged, open hall on the ground floor. We sat on a cool tile floor facing a little stage at one end of the hall. At the other end, by the entrance, a small library, an altar with a collection of photos, religious icons, flowers, and a light in tribute to Swami Satchidananda gave the space life. Two side doors led to small gardens outside.

We relished our little bit of free time to explore the city and each other. We discovered some clothing stores, markets, Internet cafes, interesting restaurants, and where to make international calls. Madalena and I went out to a salad place whenever we could for fresh vegetables. Mostly in our free time we sat around talking to the Indian teachers. Madalena had already been living at the Institute for a month before I arrived and had been adopted as a little sister by all the teachers, so through her I was introduced to their world.

One morning I awoke to severe back pain and could barely manage a smile. I decided to take a little alone time and give myself a break from the all white diet offered at the Institute–bread, potatoes, onions, *paneer*, yoghurt. I found a market and bought my own vegetables. I inhaled a carrot like a drug, shaking with desire, my body craving the orange sweetness. Preity's husband was a chef and managed to make the white food delicious, but my body wasn't adjusting to the austerity in ingredients. Again austerity. *Tapas*.

My little moment of heaven was Preity's *masala chai*–boiled down milk, black tea, cardamom, and sugar. Rich, sweet, and flavorful. As I walked by the kitchen, she would motion conspiratorially to me, waving me in to secretly share in a cup. We'd down a shot before class, giggling as the heavenly jolt warmed and quickened our pulse, our little indiscretion at the ashram. Caffeine is a stimulant that should be avoided.

The Institute was greatly respected in the community, and as its guests, we were invited to several local celebrations around the Pongal Festival. This Tamilian festival celebrates the coming harvest and the beginning of spring. The night before, one of the Institute's main benefactors welcomed us all into his family's home to participate in some rituals that are said to predict the prosperity of the coming year. At the entrance to their home, an intricate design was drawn on the earth using colored rice flour. Different patterns represent different symbolism; for example, some invite good fortune into the home, others ask for protection. These designs are common outside homes all year round.

We sat outside in the family's garden, a large dirt yard with trees and some animals, on plastic chairs anticipating the evening. Several speeches were made, some prayers and toasts given, all in Tamil. We would get some intermittent translations or, if lucky, were sitting next to a local who would try to fill us in here and there.

One of the rituals we witnessed involved boiling a large clay pot filled with rice over a wood fire. We watched to see on which side of the pot the white rice froth would overflow, the outcome would predict whether the coming harvest would be fruitful or not. Another ritual involved dragging a sleepy calf over to an area of dirt where they had dug channels, he stomped around until a channel broke and water flowed. I was as sleepy as the calf and understood as little as he did about these proceedings.

After a long night of ceremony, we feasted on blessed food, talked with new people, watched children run and play around us, and tried to keep our eyes open as the night began to fade and dawn approached.

The next morning another friend of the Institute invited us for Pongal breakfast at her home. Again, elaborate dishes were ceremonially prepared and served, and we felt honored to be included. In this more intimate setting, Pongal was explained in more detail by our gracious hosts. They felt proud to share their culture with us and to have Swami Krishnananda come to their home and share it with them.

That afternoon I sat with Leela (an Indian teacher) and Preity and listened to how they felt about "real" India–the modern experience for women–what was different and what wasn't from the traditions and the images of India we have in the West. In India, a woman is defined by her father or her husband. The marriage match she is able to obtain gauges her worth. She needs some education, but not more than her prospective husband. She needs beauty, but not so much as to invite suspicion, jealousy or complications. She must marry young because she cannot be older, more educated, or more professionally successful than her husband. Obedience to the wishes of the dominant male in her life is expected.

Women prefer to marry rather than not because usually their marital life is freer than their life in their father's house. This is traditional. With more women becoming college educated, traveling away from home, and entering the workforce as professionals, these traditional parameters have begun to change.

Both Leela and Preity worked. They were also at the Institute as yoga teachers. One was married. One lived with her parents. Both wanted to push the boundaries of their culture and expectations of them as women. Over the course of time I saw them struggle within the constraints of womanhood. Both went through some kind of identity crisis in the short time I knew them.

Leela was from a wealthy family. She was educated, well traveled, and had a job; she was running a yoga studio in Chennai. She tried to live a yogic lifestyle but at the same time was just 22 years old, had tons of friends and loved to party. She went to clubs, danced, drank, and talked to boys. She fluctuated between lifestyles, finding herself in a personal crisis, trying to meld her vastly different lives to reconcile these discrepancies. She wanted to live up to Swami Krishnananda's expectations, but also wanted to be a modern, independent woman. Much of fulfilling that modern ideal manifests in expressing oneself in a western way, including wearing western clothes and listening to western music. Beyond superficial manifestations, living as a modern Indian means practicing a western attitude about freedom and experimentation in love and relationships outside of marriage.

Leela explored a controversial expression of yoga at a well-known ashram in Pune, where they promote the practice of fully letting go of inhibitions, fully exploring desires, in order to go deeper within your self. When an understanding of the nature of the desires and inhibitions is reached, then letting go of them becomes easy. This ashram is mostly filled with westerners and caters to that western perspective. Leela wanted to quench her curiosity, a curiosity not expected of women.

Preity wanted love, she almost waited too long to marry, and felt so grateful that her husband was willing to marry her. She was already 30 years old. Her parents were getting quite desperate. He wanted her to be a housewife but she wanted to continue to work. As a spiritually focused person and regular practitioner of meditation, she found herself drawn to yoga and wanted to become a teacher. Her husband supported her but insisted on coming with her to the Institute while she did her training. At first I thought it was newlywed enthusiasm, but underneath the love in his eyes lurked possessiveness.

Leela and Preity reflected a common theme I noticed in India among youth–the lure of promised freedom within a rigid system that resists change. Young women are tugged in different directions, wanting a "love match," wanting to dance in a club, wanting to be educated, and wanting to have a job.

While that lifestyle is celebrated in Bollywood, it most definitely is not accepted in traditional everyday life. Almost everyone I met smoked cigarettes, yet if their authority figure (parent, uncle, guru) found out, they would shame their whole family by exhibiting the behavior of a "bad" person.

Bollywood images of romance and love, while considered fantasy, are longed for by the youth, and I think sometimes "love" is manufactured in a desperate attempt to experience something before their marriage arrangement is settled for them. Most young people I spoke with expressed their total ignorance of what love actually is. Instead they performed it.

It was difficult to reconcile the images of Bollywood films with everyday reality. Women smoke, drink, wear mini skirts, have high-level jobs, are ridiculously gorgeous; and have completely supportive and understanding parents no matter what the daughter wants. Life is extreme. Happiness explodes on the screen in huge song and dance numbers with the entire world exalting in the characters' happiness. They fall madly in love with their soul mate and through trials and tribulations, sometimes involving unsupportive family, their love triumphs over all. Or it is forever a tragedy with lovers separated and unhappy for the rest of their lives. This ending supports the notion that rather than traditional values, love should have been obeyed.

What is the message of these films? Are people supposed to emulate these lives, or assume this expression of love is an unreachable fantasy? Is it only for the elite? Is it like reading a comic book–total escapist fantasy? *Fantasy.*

Or is it reflecting changes in societal norms?

The "Richard Gere incident" highlights the extreme difference between onscreen life and offscreen life. He got a little carried away and kissed fellow actor, Sameera Shetty, on the cheek during a charity event. They were both issued with warrants for arrest after a public outcry and protests against her. He, of course, just left the country, but Sameera nearly lost her career and could have been incarcerated for Gere's jestful, yet thoughtless action. What's acceptable on-screen is not a reflection of real life.

In the end, most families are traditional and no matter at what age, the personal desires of the children are meaningless. Bollywood is not real life. Love is not important. Rebellion does occur and some families are more open-minded. Some children decide their own matches and some live on their own without parents or in-laws. But these alternative experiences are still uncommon.

I had a long conversation with Sanjay, another teacher, about movies, music, and relationships–the male perspective. Sanjay was my age, tall, handsome, and dedicated to his yogic practice. We talked as if we had known each other for years. He explained that there was much more flexibility about dating than I had thought and the dream of finding your "soul mate" did exist.

"I want a love match," he confided.

"Really? Isn't that unusual?"

"There are a lot of people now who want love matches, who are more independent from their parents. I'm not speaking for others, I just know for me, I want to be happy, I want to be in love, I want to feel like a child, excited and inspired, I want to be with my soul mate, the one I feel that deep connection with, a spiritual connection."

"Do you want that because you see it in the movies?" I wondered.

"I do want a big love story, but because I feel the desire inside. I know I want to love. I don't want all that drama, but I want a deep love."

I had never really thought about the desire to love as a choice before. I also wanted a deep love, not a fairy tale, nor a melodrama. I wanted my equal, my best friend, my complement.

"How do you balance that desire and the practice of desirelessness in yoga?" I asked him.

"I think they can coexist. I think the love of God and loving a person can be the same thing if it's true love."

I disagreed. "Maybe, but I guess in my experience romantic love is a distraction and causes pain and can take your focus away from what is true."

"Maybe if you meet the right person it's not like that."

"I think that's a dream."

It is not unusual for yoga students to feel a romantic attraction to their teachers. There is something about an authority figure combined with the vulnerability of spiritual opening that creates an attachment for the student. Some teachers have been known to take advantage of that situation or misinterpret feelings. The combination of spiritual practice and romantic feelings can confuse a true understanding of both. Sanjay and I shared personal encounters with this. I felt it was wrong to date a student. He thought it depended on the situation.

He shared one story of a woman who relentlessly flirted with him. She wore see-through yoga pants, which caught the attention of all the men in the class.

"Maybe she was a test to draw attention to the need to focus on the inner and not the outer," I suggested.

"I'm sure *she* was on that level but the others in class I'm sure were not!" We laughed.

"But attraction can create a distracting energy in class for everyone," I countered.

"It's just something you have to find a balance with and remain true to your own energy."

Wherever in the world you travel or live, you find souls in search of love, in search of a compatible soul to meld with. You also find the same confusion and angst, expectations, hopes, and the crash of reality, a cymbal opening your eyes wide in the shock of dashed dreams. The heart stops for a moment, reverberations are felt, and then we regain stasis. Is it such a bad idea to avoid all that with arranged marriages?

Almost two years later at the Integral Yoga Institute in New York, I attended an evening class after work, a class I didn't usually attend. We had a substitute teacher. I had arrived early and was in my own world, stretching and then meditating. When the teacher asked us to come to a seated posture to begin, my eyes closed, I smiled. Without seeing him in body, I recognized my friend Sanjay in spirit and smiled all through class.

At the end of class we greeted each other in disbelief at the coincidence of running into each other half way around the world. He had reconnected with the woman he was in love with before I had met him. They decided to marry and he had just moved to New York, Brooklyn in fact, 10 minutes from where I lived, to be with her. He found what he had dreamed of in love and allowed himself to follow that wherever it led.

The day before graduation a bunch of us ventured out to do a little shopping and have lunch at an elegant restaurant. I bought a cheap film camera, an Olympus Trip (perfect name) for the traveling we would do after the course was finished. On the way back, we all shared an auto rickshaw.

An auto rickshaw is basically a moped fitted with a metal cab with a seat big enough for two in the back. Four of us smooshed together in a space comfortable for two, Swami Arthyananda lay across our laps and the one man in our group shared a tiny seat with the driver, one butt cheek each, holding onto the metal frame of the auto to keep from falling out. This didn't deter the driver, however, from his usual aggressive, high-speed maneuvering through the chaos of Indian traffic. We vacillated between laughing and screaming.

We made it back alive. The evening yoga class was so energizing I couldn't fall asleep. Maybe it was exhilaration at having finished the training. I was up early for another class in the morning and then had a craving for eggs. I left the Institute to quell my need and wandered until I found a restaurant. They of course weren't open yet (I thought we started our days way too early) so I sat on the steps outside until they opened. The employees gave me strange looks out of the corner of their eyes as they swept and set up the tables. I was too tired and hungry to care. I was trying to give my body what it needed.

Satisfied and stimulated by coffee I happily made my way back to the Institute to pack and prepare for our Graduation day of local culture, food, speeches, and a ceremony. The Institute invited artists to teach us some Indian culture including local dance, song, and *mehndi* art. One of the yoga teachers was also a classical Bharatnatyam dancer and gave us a demonstration. Another teacher dyed our hands with intricate *mehndi* designs. These temporary henna tattoos are usually used to decorate a woman's body during her wedding ceremony, but the use has become more popular and widespread. I had my palms beautifully decorated and every time I looked at them, I felt joyful.

For the closing ceremony of our training program, we performed a few funny sketches poking fun at each other and the swamis. Anil, one of the teachers from the Institute, performed a "yoga dance" to music, contorting his body in beautiful ways and demonstrating Iyengar's idea of beauty in perfection of the physical postures. He had spent weeks choreographing his dance and playing with how to move between poses gracefully. His introduction to yoga was Iyengar's *Light on Yoga*, a book outlining the postures, which he had studied ravenously before finding an actual teacher and the Institute.

We received diplomas, applauded each other, and were motivated by our unity. We listened to speeches on the expanse of what yoga encompasses, including an address from the eldest Mataji, an American swami who appeared and disappeared rather mysteriously. I don't know if she had been traveling through India, lived there, or lived anywhere. She seemed ancient and nearly nonexistent.

We then celebrated all faiths, as is the tradition in Integral Yoga: "Paths are many, truth is one." Several of us were chosen to say a prayer representing our religious faith, or all other known or unknown paths. I was chosen to represent the latter. My expression of that was, "Divine love will always inspire the birth of ever more beautiful ways of expressing our appreciation for that love." We lit a multi-tiered brass ghee lamp with each prayer until the shiny metal radiated light and reflected in our eyes.

The Integral Yoga Yantra expresses this unity. A *yantra* is a spiritual symbol that serves as a guide, a representation, an inspiration of peace and the spiritual path. The Integral Yoga Yantra is ringed with lotus petals, each one depicting a religious symbol to indicate the belief "Many Paths, One Truth." Swami Satchidananda worked throughout his life to foster tolerance, respect, and appreciation for all the religious and spiritual paths, which at their heart speak the same truth, yearn for the same connection with the Divine, and are filled with love.

® 7

5

Affirmations, *darshan*, put on your running shoes for the breathtaking

The day after graduation we were joined by new arrivals for the South India tour and all set out on the excursion to Mysore. We formed new bonds in a short time. After the whirlwind tour on the little blue train, the big orange bus, missing the tigers, seeing a palace, up the mountain and down again ,we rested for a few days back at the ashram.

Memories of my grandfather hung heavy in my throat. I found myself unable to digest everything I had been experiencing, unable to clarify all the feelings and images; I was so full I cried just to release the overwhelmingness of it all.

We set off again from Coimbatore and began the next leg of the tour. We stopped at Perur temple, watched an elephant get a bath, made an offering, and were blessed by swamis. We visited a nearby orphanage supported by the Institute, comprised of a cluster of cement block buildings on a small dirt compound. Most of the children had their hair buzzed short to better control lice. They wore donated ill-fitting clothes, mismatched, western and Indian styles, ornate and plain, clean and colorful. They were barefoot and smiling. They performed songs for us in a room painted with rainbows. Someone from our group bought a few pairs of plastic, black-rimmed eyeglasses, the kind with a big nose, fake mustache, and bushy eyebrows. The kids took turns wearing them and laughing at each other.

The woman who ran the orphanage obviously loved every child there. They supported the children even after they turned 18, and saved a small dowry for the girls so they had some prospect of getting married and living a respectable life. When a young pregnant woman comes for help, she stays until she gives birth and for as long as she needs if her family has rejected her from the disgrace. They fulfill the role of family so she can have access to education, work, and/or marriage.

Every year a yoga teacher from the Institute volunteers to accompany the group on the tour, to help with translation and other logistical needs. Raudra was that teacher for us. He was a tall, lanky Tamilian writer, with especially long arms. He began devoting himself to the study of yoga in his forties and enjoyed talking about different philosophical ideas and perspectives. He had a wonderful sense of humor that kept the trip light.

On the bus I noticed Raudra reading a book that he then zealously described to me. He believed strongly in affirmations and practiced believing in what he wanted. He had success in experiencing his desires happening. He enthusiastically loaned me the book.

I immediately turned to the issue that had defined many years of my life, endometriosis, in the hopes of some magic cure. Endometriosis is a disease where a woman's uterine lining grows outside the uterus, on and between the ovaries and surrounding organs, causing pelvic and back pain, chronic fatigue, infertility, and depression. I had surgery a few years prior but still dealt with some physical issues, and so hungrily looked for answers wherever I could find them. In this case, from Louise Hay. Affirmations from *Heal Your Body*:

Endometriosis
Probable cause: Insecurity, disappointment, frustration. Replacing self-love with sugars. Blamers.
New Thought Pattern: I am both powerful and desirable. It's wonderful to be a woman. I love myself and I am fulfilled.[8]

"It's wonderful to be a woman." That was a difficult sentence for me to repeat. To really love being a woman has been difficult in a world that rewards more "masculine" behavior and thought patterns. Growing up with the feminist movement which encouraged women to be equal by acting like men, dressing like men, and working like men, juxtaposed against images of womanliness depicted as hysterical, simplistic, or anti-feminist, I had a confused idea of masculine and feminine, man and woman. The movement definitely encompasses many more theories on womanhood, but mainstream media is powerful and impressionable to a girl growing up in the 1980s in the turbulent backlash against the powerful momentum of the movement.

I am a feminist and I appreciate the freedom to walk through the world with confidence, to wear what I want, to try to get whatever job I want. In exchange, we have given up some of the necessary differences–men and women are different–and those differences should be respected equally. We are also free now to be exploited on whole new levels. Is it wonderful to see a woman becoming successful, powerful, and wealthy by sexualizing herself, using her body as a marketing tool to sell her talent?

I didn't want to be sexually objectified. I didn't want to be defined by my body. I didn't want to be a woman. My body reminded me that I am a woman. I had channeled so much negativity into my body, it was dying, my womb was sick. There is no denying or escaping that my body is part of me, and there should be no desire to deny or escape any part of me. Healing, peace, and acceptance. *Acceptance.*

I think these jumbled ideas of womanhood are now a strength in how we can imagine the possibilities of a future without such strict gender definitions. I see so many alternative lifestyle choices–alternative to what, I'm not sure. In my mind, I never fit into the traditional Christian, patriarchal, capitalist system that makes up much of the American experience. I live in it; I choose to stay in it. I feel freer in the United States as a woman than anywhere else I've ever been. Freedom is choice.

True freedom, maybe, is no longer needing to choose. Just being.

After a long but lush and beautiful drive and losing our way several times through the maze of winding residential streets, our driver successfully delivered us to Swami Bhoomananda Tirtha's ashram. We tumbled out of our bus to a peaceful oasis softly hidden among thick trees on a hilltop overlooking the state of Kerala. The ethereal hush made even our own footsteps difficult to hear.

After removing our shoes and washing our feet at the water spigot outside, we shuffled into the silent meal hall, where the residents served us with radiant smiles and vows of silence. We then convened, cross-legged on cushions, in a bright room lined with windows for a private *darshan* with Swami Bhoomananda, a man known for his ability to communicate spirituality through intellectual levels and with those intellectuals who find it difficult to get out of their heads. He deftly waded through mundane questions, finding the deeper root and intention that had motivated the initial question, taking us to another level of understanding in how to delve into ourselves.

What is *darshan*? Swami Nirviseshananda Tirtha, a disciple of Swami Bhoomananda gives a wonderful description in the introduction to Swami Bhoomananda's book, *Morning Rays*, when he describes being in the Swami's presence and listening to his words.

> The profound words on *sadhana*, like the effulgent morning rays, would often illuminate many a dark corner in the listeners' minds. At other times, like deep whispers from eternity, the words would create a meditative mood in the listeners and take them straight to the taintless sky of Soul-experience.[9]

Darshan is being in the presence of one inspired by the Divine, filled with divine connection and oneness. That person is a divine river;

just being in their presence is cleansing. Their presence inspires the stirring of divine consciousness within.

We are always vibrating, our body is energy and movement, our existence, life is sensed through vibration. Our resonation reflects what is around us. We can choose to put ourselves in situations and around people whose vibration we want to resonate with. The guru is like a pebble dropped into the pool of life, the resulting pulsating waves ripple through us at the same rhythm, moving us the same way he or she moves.

It is important to be aware of which energies we choose to surround ourselves with, and the interplay of vibrations between everyone and everything in our lives. We all affect one another. I believe this is why people are attracted to spiritual and religious services or environments. They want to immerse themselves in the same vibrational frequency.

How do you want to be affected and how do you want to affect others?

The idea of being in the presence of someone whose energy rubs off on us is familiar. We can in a sense, be opened to the ability to receive by being with someone who is actively receiving. This is *darshan*.

Sometimes *darshan* includes a talk or conversation with the swami or guru on the subject of living the spiritual path in our everyday existence or understanding the path or any subject praying on the minds of those present. Sometimes it is sitting in meditation together, and sometimes it is just being in the presence of that person.

Places can have the same effect. Sitting in a place of worship, filled with the vibrations of spiritual feeling, can change our bodies, change our vibration, and bring our state of being into resonance with the energy around us. People find peace in a forest, in a cave, a church, temple, mosque, ashram, or on a surfboard in the ocean.

After the peace of the ashram, we sat through another long bus ride, arrived late in Kochi, the state capital of Kerala, ate quickly at the hotel restaurant and went straight to bed. The next morning we continued south on the bus for endless hours. Finally we were let out on a dirt road near a body of water. Glad to stretch our legs, we weren't sure what was in store for us. We walked down a muddy path and encountered a fat, thatched-roof bamboo houseboat. We stepped aboard and pushed out into the backwaters of Kerala.

Heaven.

Our spirits jumped as we settled luxuriously into the calming rhythm of water gently lapping against the sides of the boat. Rural life floated by. Muscles melted, satisfied smiles appeared in the lovely quiet. We were served a delicious vegetarian lunch, my first encounter with the variety and freshness of Keralan cuisine. We lounged and laughed. A few of the ladies took naps in the quiet bedroom bathed by the soft shafts of light wafting through the wood slatted windows. We took turns laying on the red cushions at the front of the boat, jutting out over the water, feeling like a seabird gliding just above the glistening ripples.

It was over too soon. We reluctantly dragged our feet back onto the bus and headed farther south down the west coast of India. Rice paddies stretched to the horizon. Rivers spilled into the ocean.

We arrived at the resort town of Kovalam to a comfortable hotel painted in bright colors, with sunny open windows, whirring ceiling fans, and verandas facing the ocean. We all split up to explore, shop, get Ayurvedic massages, and go to the beach. Little groups formed, scattered, re-formed, grew and shrank as we ran into each other on the beachfront or among winding backstreets.

On the beach local men and women sold tourist trinkets, wool blankets, and fruit. When we insisted we weren't interested in purchasing their product, they lowered the price. And lowered it, and lowered it again to nearly nothing until finally they left in disgust. About every 10 minutes another vendor came along to repeat the process. We witnessed a feud between two women fruit sellers, each claiming the other was encroaching on her territory. Young Indian men sat around watching western women in bathing suits. A couple of young Army cadets told us about their training as we bounced rhythmically in the calm ocean waves. Swami Krishnananda went into the ocean fully clad, grinning. Only men and western women went into the ocean.

The beach was lined with tourist shops and small restaurants. The German Bakery buzzed with foreigners enjoying the panorama view from the terrace, eating bacon and eggs, espresso, French bread and chocolate cake. After exploring the maze of back streets lined with more shops, tailors, spas, and the poverty of the locals, I felt my usual resistance to the choke of capitalism. The dichotomy between rich and poor, foreign and local, was vast. The entire economy seemed to depend on foreign currency, a relationship tense with disdain for that need.

The next morning Madalena and I decided to find a more secluded, less touristy beach and set out with adventure in our hearts. A dirt road stretched before us along the coast. As we walked, first a barrier of rocks and then a wall rose next to us, blocking our view of the ocean. We kept walking. The dirt road turned into a trail and then a beaten path through heavy brush. We found ourselves in a village. Kids ran up to stare at us and then ran off somewhere to tell their friends. We came upon a group of women making twine. This twine would become the rope used in the fishing industry and sold as the villagers' main financial support. The women showed us how they spun the material that had been pounded by hand for hours. They used a machine to twist the spun lengths together into rope.

We continued on our journey to the point of exhaustion and overheating. We couldn't decide whether to go back the way we came or head inland to find a road and a bus or an auto to take us back to our hotel. We turned another corner on our winding path and grins spread over our weary faces. A paradise greeted us. A long expanse of white sand, deserted but for a few fisherman. On one side, the sea, on the other a peaceful lagoon. We giggled and ran, unable to believe the beauty.

We walked along the softness, listening to the fishermen singing as they hauled in their nets on the beach. Crossing the lagoon was a small canoe, a single boatman with a pole and umbrella. He smiled. He offered to ferry us over to an invisible resort on the other side of the lagoon. We quietly floated across and arranged for him to pick us up later and take us around the waterways for an hour. He dropped us at a stone wall with steps leading up to a heavenly patio of flowers and a small café canopied in colorful fabric where we lunched on fresh salad and juice and felt like royalty drinking in the serenity.

Our boatman reappeared, we climbed back under his umbrella, and floated amidst birds and palm trees in our little boat. Alone and quiet.

Madalena lay on the bottom of the boat looking up at the passing palm fronds and sky above us. I watched the beautiful sea birds and eagles perching in the lush trees. I let the glisten of the placid water mesmerize me until my mind cleared.

I don't remember how we made it back to the hotel, I'm sure we must have found an auto or taxi. It was so inconsequential compared to the journey we had just been on. While members of our group compared their Ayurvedic treatment experiences, we felt refreshed at having avoided the unmemorable tourist traps and instead experienced unforgettable serenity and beauty.

Details were becoming hazy. My eyes felt heavy. Images of softly spinning ceiling fans and my *mehndi* decorated hands bringing a smile to my lips stay with me. I cried often; I think as a deep release or a cleansing. I thought of returning to the peace of Swami Bhoomananda's ashram. Everything felt emotional, challenging, and intense.

The days blurred together and somehow we ended up in Kanyakumari, a city located at the southernmost tip of India. In the morning, we took a ferry ride to the giant statue of the Tamil poet and saint Thiruvalluvar. Like the Statue of Liberty, it stands majestically on its own little rock island. On the next rock over is the Swami Vivekananda Rock Memorial, a tribute to an inspiring man who spent solitary time in meditation on that lonely rock and went on to inspire Indian revolutionaries. We braced against the wind and walked around the little temple complex dedicated to him. We watched high school kids on a field trip take photos and make fun of each other, all clumped together in their school uniforms. The little ferry took us back to shore, rocking to and fro in the turbulent waters.

That evening we visited a Hindu temple that smelled of ghee, flowers, and the mustiness of the centuries. We shuffled in with hundreds of others over dark stone, smooth from millions of bare feet massaging oil into its surfaces, and gave a small offering before being spat out again into the corridor where we had left our shoes.

The group split up at this point and some of us went down to the beach at sunset and watched as locals let the ocean cleanse their feet and hands. There was a memorial to Gandhi jutting out into the water. The beach was strewn with strolling families and friends. Festive lights and jovial vendors hawking colorful souvenirs created a carnivalesque atmosphere. A wave-like sculpture overlooked the sea in memoriam of those who had lost their lives in the 2004 tsunami.

The next morning we watched the sunrise from the roof of our hotel overlooking the powerful convergence of the Indian Ocean, Bay of Bengal, and Arabian Sea. Stunning. We waited for a late arrival of the sun above the mist–then the red orb appeared, turned orange, and finally dripped golden liquid from top to bottom as it rose higher. Sunrise makes us wait while sunset goes quickly. I forgot how energizing and still the early morning could be.

We visited the Gandhi Museum. I felt myself starved for accounts of the struggle against British occupation from the Indian perspective. While the group rushed through the museum, I stopped to feed myself ravenously with information from every placard and stared into the faces in every photo. I struggled with my family heritage, and struggled to accept the reality of cruelty in human beings. Gandhi's museum was a museum of war. It's easy to simplify history, to forget the tremendous cliff that was scaled in the hopes of peace, to silence the pain, the agony endured in war. Gandhi's accomplishment is beyond inspiring. It still feels impossible.

We set out again on our trusty orange bus to Madurai, an ancient city in Central Tamil Nadu that is home to one of the most renowned temples in South India. We settled into a generic hotel. In the evening, I ventured out on my own to the Meenakshi Amman Temple. Several men approached, attempting to convince me to follow them to their rooftop, which offered an incredible view right over the towering temple walls into the heart of the temple. I declined.

There was some sort of special event happening and the temple was packed. I wandered around and dragged my fingers along the temple walls, feeling the ancient carvings until I found the Golden Lotus Tank, a sacred pool of water in the center of the huge temple. I sat for a while on the wide cement steps that ran around the tank, looking at all the other people doing the same thing, and contemplated the energy surrounding me and the meaning of it all. I had a moment of great wonder, looking outside myself, seeing my place in my surroundings, appearing as if I belonged somewhere that felt so foreign. I felt incongruous and natural at the same time. It all felt a bit surreal.

The next morning, I woke up at 5am, which is not natural for my body. I taught our morning yoga class completely disconnected from myself. Even my voice didn't sound like my voice. I mumbled my way through and as soon as it was over, I couldn't remember a word I had said, just like when I used to perform on stage. I felt disconnected from the Divine, disconnected from the practice itself. My voice became routine, my words sounded superficial–full of air and pretend substance.

Packed once again onto the bus, our second home, we set off for Tiruvanamalai. On the way we stopped at an incredible ruined fortress that sprawls for miles on a large plain and up into the nearby rock formations. As we pulled into the dusty dirt road entrance, Swami Krish-nananda told us all to put on our running shoes as we were going to do a running tour. We all laughed. She laced up her Keds.

We congregated at the entrance to the ruined city; she stretched her thighs and calves as she quickly related the basic history of the place. Then, to our surprise, she actually started running. Some of us kept up (I had on sneakers), others gave up, sat in the shade with the monkeys, and found a vendor with cold drinks. Some wandered into the ruins resigned to only receive a fleeting impression of the site and some made it part way up the dusty gold steps of one of the largest ruined structures.

Most of us found secluded walls to crouch behind for a pee before setting off again. This was a major logistical effort throughout the trip, as Indian buses don't have toilets on board. We constantly had to take votes on how many of us needed a stop. When it was either extremely urgent or a majority vote, we would tell the driver to find a spot on the road with cover, which wasn't always easy. Then we'd fan out and do our thing. It would invariably take longer than expected, someone would disappear, and we'd get anxious to get going on the ridiculously long stretches of distance that we covered each day.

6

Arunachala quiets the soul, strolling elephants, kholed eyes, The Mother

We arrived in Tiruvanamalai after nightfall. I requested my own room for just one night and my roommate kindly agreed to share with a few other women. I was overwhelmingly exhausted and needed some space. I didn't join the group for dinner or morning Hatha practice or breakfast. I slept until I woke up. I took a long shower and dressed slowly. Nowhere to run to, no schedule to keep but my own.

Coincidences began to happen more frequently.

In the lobby of our hotel I was about to ask how I could get into town when a woman breezed past me, noticing that her auto rickshaw had just arrived outside. I asked if she was going into town and she invited me along. We chatted. She was from New York and was just going back to do her Yoga Teacher Training course with Swami Ramananda who was also my teacher at my first training. She wouldn't allow me to pay for half the auto. We arrived in the bustling town center and said our goodbyes hoping we would run into each other at the Integral Yoga Institute in New York (and a little over a year later we did, sharing a laugh at how small the world is).

I wandered to the temple. I left my shoes in the pile outside the gates as usual. The stone was intensely hot in the midday sun, burning the soles of my bare feet. I skirted walls for shade. The inner sanctum was closed to non-Hindus. I knew I wasn't in Tiruvanamalai to see another temple, so I reclaimed my shoes and continued my journey.

I asked several water vendors where the path up the mountain began and tried to follow the direction of pointed fingers. The fingers led to a small paved path hidden between cement-block houses. There were no signs indicating if I was going in the right direction until my young guide Uma appeared. I had never said yes before or after to such solicitations, but that day and to her, I did. We introduced ourselves and she said I had a "super name."

We silently climbed, from a narrow path to steep stone steps. I had to call ahead to her many times to stop so I could catch my breath. I looked behind me at the town shrinking far below. She skipped along with her little legs and bare feet on the hot stone. We arrived at a silent shroud of trees covering a small patio. Uma waited outside among the trees while I opened the little gate, took off my shoes, and stood in front of the unassuming opening to a cave. This was the famous sage Sri Ramana Maharshi's cave. I steadied my breath and entered. The cave consisted of two tiny painted rooms–a bright entry with photos, books and biographical information, and the inner cave where Sri Ramana Maharshi had lived, meditated, and remained silent for decades.

I ducked into the shallow inner cave, sat in a dark corner, and closed my eyes. At first, I felt a demon presence, maybe brought in by all the people who had been there before, but it gradually turned into peacefulness. Maybe it was my own demons being calmed. I felt a great healing energy and my palms came together to share their energy with each other. I sat in meditation. I understood the peace that comes from being so removed in a cave, a place of solitude and quiet.

Time didn't exist. I was filled with peace.

Uma reappeared like a spirit guiding me to the next stop along the path. At Skanda Ashram I paid her generously and she was gone as quickly as she had appeared, as if she had jumped in a light skip right into the ether.

Skanda Ashram was built from a cave hidden in a cluster of trees and was where Ramana Maharshi moved when his group of followers began to overwhelm the tiny cave. I was drawn to the little side room adorned only with a photo of Ramana Maharshi's mother. Through his touch, he gave his mother the gift of enlightenment in that room. What a gift to be able to give your mother. I meditated there alone again. The room was filled with life and power.

I explored the main room but it felt heavy to me, unwelcoming, and filled with male energy. I left after only a few minutes, strolling into the small garden, and breathed in the incredible view of the town and valley far below.

The path continued along the entire side of Mount Arunachala. The mountain was alive–every stone, every root, every branch–each rock a spirit, each tree singing. I felt the presence of thousands of pilgrims silently contemplating the Divine. Tears came to my eyes as I encountered that energy of devotion, the life energy of the mountain feeling their presence and being felt in return.

The path ended at the unmarked back gate of the newest Ramanashram. The iron-gate creaked open at my touch and peacocks greeted me as I took off my shoes and let my toes sift through the soft dirt. I wandered the large ashram, floating through its many halls, dorms, and shrines. I spent time in the bookstore stocking up on books unavailable in the US for my mother, who I remembered loved Ramana Maharshi. I came to a courtyard and ran into my fellow travelers. I sat silently for a while listening to them chat. I was in another world. Then we all clambered back on the bus to refresh at the hotel. Sitting on the green lawn outside the rooms, everyone reflected on their day.

Swami Arthyananda mentioned she wanted to go back to town and I asked if I could join her. She wanted to visit the place of Ramana Maharshi's *mahasamadhi*. This is the actual resting place of the body of an enlightened being, someone who has reached the ultimate goal of oneness with the Divine, or *mahasamadhi*.

She asked if I wouldn't mind circumambulating the shrine for a while. I didn't. I followed behind her, my eyes glazed over, just aware of her feet, with which I mindlessly flowed. We circled for a long time. Time didn't exist. I mindfully placed one foot in front of the other in time with her slow rhythm, only aware of that steady movement. Eventually one of us broke the spell and we said a final goodbye to this powerful place.

Afterwards we had dinner together at an ex-pat hang out with checkered tablecloths, a party atmosphere, western food sold by weight, surrounded by western seekers. The sounds of foreign-tongued chatter sharing deep and not so deep experiences filled the big, open, thatched-roof restaurant. We went back to the hotel satiated.

I felt like I had come back into myself that day.

Pondicherry, the once French colony, was the last stop on the tour. We stayed in a beautiful resort just outside of the city, surrounded by an orchard, and within walking distance of the beach. Our eyes widened at the sight of the beckoning swimming pool. The rooms were cool and comfortable. It was a wonderful way to end the exhausting tour. We relaxed into poolside service and had fun exploring the city.

Pondicherry felt split in two, with one section retaining European architecture, French street names, cobblestones, and a healthy ex-pat community, and the other resembling the South Indian cities we had so far encountered, bustling with life, noise, dirt, and color.

We lined up to deposit our shoes across the street from the Sri Aurobindo ashram, entered barefoot through a doorway along the tall white wall, and wandered along a narrow pathway bordered with delicate flowers to the open courtyard. We sat on smooth marble, dotted haphazardly among other quiet beings, and meditated.

As our journey progressed, I felt more and more detached, wanting to let go of the social aspect, the group aspect, and concentrate on my own journey. At some point, I realized the others had left, disappearing with the big orange bus to the Chennai airport. I remember a day when many of us swam in the pool, sun bathed, and ate, lounging in the sun, but that day melds in my mind with a day when only Lucia, Madalena, and I were left, deciding to follow our own path rather than getting back on the bus. We stayed an extra night at the resort to let our muscles melt in the heat and stretch in the clear water.

I wrote in my journal, lost track of time, and wondered about the next segment of my journey. I was anticipating our visit to Auroville and really seeing if that was where I wanted to settle for a little while, if I wanted to participate in the experiment.

Auroville was founded by The Mother. Born Mirra Alfassa in 1878, a French woman of Turkish and Egyptian descent, The Mother met Sri Aurobindo in Pondicherry, at the time still a French colony in the state of Tamil Nadu, recognized him as her spiritual mentor, and moved to India permanently in 1920. She founded the community of Auroville with the desire to create a place in this world where everyone lives harmoniously together guided by a dedication to the Divine. An urn, made from the earth of every continent and country, sits at the foundation of the community's spiritual center, representing both symbolically and literally the formation of the Auroville international community. Here she beautifully describes the mission of Auroville:

> There should be somewhere upon earth a place that
> no nation could claim as its sole property, a place
> where all beings of goodwill, sincere in their aspira-
> tion, could live freely as citizens of the world, obeying
> one single authority, that of the supreme Truth; a place
> of peace, concord, harmony, where all the fighting in-
> stincts of man would be used exclusively to conquer
> the causes of his suffering and misery, to surmount his

weakness and ignorance, to triumph over his limitations and incapacities; a place where the needs of the
spirit and the care for progress would get precedence
over the satisfaction of desires and passions, the seeking for pleasures and material enjoyments.[10]

Auroville was inaugurated in 1968, a fitting time for the western
world with the popularity of the peace movement at its height. The
idea of achieving our greatest humanness, by overcoming our animal
instincts and tendencies, is appealing and feels like a noble pursuit.
But we are animals. We are confronted with that daily message in the
media, in government actions, in wars, in the causes of poverty and
sexual exploitation. A community would have to be united in its commitment to follow the direct individual guidance of the Divine, not the
guidance of a leader.

This was the ideal of Auroville. If everyone was motivated by
truth–which is essentially love, then suffering could be alleviated. Peace
and love, man. Sounds like my hippy parents back in the day and their
former spiritual community that has been forever plagued by human
politics. But that is what I believe, and that is how I try to live my life.
Love and peace.

I was inspired by the intention of the founder and intrigued but
confused by some paradoxical issues that filled me with questions. My
critical mind awoke. Everyone at Auroville was supposed to be productive and giving. You have to know what you have to offer and know
that whatever it may be is valued, respected, and appreciated for its
contribution to the community. Pride in what you offer. Joy in offering. Out of love.

I see trouble brewing when someone professes to be some kind of
intermediary or translator for the Divine and someone else decides to
unquestioningly follow that person's guidance. I believe the truer focus
would be on the guidance provided for followers to experience the
Divine on their own, through prayer and a life lived according to basic

universal principles that are present in most religions as well as spiritual philosophies like yoga.

These are the same principles taught by Jesus. Many Indians believe Jesus received these teachings from enlightened sages and yogic monks during his "missing years" that are unaccounted for in the Bible. Most of Jesus' ideas on how to treat your fellow humans, how to love, and how we all have the Divine within us, are the same as yogic principles on living in peace.

One proponent of the theory that Jesus developed his philosophy from yogic philosophy is Paramahansa Yogananda, an Indian monk who was fascinated by the connections between eastern and western thought and was inspired to come to the west to teach eastern thought using a western framework. He discusses the similarities and connections between Christianity and Yoga in many of his books. In *The Yoga of Jesus* he interprets Jesus' teachings in the Bible from a yogic perspective, that they are rooted in the teachings Jesus received in India, the teachings that awakened his own realization and molded his own divine knowledge.

The spiritual techniques of Jesus' teachings and yogic teachings are complementary and of the same goal–communion with God, the Divine. At times it seems the Church impedes its own teachings. The institution confuses, convolutes, and distracts from the true message, which leads to further divergence and separation. Hierarchies and exclusivity are created, us verses them, right and wrong judged on inclusiveness and surrender to an institution as representative of God. Was this what Jesus taught? To worship an outer representation and interpretation? To look outward rather than inward? Is that where love is?

Love is union, not separation. True love is union with the Divine. Faith and surrender, purity and contentment, compassion and truth lead to knowledge of our own divine selves. We are all one with God. We are all one. There is no separation between the Divine and us. All we have to do is believe and surrender to the inner truth. The Mother describes surrender in this analogy:

> It is as when a drop of water falls into the sea; if it still
> kept there its separate identity, it would remain a little
> drop of water and nothing more, a little drop crushed
> by all the immensity around, because it has not sur-
> rendered. But, surrendering, it unites with the sea and
> participates in the nature and power and vastness of
> the whole sea.[11]

This is yoga.

I do believe in teachers, gurus, and guides who help the individual
discover truth and love in his or her self, who provide a supportive
community for that exploration without judgment or any expectations.
They are the heart of a *sangha*, a group of people dedicated to the
spiritual path who support each other's efforts and, as a group, magnify
the pulse of the heart. Gurus can be an inspiration and take us deeper
into our minds and our hearts. They share the path that led them to
their goal and provide a direction if one is lost. They are in a position
of great trust and I think these positions are unfortunately sometimes
abused or misunderstood.

Yoga is a personal journey. My motivation is to further my own
practice as well as the hope that I might inspire my students to em-
bark upon that personal journey in their own ways. Yoga is a joyful
path and teaching brings me joy. That may be selfish, but I believe by
walking through the world in joy I bring joy to others, or at least I try
to not add to the myriad experiences of negative confrontations and
distractions that surround us. It's easy to lose focus of the positive, and
instead become overwhelmed by negative experiences. For me that
heaviness brought me down into depression.

If I can be a small light, even just to myself, maybe dawn will break
and the sunlit path will be revealed.

Lucia was a Spanish Film Studies professor from Philadelphia with a wiry body of pure muscle and wild, curly brown hair. She was an intellectual who never wanted to be an academic but had become just that. She loved to discuss everything and anything, curious to learn and engage, to be critical and meticulous, which drove Madalena crazy. Separated by twenty years of life, they were an interesting pair of opposites—one driven by the mind, the other by the heart.

Madalena was walking positive energy, smiles, and an openness to life; she possessed that innocent truth of youth. Clear, trusting, and joyful. She spoke deeply as youth often do before they are complicated by life. As children we seem to have an understanding that comes from a clear path to the Divine, and then years later, if possible, we come back to that understanding after clearing ourselves of life's disturbances, the barriers we construct. In between we suffer.

Lucia, Madalena, and I took an obstacle-filled ride in an auto rickshaw into town—our driver encountered traffic, a broken down bus, bricks laid across the road, and finally a herd of cows. The bull tried to ram the front of the rickshaw for getting in its way. He squared up, sized us up, and ran full force into us. We all reacted loudly, making the whole neighborhood stare and laugh. Seeing that we hadn't moved, the bull dropped back and rammed us again. We screamed each time to the delight of those around us. He finally gave up and wandered on, letting us pass.

We made it to one of the Sri Aurobindo Ashram guesthouses and shared a room with a little balcony overlooking the promenade and sea. It was simple, clean and airy, with a hot shower, western toilet, and ceiling fans.

In the early morning, I joined Lucia on the balcony and watched the newly risen sun shining on the ocean, which crashed gently into the rocks protecting the promenade. She had already greeted the day with her sun salutations.

A few exercisers sporting sneakers and round bellies huffed below at a brisk walk.

"Look, there's an elephant!" I said.

Lucia laughed, used to my silly humor by now, and ignored me.

"No, really."

She reluctantly turned around and was surprised to indeed see a temple elephant strolling along the promenade, also taking in a little exercise, watching the ocean waves. The elephant blessed a few coin-toting individuals by raising her trunk and tapping them on the top of the head. Then she spied an ice-cream cart and became determined. Her trunk found the back of the seller who turned around in response to her tap and nearly jumped out of his skin at the expectant customer. He tried shooing her away. She tried digging into his cart with her curious trunk. He flung his arms around in protest. She gave up and with a short trumpet continued to saunter along the seashore, the salt air flapping her ears, the breeze gently tickling her little hairs.

In Pondicherry, we connected with some friends of a friend of Lucia's. They owned an art gallery and invited us to a performance that night. Two European musicians performed a comedic chess game that is difficult to describe. It was so absurd even the performers busted up laughing toward the end. We had a meal with them afterwards at the friend's home. They were a couple on a world tour, in love with each other and in love with classical music.

Through these friends, we were introduced to Vimala, a medical professional who lived at Auroville. She invited us to stay with her at her house. When we arrived by taxi, we were greeted by several huge dogs and noticed what seemed like hundreds of cat eyes peering out at us from unlikely corners. Vimala was a great animal lover. She pulled the dogs back and walked us into her world.

She showed the three of us our shared room, pointing out where to avoid broken furniture, and informed us the toilet in the house wasn't working. The house smelled of mothballs and neglect. She led us outside to a small cement building with a shower and working toilet. She talked incessantly with an energy filled with desperation and loneliness, until she finally paused, leaving us to freshen up and rest.

My mattress was the one on the floor, Lucia and Madalena claimed the beds, and as I dropped my bag onto it a centipede crawled out from underneath. Lucia helped me carry the mattress up to a loft in the room. I took a cold shower, standing basically outside, naked, with little green frogs keeping me company, hopping around my feet. Ants crawled around the toilet. I swatted fat mosquitoes as I shuffled back into the house. I felt like I was attracting all these creepy crawlers.

I noticed immediately that when my attitude and energy changed so did my surrounding environment. My thoughts were critical and petty. I had had trouble changing money, I missed meditation because they changed the location and we didn't make it in time, I couldn't figure out how to book a train ticket. I was getting frustrated rather than accepting things as they were. Small, annoyed reactions became small insects and creatures hovering, jumping, and crawling around me. I was attracting the physical manifestation of how I was feeling.

Vimala filled us in on how to get around Auroville, where to go and how things worked, and shared with us her personal story. I had so many questions. I wanted to know what it was really like living there, why someone would choose to come, and why you would stay–what did people see as the future? Auroville didn't feel like India. It was other. That fascinated me.

Lucia, Madalena, and I rented bicycles and then separated to explore Auroville at our own pace. In the morning, I met a young couple who grew up there. They were critical, but also defensive of Auroville. Yet with all its issues, they still wanted to raise their own children there. They explained how they used an account system to pay for everything–no cash–but there was a monetary system. I wondered where the money came from.

I then had brunch with a Subud couple whom I had emailed from the US and arranged to meet. Susila Budhi Dharma (Subud) is a spiritual organization I had been involved with since I was a child, initially through my parents. Subud was created around a spiritual exercise that provides inner guidance from the power of the Divine. It isn't a religion; one chooses how to worship according to one's own beliefs or religious background. Members live all over the world and always seem interested in meeting one another and sharing experiences. We had a wonderful four-hour brunch filled with great conversation and lovely energy. We also talked about how they thought the initial dream of The Mother was actually manifesting (a popular subject). It was interesting to hear locals' perspectives.

The land of Auroville was red, dry, dusty earth. Over the years, the community had planted tens of thousands of trees and created arable land out of desert. Cattle roamed in small ravines. The roads were unpaved, the main road was fairly flat, but those on the outskirts could hardly be called roads. I tipped over on my bike amidst the bumps and gashes and felt eight years old, laughing at myself like I was the fourth Stooge; glad no one was there to see.

I cycled by beautiful, creative homes and buildings, modern designs, little works of art hidden between trees, little enclaves of human life. It was a much larger community than it first appeared. Visitors were generally shuttled between the tourist center with its shops, and the *matrimandir*, the spiritual hub and heart of Auroville. The silent meditation chamber was a giant gold dome with a skylight at the top that let in a shaft of light directed at a crystal that floods the room with refracted sunlight.

Madalena, Lucia, and I met up at the cafeteria for dinner and shared our adventures from the day. We all really appreciated having a day on our own finally. Lucia even managed to make hotel reservations and book a taxi for when we left. I had as yet seemed incapable of making those kinds of concrete plans.

The next morning we all went to the tourist center to get information on what else to do in Auroville and to look around the shop. Among the locally produced incense, hand-made paper, and loose flowy clothing, Madalena ran into her old friend Jan from the Institute in Coimbatore. Their separate trajectories converged at a single point, randomly coinciding. Is there some larger vibrational connection we make with people that allows for such convergences? Is the world really so small? When we think of someone do we really draw her near?

Madalena left Auroville (and us) to continue her adventures with Jan. Lucia and I stayed, undecided on our own course. Paths crossing and re-crossing. Interconnected beings.

I walked down a dirt path to the Auroville beach, a segregated area, roped off on the sides, for residents only. How can you segregate the ocean? Small herds of young Indian men took turns patrolling the nearly naked women. Naked babies ran around, their fat, white bodies exposed. I was a tourist attraction for a couple of Indian women who wanted a picture with me and asked about my life in general.

The disparity was so drastic out in the open like that–Europeans in bikinis and Speedos laying on towels, wet from a swim or sweat, Indians fully dressed and sitting on the sand or walking, staying away from the ocean. I felt in between cultures, shocked at the blatant disregard for local custom and at the same time wishing I could throw on a bathing suit and go for a swim. I walked up to The Beach Café and they were blaring Bob Dylan. What a trip!

I met Lucia back at Vimala's house in the afternoon. Vimala made tea and we sat on her porch sharing. Vimala opened up about her life. When she married, her French husband convinced her to leave her family and friends and move to Auroville. After two children and 20 years of marriage, he cheated on her with a woman half his age. He left Auroville and he left her. Their children were both at university in the

US. Vimala was alone and unhappy, as unhappy and angry as the day he left five years before.

Lucia and I convinced her to go out to dinner in Pondicherry. We wanted to give her a feast as a thank you for her hospitality. She instantly became excited, insisting that we should also dress up. She provided each of us with a *sari* and dressed up in the one she had worn to her son's high school graduation a few years before.

Lucia and I kohled our eyes, put on dangly earrings, oiled our hair, and posed, imitating the photos young women present to the family of the man they want to marry.

Vimala hired a car for the evening; we drove into Pondicherry, and walked into an elegant restaurant on the promenade. We talked about men, love, and life choices over rich and delicious Indian food. Vimala brimmed with pride and strong beauty.

We walked arm in arm along the promenade after dinner and watched everyone watching us. We listened to the breaking waves, smelled the salt air, and felt the breeze against our skin. We had to wrap the end of our *sari* under an arm so the wind wouldn't whip it off our shoulders. Wearing a *sari* felt soft and light. We rustled back to our waiting car and retired, full from the evening.

The next day Lucia and I said goodbye to Auroville and traveled on a few hours north to the coastal town of Mahabalapuram for one day and night. We found a little basic hotel on a street lined with shops and Internet cafes. Just a handful of streets, the town caters to tourists, foreign and domestic, who come to view unique temples carved into giant boulders.

Together we explored the famous rock formations and countless artisan stalls filled with stone carved gods and goddesses. Millions of god eyes followed us from every corner. We walked in the blistering heat among the giant rocks and carved temples. While the rocks had a heaviness of history, the ubiquitous carvings felt cheap and meaningless in comparison. The masses of identical god representations felt empty. I suppose they are vessels waiting to have meaning imparted to them by their owners.

On a shady wall we sat to catch our breath and cool down, when a young monkey scampered over to us. He had spied my water bottle and became determined to capture it. He wasted no time knocking it out of my hand and we watched curiously as he tried to drag it away. It was nearly full and I'm sure weighed more than his slight body. He pushed and pulled, it rolled down a little hill; he dashed after it. Finally, he hunkered down to try opening the bottle to get at the good stuff inside. I almost wanted to go over and help him. A few adult monkeys felt the same way and he had to push and pull and drag his prize away a few more times. When he managed to crack an opening into the bottle and drink what hadn't spilled, I was happy for his success.

Then he came back and thought he'd have a go at my guidebook. We decided it was a good time to leave.

We split up for the afternoon; I went for a long walk on the beach while Lucia did some last minute shopping and emailing on her last day in India. I unexpectedly ran into Madalena and Jan on the street. We made plans for that evening. I found Lucia online at an Internet shop and told her where to meet us later for a great bon voyage party. We met up for beers at a restaurant on the beach, along with some other friends they had made along the way. We listened to the waves caress the beach, smelled the salt of a foreign sea, and shared stories of our travels in India.

We laughed wildly.

The next morning Lucia took a taxi to Chennai and I took a local bus back to Pondicherry. I couldn't spend one more day talking. I was so happy to finally be on my own, to be quiet and go within myself. To find myself again.

On the bus–moving by so quickly in opposite directions someone will catch your eye–not for a second–but for an impossibly long time. The intensity with which Indians look instantly into your eyes amazed me. It seemed as if you could see deep into each other in the smallest moment. My breath deepened as I watched the film of life fly past the open doorway of the bus: a sea of lotus blossoms, fields of rice, beaches in the distance. Every few moments the horn of the bus squawked as we careened around motorcycles, tractors, and oxen plodding along steadily, pulling their load as their driver tapped them with a stick while he laughed into his mobile phone. The door was just a hole in the side of the bus, I was afraid my suitcase was going to fly out at any moment.

It was my escape. Or, more accurately, it was my new beginning.

After five weeks of group socializing–yoga teacher training course, two weeks on a South India temple tour, then one week traveling with two fellow adventurers–I was done. I had turned mute with a jumbled personality. Dominated by the wills of others I had just attempted to follow the flow. Sometimes we can fall into someone else's flow like a riptide and before we know it we're so far from shore we don't know which way to swim. Drowning isn't an option. So I waited. I let the current take me without external struggle until I found its end and was now swimming in a tangential direction.

The bus stopped for a break. The flies invaded through the glass-less windows while we waited. Bulls meandered past, followed by a herd of goats. I saw the resemblance between goat and human kids–energetic, running here and there, jumping out of line and being herded back into place, getting excited and then complaining about the lack of freedom. On the road again. The driver was flying; we made good time. The road from Mahabalapuram took me back past Auroville and I reminisced about their delicious *kulfi*–frozen, spiced, boiled milk with almond, pistachio, cloves, rose water, cardamom and other rich, complex flavors. I'm sure I imagined even more ingredients than actually existed from the distinct flavors playing together in my mouth.

As we rolled along daydreams of ex-boyfriends pervaded my

mind. I had never been capable of fully letting go of someone I had loved; they always live in me somewhere. I wondered about the modern experience of having many relationships–an endless string of monogamous relationships, some producing children, some lasting decades, some a year or two, some legal unions, some casual. What is the extent to which we are affected in body, mind, heart, and spirit? How has this normalcy affected our concept of love? Of relationships? Of individuality?

Were these thoughts appearing because I was again alone?

Lucia said it was nice being with me because I seemed to be in a monk state–asexual. I had become more like that through the weeks. Being so in the present with all the constant newness and immediateness of everything we did in the program and on the tour, I had little space left for desires. I was unintentionally practicing *brahmacharya* (abstinence); experiencing that letting go, that detachment. The deep needs, wants, and yearnings had nearly disappeared and were therefore not in the energy I put out in the world. I came across as asexual. My needs had become basic.

Now that I was on my own and alone with my thoughts, I began being less present and all kinds of things crept into my mind.

Back in Pondicherry, I stayed at one of the other Sri Aurobindo Ashram hostels, a large cement block building in the middle of the city. My simple room–single bed, ceiling fan, attached bath, no shower–was 100 rupees a night ($2.25) including a meal. For 10 rupees extra, a plastic bucket of hot water appeared outside my door in the early morning for my bucket bath. The ashram's dining hall was large with rows of long tables to be shared by everyone like a cafeteria. My ticket was taken, tray given, and food dispensed–simple rice and dal with a vegetable, bland and nutritious. After eating I was instructed to wash my own metal plate and return it to the kitchen.

I dropped off my shoes with the attendant outside and sought solace at the Sri Aurobindo Ashram. The path inside was bordered with sweet scented flowers. I joined the line of those wanting a moment at the *mahasamadhi* of The Mother, a large marble rectangle low to the ground. Kneeling down and putting my forehead to the stone was like magnets attracting, a force pulled me down to connection. I couldn't move, feeling an energy flowing between us, me and The Mother. I felt her vibration. Pulling away from the cold marble was an effort. *Effort.*

I sat on the ground among the other visitors and easily slipped into meditation. Stillness entered my body and mind. I could have stayed there a long time; I felt a healing energy.

Why did I feel such a connection at that ashram? Was I in India to find this place? Was that my answer?

My only answer at that point was intuition. I was drawn to India from a feeling that it was the right time for me to be there. And that was it. I'm the kind of person that follows such remote and vague draws. I knew I would learn and broaden my mind, perspectives, and experiences of life. But honestly was I also running from something? Searching for some magic answer to the big questions in life? Finding happiness? Being special?

Was I in India following some fantasy of who I thought I was or could be? Could I be free enough here to dare to dream? To open up to my secret locked away desires? Could I admit even to myself the ridiculous dream of becoming a Bollywood star? Its singing, dancing, melodrama, and happy endings delight as pure, distracting entertainment. There were times I needed a break from reality, from my loneliness, from my aloneness, and growing up, musicals filled that void. I acted, sang, and danced my way through school. I wanted to perform living such an adventurous, fun filled life with love and friendship and the ability to freely express feelings. My penchant for fantasy was encouraged. *Fantasy.*

I opened my mind up to allow for any and all thoughts, rational or not, to try to find some guidance. I didn't have any answers. I was on my own and all I could see was myself, truly, in an honest and free way. I knew this was an unusual chance to change my life in any way I wanted to, to go for it. I of course wasn't sure what the "it" was. But being so far from the known did give me a freedom to believe in possibilities.

My father wondered what world I lived in making decisions week to week in a foreign country. Talking to my Dad felt like he was just down the street, even though I was half way around the world. For me, foreign countries didn't feel so foreign. In some respects, everywhere feels the same despite cultural differences. Underlying everything, we are all people trying to find happiness, health, a family, and larger community. How we go about it can vary drastically and sometimes not at all.

So why do westerners go to India to find the answers? What's it all about? The search for the connection with our souls? Surrounded by spirituality, do we believe that somehow it will be infectious?

We want to be infected by spirituality, not have to work at it. To be given a recipe to follow for instant God:

1 part India
1 part purifying illness
1 part delusion
Mix with 1 monsoon.
Let simmer.

Has spirituality been so erased, so removed from western society to warrant such a long, tremendous journey? Or do we only perceive its disappearance? To me spirituality is invisible. It doesn't go anywhere, disappear, or reappear. Our relationship with the Divine is truly only visible within ourselves. It is an inner experience. The inner journey is the most difficult and scary. We prefer to distract ourselves with outer journeys as if that is somehow an easier path.

I went to meditation at the ashram again in the evening. I felt a hand on my shoulder and opened my eyes but there was no one there. I felt a presence next to me. I closed my eyes and started to cry. I don't know who it was but I was deeply moved. When the ending bell rang, I was surprised the time had flown by. I walked in a bit of a daze down to the ocean; I felt the presence accompany me.

The next morning I tried to buy a private bus ticket again but was again told there were no available seats. I found out why–there were only two "ladies only" seats on each bus. I said I would take any seat on the bus; there must be other women traveling. The ticket agent said there were no other unaccompanied women on the bus and he wouldn't sell me a ticket for fear for my safety sitting next to a man. I thanked him for the information and banged my head against the wall. I tried to book a train ticket but all seats were booked a week in advance.

I couldn't figure out how to travel alone. No one could seem to help me with the answer.

I walked to the local bus terminal to find schedules and maps. I asked one attendant who yelled at me for being at the wrong window. I asked at another window and was told I couldn't get a direct bus to where I wanted to go and there weren't any buses that stopped at the major city where I could change buses. It didn't make any sense to me. As I stood in a third line for another twenty minutes next to a rank pool of urine and trying not to engage with the hundredth hungry child who begged me for money, I started to cry.

I stood and cried, indifferent to the stares. This third attendant took pity on me and sold me a ticket all the way to my final destination, stopping in the major city where he assured me I could change to another bus. I had to be at the station at 4am the next morning.

Exhausted and relieved, I went back to my room to recover and pack. I had a destination but still didn't know my path. I closed my eyes, put my forehead on my fat India guidebook, opened it to a random page, and found a list of Bollywood websites and information on cinema. Visions of Bollywood. I knew I wanted to dance.

I visited the Sri Aurobindo Ashram gift shop to find some books before I left. I also bought a little pinky ring with The Mother's symbol on it as a colorful reminder of her path. Her symbol is a rainbow of colors. I think of the beauty of rainbows that my mother always told me was God providing a reminder of the divine in our everyday lives. A beautiful miracle.

The following qualities are represented in The Mother's symbol– each by a different colored petal on a circular flower:

o Sincerity: To be constantly the true flame that burns like an offering.

o Humility: We are nothing in ourselves.

o Gratitude: The whole being offers itself to the Lord in absolute trust.

o Perseverance: The decision to go to the very end.

o Aspiration: We must aspire with all our being for the manifestation to come soon and complete.

o Receptivity: The whole being is aware of the Divine Will and obeys it.

o Progress: The will for progress by the urge towards perfection.

o Courage: When we trust in the Divine Grace we get an unfailing courage.

o Goodness: Good is all that helps the individual and the world to-wards their Divine Fullness.

o Generosity: Gives and gives oneself without bargaining.

o Equality: The Supreme Divine Nature is founded on equality.

o Peace: The Divine is Supreme Peace. Be with the Divine and you will be in peace.

I left the shop and walked back to the ocean, sat on a rock, and looked out into the waves. In my life, I have been mostly lost with moments of peace and comfort. During my depression, I experienced very little of either. Now, I am mostly content and at peace with moments of feeling lost. Even if that isn't completely true, believing so helps me manifest it. That change is due to practicing a healthier relationship with myself. Yoga proposes a healthy lifestyle, not just physically, but mentally and emotionally, and in how we walk through the world. It is a healthy way to see ourselves, to truly know ourselves. Yoga provides a practice in healthy living.

The simplicity of the yogic lifestyle belies the difficulty of simplifying one's life. It is as if we have a natural compunction to create difficulties, to complicate our lives. So this very natural lifestyle becomes unnatural. The thought of such openness instills fear. The thought of no attachments feels empty and creates a feeling of being lost.

To surrender is to lose control, discipline is boring, God is unreachable. In reality, the opposite is true. All those things we fear bring joy and quiet and comfort.

But fear is a powerful inhibitor–it self-perpetuates, growing stronger with each recognition of its existence. Fear closes us off. It creates defensive behaviors and walls that separate us from everyone else. These perceived separations grow, and the experience of our oneness is lost. Ego is enhanced to protect our fragile sensibility, furthering us from the truth, increasing a distorted worldview. Ego is our sense of self as separate. It is a created identity that separates our true Self from the perceived notion of our self. It is the "I" of the outer world.

At a workshop in New York City, Yogi Amrit Desai, the highly respected developer of Kripalu Yoga and teacher to the West since the 1960s, described a change of perspective. He asked, "How long would it take to paint the entire city of New York red?" We imagined a bucket of red paint and a paintbrush and going wall-by-wall, fence-by-fence, sidewalk-by-sidewalk, painting. Lifetimes.

How long would it take for the city to become red if you put on red-lensed glasses? The change would be immediate. Simple.

How we go about change is important. We can struggle forever with the wrong tools, but with the right tools, our eyes open to a new perspective. Recognizing the filters through which we see, the lenses, the ego produced perceptions and removing them takes us deeper into our true selves. An understanding of the ego, of the distortions of the mind, leads to an understanding of our perception of the world. *Perception.*

I had a coffee at Le Space, a rooftop café and wrote in my journal. I stared at my new ring and found my own interpretations of each petal, each quality, each reminder on how to walk on this path.

o Sincerity is lightness. It is not only trust between people, but also possession of a clean spirit.

o Humility is honesty with our selves. Deep honesty is the truth that we are all the same. There is no separation between you and me— you are me and I am you. You and I don't exist.

o Gratitude is worship through surrender.

o Perseverance and receptivity are discipline. It takes practice to become open, open enough to truly surrender.

o Aspiration and progress are determination, setting your intention with purpose.

o Courage is being without fear. Surrender aids in dispelling fear.

o Goodness and Generosity are love and compassion.

o Equality is feeling oneness, knowing oneness, living in the expression of oneness.

o Peace is God.

I flipped through my new books and noticed a section on charity work. The Mother explained how it is essentially egotistical, done to make ourselves feel good, to serve our own spiritual practice, to create a self we want the world to see. I had a hard time reconciling her perspective in my mind although I could see how it wasn't truly selfless. I let myself let go of my original idea to volunteer at an orphanage, to do charity work as my purpose here, and I suddenly felt lighter. I had thought India was supposed to be where I delved into my inner spiritual life and developed my yoga practice, but I felt like I was having a much more difficult time doing that there than I had at home. My enthusiasm and energy in India was coming from the idea of studying Indian dance and experiencing the culture.

I splurged on dinner and ate at Madame Santhé, a French restaurant. The fish dishes were Indian and the music playing was Cuban. Everyone was a tourist, and as I observed more closely, every one of us was reading our Lonely Planet India, sitting alone, one to a table. I stifled a laugh.

It felt like home to be sitting with a guidebook open before me, far from what I knew, far from the recognizable, excited to explore, excited by all the possibilities of life unfolding before me. This feeling of being on the precipice of possibility was familiar and comforting. I was so thankful for the privilege–the privilege of freedom, means, and opportunity–a rare experience in this world. Grateful for my health and my supportive family and friends.

On my own now, in the "travel" portion of my trip, my notions about who I was began bubbling up to the surface. My secret dreams, my suppressed desires, my self-definition. Where had I come from? What made me who I am? What makes me feel like me? What symbols and ideas do I surround myself with? Why does the unfamiliar make me feel at home?

7

***

Sweaty buses, deep aloneness, elephant eyelashes, dance, trusting openness

I was packed and ready to go before 4am, I was at the bus station by 4:20am, and minutes later on my way to Trichy in a packed government bus. I had managed to find a women-only seat at the front of the bus on the aisle where you share your space with all the people leaning into and over you to fit in. Next to the driver, there is an empty area where people put large duffle bags, shopping bags, boxes, and luggage. That's where my little suitcase snugly fit, leaving me free to squeeze into a row unencumbered.

No one seemed bothered by a foreigner on their bus. I wore my new *salwar kamise* from Pondy and was left alone. It was nice to be ignored. I didn't think this was how foreigners traveled.

For the first few hours most people slept. As the hours passed, I watched people get on and off, I watched the sun rise, and I watched India roll by outside the windows. I sweated. I thought. I did a few Sudoku puzzles to the amusement of the women next to me who wanted to know how to play, but I couldn't communicate the rules with hand signals alone. We smiled a lot.

After six hours, we stopped at the major bus station in Trichy. I followed the women to a soaking wet bathroom with holes in the ground for toilets. Then I found my next bus to Kodaikanal and negotiated my way into another seat for the next six hours. It was a long trip that only cost a few dollars. I nearly crossed back over the entire state of Tamil Nadu.

I arrived beleaguered at my hotel, hoping for a hot shower and a little solitude, but was informed they still had to clean my room. Too tired to move, I waited in the lobby and made a plan for the sites I wanted to visit. They rushed to get me into my room and out of the lobby; I made them uncomfortable sitting there alone. I collapsed for the evening. They brought extra blankets and informed me there was no hot water.

Kodaikanal is a hill station that was once a colonialist refuge from the sweltering heat below. Like Ooty, it sits atop hills of tiered tea plants and lush forests. Jan told Madalena and I that somehow Kodai was going to be the only place left standing on Earth after the arrival of the second coming or some kind of world destruction. She thought she'd pilgrimage there along with thousands of others...just in case. I don't know where that story came from, but the predicted date of the end of the world came and went and this little planet that could is still here.

The town seemed to radiate out from a hilly botanical garden that surrounds a large lake where several antiquated boathouses still pre-side. Streets lined with hotels, some little shops and restaurants branch out from this center. Coaker's Walk, a breathtaking path along the mountaintop, provided incredible misty views of the mountains below. I felt as if I were walking in the clouds. Kodaikanal was unusually quiet and felt isolated. A deep loneliness ached in my heart.

I took a long, lovely walk around the lake. I walked through the local market full of dried coconuts, spices, salted fish, butchers chopping chickens, grains, shoes, tomatoes, cilantro, potatoes, jack fruit, flowers—everything I could imagine. It was a sea of colorful people and vibrant energy. I noticed how they wrapped everything in newspaper or recycled papers of some kind, food, goods, gifts, anything. The other hill stations had programs against plastics as well.

I came across a psychiatrist's office with a mural of Jimmy Hendrix painted on the door. I found a Catholic church with a towering statue of Jesus of the Bleeding Heart standing aloft, gazing beyond the cliff, and below into the clouds. I walked by countless chocolate shops and stopped at The Pastry Corner, apparently the place to be on the international map. I encountered only foreign tourists. I ate Tibetan food.

My hotel had no heat–not unusual there. And I rarely had hot water. I was given a pile of wool blankets to stay warm. I layered on most of my clothes, even to sleep in. I sometimes woke up shivering and had to rewrap myself tightly in the blankets like a cocoon. In my little cocoon, I felt even more alone. I wrote in my journal as my companion.

February 11 — I'm trying to walk with God. Otherwise, everything is feeling pointless. I don't know where to go to dance. So I'm rambling. Seeing some Bollywood stuff on TV made me wonder how I imagined that could be me. I don't even speak Hindi. I do feel a little refreshed — walking a lot, clean air, Tibetan chicken noodle soup. I had a hard time getting up this morning. I realized tomorrow is Sunday and then I realized that didn't mean anything.

I met Germans last night, French and Australian today. I miss talking to people because now it seems the Indians I meet want money in exchange for everything. Friendship feels false. Sad.

My horoscope said maybe I should keep the person I'm with as a permanent travel companion — but I'm not with anyone — and I would like to share moments like this. I woke up lonely.

I should stay longer in India and study dance. Going home would be frustrating, disappointing, and I'd have grown little. How to stay here despite my financial situation is the issue. I feel a strength and centeredness thinking about staying and studying.

Alone and within myself I walked to a garden. On the way, I encountered stares and comments, men and boys following me reeking of deprivation of female visuals. I should have been able to handle it. It shouldn't have affected me or changed my felt right to walk the world. But I succumbed, turned back, and hid in my room, chased away from the world into my proper, unseen place. We wouldn't want men to have to do any work, put any effort into the way they walk through the world, learn how to control themselves. No, the world is their toilet. They can piss where they want, whenever they want. Where was my defiant feminist strength?

Lurking deep within was the bloodthirsty fury of the goddess Kali. My anger had been summoned, my desire to embrace chaos in vengeance against an order that demeans me. The anger can become all consuming, the flames destroying all sense of control and clarity, engulfing the complexity of me, of the world, and leaving nothing but angry action.

I removed myself from exposure to this behavior but it was the anger itself that was drawing them to me, instinctual moths caught in a tractor beam to the fatal flame. I had cooled myself so well before. Now negativity was drawn to me like a magnet. I needed to reverse my polarity.

I re-centered in my room alone. I doused the flames with prayer. I cooled the mind with chants. I meditated on joy. I remembered Swami Satchidananda's words:

> If you repeat, "war, war, war," one day you will be at war. Think, "monkey, monkey, monkey," and probably within a week or two you will be jumping here and there. Yes, "As you think, so you become." Knowingly or unknowingly, you imbibe the qualities of the thing named.[12]

I smiled and quelled the flames with breath and joy. *Joy.*

From my expansive window I saw the town and hills awash in

pinks from the sunset, the bright full moon lingered in the pale blue sky, a purple haze topped with rolling white and pink clouds hung just above the mountain peaks. The hills turned shades of blue as the sky turned lavender and the moon became the brightest white. Lights twinkled in the waning light.

In the new day, I found a new energy, an openness that seemed to have people running after me to talk. I shared a lunch table and stories with engineering students over Tibetan ginger chicken; I talked about yoga *asanas* with a jewelry store owner and even showed her some poses to strengthen her back; then the attendants at the bus station were helpful and clear and informative. I met a French freelance cat photographer and not knowing really how to respond repeatedly said, "wow." I walked the entire town and even called my friend Raudra at the Institute for a sweet familiar voice. We always made each other laugh, and I needed a laugh.

February 13 — I had another dream about an ex-love. There was a sad depth. I woke up wondering: If we had stayed together, what would it have felt like? I crave that closeness — not with him — the feeling itself, with someone. It feels so far away. There was a sense of sadness in the dream on both our parts. Did we let go of our greatest love? I guess travel brings out all the issues you're processing and I still obviously process my relationships — probably forever. But I'm still too afraid to actually fully open up when I'm in one.

I cried and then cried some more about another ex and my choices in men and being single again at 30. Alone in India, on my journey.

One of those "I could stay in bed all day" days.

I did sun salutations facing the sun as it rose outside my window. I meditated awash in the colors of dawn. The misty blue mountain peaks still slumbered in the early morning. A hot shower felt amazing after another freezing night.

I contemplated a dream that filled my thoughts as I woke. In my dream, I picked up my suitcase and realized it was only half full. Everything was so light. I knew then that I had left some of my things in different places as I was traveling until I hardly had anything left. I was on my way to go back to find them.

I let go of so much when I left New York. I gave away almost all my possessions: furniture, clothes, television, things; I only kept my grandparents' dressers, my mother's wedding china, my books, and personal items, reminders of my travels, and childhood photos. I put those few precious items in storage. I let go of the baggage of my dark years, my difficult and unfulfilling Master's degree, my disappointments, and began a new life.

I took one small carry-on bag of clothing to India. I had literally lightened my load.

In India I began to dream of my past, to reclaim my past, to process relationships that defined periods of my life. I was sorting through my "baggage." By letting go of so much, I was in an emptier place, which allowed for the room necessary to process what needed to be re-visited. This was one interpretation of my dream.

The other interpretation was more rooted in India. I had encountered so much profundity on a daily basis that it had overwhelmed my ability to absorb the fullness of the experiences. I was now able to begin going back–to gather each one, to take them with me as a part of me, to find a part of me within the experience.

I moved forward on my journey. I found a two-week dance program south of Kochi. I had a week to fill before it began and had an inspiration to go to Thrissur–the cultural heart of Kerala. I finally had a direction.

I checked out of the hotel and walked to the bus station. My bag joined the pile of luggage at the front of the bus and I sat in a ladies-only row at the front. A woman gestured if she could sit next to me; I gestured yes, and she plopped down. Quite ample in the hip region, she then squeezed even closer to me to let her equally ample husband also sit in the row. Her sweaty thigh soaked mine and where to put our elbows became anyone's game. The driver barreled down the hill with its amazing views of cliffs, waterfalls, and the vast stretch of valley below. We stopped for a tea and a "go in the bushes where you can" break—easy for the men of course. It was three hours from Kodai to Palani.

At the bus station in Palani I had an hour before my connection and made sure to get on the bus early. It would be four more hours to my destination of Thrissur. I secured the very first seat on the bus, a single chair next to the window; I was practically sitting next to the driver. I had an unobstructed view and wouldn't have to fight over elbow room or access to air from the window.

The bus was intensely hot as I waited for our departure, but it was better than waiting outside and being barraged with constant requests for money. I had paid an extra five rupees to "reserve" my seat, although I just sat where I wanted because there was no one else on the bus. The government buses were convenient, cheap, and frequent although they were also filthy, loud, and crowded. I had tried to book private buses, but they only seemed to run overnight and drop you off at 2am or some other unreasonable hour for a woman alone. The trains seemed to be fully booked weeks in advance. I still hadn't figured out the best way to travel.

The state of Kerala was alive with culture. A multitude of festivals seemed to be happening continuously in every corner of the state. One amazing advantage to taking a bus was driving through the middle of life, getting a sense of each town, seeing everyday activities and how people interacted with each other.

As we rumbled along the road, I began noticing a few lone walkers wearing orange on the side of the road, then a few more, then a small cluster until the trickle grew into a large mass, a sea of orange.

A long parade of strolling revelers. A few precariously balanced huge headdresses of statuary, flowers, and fabric on their heads. A battery of drummers traveled in a pack, dancing with their feet, pounding with their hands. They seemed unconcerned with traffic or any other impediments along their trajectory. The bus followed alongside for a while and then we were gone. It all seemed very normal.

I noticed many political posters in support of the communist party. I was informed that Kerala had the largest number of democratically elected communist party representatives in its state government. At one point, during a period of huge social change where unemployment rates dropped, perceived general prosperity increased, and quality education was more available, they were the majority. Kerala is the only state with nearly 100% literacy. It is said that Keralans travel throughout the country the most; you can find them working in every state. In fact, the hotel workers in Pondicherry were from Kerala.

The bus wound through villages and fields, up and down rolling hills, around bull carts, past motorcycles carrying entire families, and careened around rumbling trucks, trumpeting its high-pitched horn incessantly. We finally arrived in Thrissur, the heart of Kerala.

I checked in at my hotel, a decent mid-range place with room service, an attached bath with shower and hot water, and a television. I stayed in my room, watched TV and rested. My tooth hurt from clenching my jaw during the raucous bus ride and my head ached from the constant honking. I climbed into my homemade sheet sleeping bag and tried to sleep, but couldn't due to a few restless buzzing mosquitos in my room.

In the morning, I encountered little streaks of blood and many, many bites on my legs. The mosquitos had infiltrated my sleeping bag. I had to start killing. I set out in search of a drug store and bought a portable mosquito killing device that plugs into an electical outlet and emits some kind of chemical. I had seen them before, but now I needed to carry my own. Ah, *ahimsa*.

My first impression of Thrissur was a sense of modernity. The city was cleaner, more organized and structured. There were traffic lights, modern shopfronts, movie theaters, many schools, and public buses everywhere. Unlike other cities where I had observed that pedestrians walked on the side of the street, in the dirt, inches from vehicles, Thissur had actual paved, raised sidewalks. I saw few foreigners.

I found the local tourist office and asked about festivals, especially one I had read about that featured an elephant race. The woman had no idea what I was talking about and gave me a big book of events to sift through. I jotted down some possibilities and thanked her.

I went back to my room and plugged in my device. I took a rest as well. For some reason it was quite exhausting going out, maybe it was the size of the city, the heat, or being on my own and in a state of constant alertness.

I set off again to visit an old palace. It was small and sparse, a lovely building with simple historical exhibits. In each room a new guide greeted me at the door and accompanied me through the room. Each one asked, "What is your good name? From which place are you? What do you do? How do you like Kerala? How long are you staying? At what hotel are you staying?" It is a kind of hospitality and friendliness that is meant with all goodwill but ends up being exhausting for the recipient. To avoid the length of each interrogation, I began skipping through the interesting exhibits more quickly to move on to the next room.

I tried to be polite as I answered the same slew of questions eight times in a row, until I finally escaped out into the garden where I could wander unaccompanied. I walked down the dirt paths in peace, found a little round fountain filled with lily pads, and sat on its edge. There were butterflies everywhere. The canopy of trees kept the garden cool in comparison to the outside world.

I explored the streets on my way back to the hotel and found a stationary shop to buy a new journal and pen, mine had finally ran out of ink from the pages and pages I had written–my only outlet for all of my experiences. I had a late lunch at a *thali* restaurant. Simple, small vegetarian dishes served with a mound of rice. A satisfying, cheap, and quick meal.

I collapsed onto my bed, somehow exhausted again.

Feb 15 — And then there is being stared at on the street, the heat and the noise, the constant hellos from men — it's tiring. I'd definitely come back with a man. I'm trying not to notice or care about the stares but any time I slow down or, heaven forbid, _stop_ to look at something, someone tries to start a conversation, going through the same questions, offering help, or wanting money for something.

Ok — that stuff hasn't happened today, but now I'm defensive from encounters over the past weeks. It does get hard when 90% of people on the street are men. At lunch, the restaurant was filled with all men except for one married woman who was with her son.

All men.

Imagine ALL MEN.

Men everywhere, all the time. And not just a few, but crowds of them hanging around tea stalls, shops, parks, corners, walking, driving motorcycles, hanging off the side of buses, filling restaurants, surrounding *chaat* stands in the street, working on a building, transporting goods on carts, by bull, or on their heads, careening around in auto rickshaws or sleeping in the back seat.

Every job outside of the home appears to be done by a man. Women are not seen or heard. It was claustrophobic.

My presence was a curiosity and apparently had be addressed. I had to answer for my audacity–why was I outside alone without a male family member? I must have had a story and everyone had to hear it for himself.

"Just a Girl" by No Doubt blared in my head.

I watched the sunrise from my window–an orange red orb rising up from the spire of a cathedral. I was too exhausted to keep my eyes open. I awoke again at 11am and forced myself at least to sit up in bed, my head filled with a crowd of dreams. I wasn't sick, just plain tired. The heat was intense and the lack of fresh vegetables seemed to keep me feeling weak. Mostly I was feeling weighed down by not having any fun. Nothing felt fun. I couldn't relax. I was on high alert at all times except in my room. I had been clenching my jaw and had to conscientiously release it whenever I noticed.

I smelled food and suddenly my stomach lurched and pulled me out of bed. I passed a fancy Chinese restaurant and my hunger drew me inside. It was empty and cool. The waiter smiled as I looked at the menu.

"I'll have this," I said pointing to a dish.

"No, that's not possible." He shook his head.

"Oh, ok, what do you recommend?"

"Everything is very good," he assured me.

"Um, then I'll try this one."

"So sorry, that also isn't available," he smiled nodding yes and no at the same time.

"What *do* you have?"

"Anything you like."

I scanned my finger slowly down the menu until he said, "yes, that's very good."

"Ok, that's what I'll have. Thank you."

A few minutes after he disappeared into the kitchen, the power went out. This wasn't unusual. I wrote in my journal in the dark. My waiter reappeared to assure me my food would arrive and not to worry about the power. He asked me questions as if reading from a script.

"Are you traveling alone, miss?"

"No, with friends." I responded. I twinged at the lie but felt it somehow protected me.

"Where are you staying?"

"Not far from here."

"How do you like Kerala?"

"It is very beautiful."

Maybe he felt the need to entertain me to compensate for the lack of soft background music.

"Where are you from?"

"The United States."

"Oh, very good. You have Indian features I see."

"Really?"

"Yes, ma'am. Your meal will be ready now."

He went back to the kitchen and brought me spring rolls, carrot soup, and pepper chicken. In total, there were maybe half a handful of actual vegetables, just cabbage and carrots. I longed for vegetables as though they were my unrequited love.

I studied my map of the city and tried to figure out where the travel agency was in reference to the restaurant. I needed advice on how to travel as a woman with more ease, and I had learned the hard way that booking in advance was vital. I followed the map as best I could but without street names or landmarks, I didn't find the travel agency. It didn't surprise me. A man offered to help–that didn't surprise me either–he took me to the wrong place–again, not a surprise. I thanked him anyway and went on my way.

I passed a movie theater and thought I would avoid the afternoon heat at a matinee. King Kong was playing. I bought a ticket and made my way up the grand red-carpeted stairs to the balcony of the huge theater from a bygone era with gilded banisters, ornate wall decorations, heavy velvet curtains, and chandeliers. There were only three other women. One sat behind me in the balcony with her husband and child, the other two were below with boyfriends. Then there was me. It was quite claustrophobic and a little scary. I relaxed as the movie began until I realized how incredibly violent it seemed, at least in my current state. I was actually glad the projectionist skipped two reels.

After all that testosterone, walking the male dominated street got me angry–angry at being uncomfortable and feeling a little scared. Angry at a world where women don't feel welcome. I headed straight to my hotel; felt light headed, and realized I was continuing my recent habit of clenching my jaw. I lay on my bed and breathed, trying to relax. My muscles were heavy and tired. I let my eyes float closed. I felt totally lost. *Lost*.

What does that really mean? No sense of belonging? No sense of purpose? Expecting existence to be meaningful and failing to find that meaning? Do we expect to be found? We can only find ourselves–our location is inconsequential, our outward existence will not lead us to discovering ourselves. Our physical journeys lead nowhere but around the world.

We may grasp a better understanding of others culturally and socially, of how people interact and create a structure of existence. We may grasp a better understanding of the greater human experience, of the interconnectedness of the world materially. We may see how in essence we are all the same. But none of that necessarily means we will see into our true selves. So we keep searching outwardly for what is too hard to find inwardly.

The hotel manager was worried about me. He wondered if I was eating or sick. Either I was an oddity or he sensed my mixed up energy. He took it upon himself to help and introduced me to a distinguished older gentleman exuding propriety. C.A. Menon called himself the cultural ambassador of Thrissur. He was tremendously concerned that I had the opportunity to experience the richness his city had to offer. He decided to take a personal interest and be my guide. He lent me a copy of the book he had written on the subject.

I had decided that morning to rally, to focus on faith and trust, not fear. I was up for adventure and found a fount of enthusiasm within me again to sip from. My feeling of being lost was part of my inner journey, it didn't have to be part of my outer journey. I let go. Whatever was to come I would enjoy for what it was.

C.A. Menon picked me up on his scooter with the agenda of seeing a dance academy and an elephant procession. I let go of all expectations as we spent the first hour or so running errands. Around lunchtime, we finally pulled into the dance academy just after everything had closed for the hour. Luckily, the theater was open for us to walk through.

Keralan architecture utilizes curves and slatted openings to let in cool air, release hot air, and collect water in inner courtyards. Lofted roofs encircle each courtyard. Light is diffused creating a peaceful atmosphere. The theater was created as a replica of the inner sanctum of a Hindu temple where religious performances are traditionally held.

It was a rare opportunity for a non-Hindu to be in an inner sanctum (albeit a replica) and feel the powerful and spiritual essence from worship through dance. The connection between art and spirituality felt clear. In ancient times the temple dancers danced there. In this theater the dancers were still there, frozen in the stone pillars surrounding the room. I could imagine each woman dancing, using her body to form a beautiful shape, and posing in stillness. So no one would forget, she was immortalized in stone, creating a visual history. I imagined these women coming back to life, dancing off the pillars, and living again to share their movement.

C.A. Menon had another appointment. He had organized for an Israeli couple that had hired him as their guide to meet us at the school. They arrived in their hired car after a long drive, cranky from the heat, jet lag, and loss of their mobile phone. I tried to smooth things over when they also noticed that the school was closed. They had just landed in India a few hours before and hadn't acclimated yet to the flexibility of schedules, subjectiveness of plans, and inaccuracies in time.

C.A. Menon took over and sent me on my way back to Thrissur by bus. No festival, no elephants. As I walked back to the hotel, a bird apparently saw my *salwar kamise* as a bullseye and aimed perfectly to hit it. In my room, I scrubbed the *kamise* in a bucket and hung it out the window to dry. Then there was a knock at the door—I had a call at the front desk. I dressed quickly, rallied again, and ran to the phone. It was C.A. Menon with instructions to take a bus immediately to where he'd be waiting to take me to a *puram* festival. The manager wrote down the name of the town in Malayalam for me to give to the bus conductor. I found the bus stop as instructed, jumped on the first bus, handed the driver the paper, and he waved me on. I stood near him with a question in my eye at each stop. When my stop came, he pointed to me and indicated it was my stop. I smiled my thank you and found myself in a little village surrounded by shops.

I was told to look for Mr. James's shop. Two lovely older gentlemen were in front of a little bookstore holding C.A. Menon's new book as a marker. They explained to me that Menon had had to leave early but put them in charge of my care. They led me behind the main shops to a large open yard filled with onlookers, musicians, and elephants. The women and children stood at the back apart from the men and the ceremony itself. Little girls were dressed up and had their eyes lined with black kohl; even the baby girls were wearing their gold earrings and painted eyes. I stood a bit in front of them with my two male chaperones. The girls didn't run and play with the boys. They held onto their mother's *saris* and watched, still and wide-eyed.

The drumming was mesmerizing and the horns sounded like trumpeting elephants a tribute to the giant pachyderms standing at attention behind them, dressed in gold and garlands of orange and white flowers. Well, not so much at attention as they kept closing their eyes, the one closest to me yawned several times. I imagined we were affectionately blinking at each other, flirting with long eyelashes.

I was shocked by how motionless most people were during the fantastic drumming; I couldn't keep my legs or head still. Subtly I let myself fall into a shallow trance. The finale escalated into insane speeds and rhythms, punctuated by a string of explosions. Puffs of smoke lingered as we followed the procession of musicians and elephants out of the yard.

My gentlemen led me back to the bus, I thanked them, and we

smiled our goodbyes. I was overjoyed on the ride back, truly happy in that moment. Standing next to those giant creatures was awe-inspiring.

I stopped at a Kashmiri restaurant near the hotel for dinner and enjoyed a mango *lassi*, tasty ginger chicken, and Kashmiri *naan*, which was filled with pineapple, nuts, cheese, and *ghee*. I didn't expect the dishes to go well together but was pleasantly surprised. I met a German couple who invited me for a drink, but I was full from the day and went back to my room to shower, write, and enjoy the rare occasion of having a TV to watch.

Even though my motto for the day was, "say yes," I said no. I thought about how I had shifted my attitude, took charge, rid myself of fears and expectations, and really enjoyed the day.

The next morning I decided again to enjoy each moment and try to truly be in the present. I explored the city, finding my way along the streets and through some markets. I found my main destination, a modern Catholic Cathedral. The architecture was European, vaulted ceilings, stained glass, religious murals covering the walls, and at the altar Jesus laying in Mary's arms, off the cross, bleeding, with daggers in his heart.

I shuffled into an empty pew and allowed myself to absorb the energy and calmness. After a while, I noticed that the pews had filled around me and a ceremony was beginning. A young woman sat down next to me. We smiled at each other and she began to chat.

"Do you know the couple?" she asked.

"No, I'm actually a tourist. I just came to see the Cathedral. I should probably leave." I felt a bit awkward.

"Oh, no don't! Where are you from?" She smiled.

We filled each other in on the basics of our lives and she explained that what was happening was a betrothal ceremony. She was a school friend of the woman. It was an arranged marriage–the couple met less than a month before and the wedding was to be in a week. They both worked in Dubai and her friend was pleased with the match because her betrothed had agreed that she could continue working at her job in a bank after they were married.

"I think that's more modern now. She shouldn't have to stop working. My search is on. I can't wait."

"Really?" I was surprised.

"It's better. At home, I have to listen to my parents. With a husband, I can have some independence, especially if we worked in Dubai or something. Away from here. Anyway, I'm already 22. I've already had a boyfriend."

"Is that who you want to marry? Would your parents approve?" I asked.

"Oh no! They wouldn't, but neither would I. We were together for three years but he was studying in another city. I go to college here; I'm getting my degree to do accounting. Anyway, I found out he had another girlfriend in his own college for the last two years! I'm glad my parents never knew."

"I'm sorry, that's terrible."

"No, it's ok. I have to focus on a husband now anyway. He was just a boy."

She filled me in on some of the people in the ceremony–she loved to gossip–and I asked if she wanted to join her friends.

"I hardly know anyone, just some boys from school. I'd rather hang out with you. Oh, you have to come to the lunch after! Please. I don't want to go alone. It'll be so boring."

So we walked over to the celebration hall together and found many things to talk and giggle about. We managed to have a lot of fun together even though we had started out as complete strangers a short hour before.

There was a huge buffet spread in a large private hall filled with tables dressed in white tablecloths and flowers. I ate and ate from huge platters of delicious chicken, beef, fish, *pulao*, salads, *chapati*, mango ice cream, and cake. Family members made speeches from the stage, the couple was adorned with wreaths of flowers, and endless photographs were taken in different family configurations. My new friend translated some of the speeches for me and introduced me to the bride to be and I congratulated her.

The celebration was winding down and as we walked outside my friend said, "Thank you so much for coming. That was fun! Everyone must have thought it was crazy I brought an American. I'll say you were famous or something." We laughed.

"Good luck with your search, I hope you find the perfect match."

"And when you write a book, put me in it."

"I will," I promised.

I gave my friend a hug, she got in an auto to go home, I got in an auto to change money, and we parted with sweet memories of a wonderful random encounter.

I took care of some business, cashed traveler's checks, called Singapore Airlines about changing the date of my ticket, bought water, and then took a siesta back at the hotel in the brutal heat of mid-afternoon. Refreshed, I got ready for the evening dance performance C.A. Menon had suggested I attend.

I set out at dusk. I walked the short distance to the Vadakkunnathan Temple in the center of the city. In the dusty grass park outside, a long, open canopied tent stretched all the way from the road up to the temple, covering a stage and rows and rows of plastic chairs. All the chairs were filled with anxious bodies. The performance was free, open to all. People came and went; chairs were moved. A little girl in front of me, maybe 10 years old, with kohled eyes, arched her back, lifted her chest, and waited with an elegant poise. She definitely was studying Bharatnatyam.

There was a contagious air of excitement around me at the prospect of seeing one of the most famous Bharatnatyam dancers perform live. Dr. Padma Subrahmanyam is legendary not only as a dancer but also for her immense contribution to the art form as a choreographer, musician, and scholar. She is also the director of the highly respected dance school that her father founded.

Important men spoke; the audience was restless. Little girls jumped in and out of their seats in anticipation. The musicians were introduced and took the stage. A woman began to sing. The audience became mesmerized as the rhythm flowed through us and into us.

Bharatnatyam is a traditional dance style of southern India. The basic stance is bent kneed, turned-out feet, arched back, chest and head held high. The movements include rhythmic footwork, pounding the flat foot, ball, or heal on the ground, quick arm movements, many hand positions or *mudras*, and head and eye movements. The expressions have been perfected over centuries, from ancient texts, from the stone figures of dancers on the walls of temples, from oral histories and tradition, a language understood by the audience.

Mudras are hand gestures formed in a particular way to convey, for example, a god, a feeling, a location, or an object. Each hand gesture has many meanings that change by sequencing, by the story being told, or by its combination with other movements and gestures.

Mudras are also energy seals. The hands have many sensitive energy connections with the entire body. When these energy flows are manipulated in certain ways they affect their corresponding areas of the body. This is similar to using pressure points. In yoga, *mudras* can be used to create a sealed energy circuit to intensify the experience of the particular energy that has been cultivated through *asana* or *pranayama* practices. Other *mudras* are used to increase receptivity of the divine energy or to offer one's own energy outward. A common *mudra* is *anjali*, or prayer position, with both palms pressed together, fingertips touching, in front of the heart to show greeting toward and reverence for the Divine.

Padma Subrahmanyam danced with amazing facial expressions and body control. She had a slow, deliberate style of grace and power. Before the finale, her grandniece performed, filled with the energy of youth. She was lively like a playful monkey jumping around the stage, flexible, wiry, and fast. One day she will also embody the wisdom of her aunt and learn to convey the stories with the same depth.

I saw the musicians back at my hotel and told them how much I had enjoyed and been inspired by the music. Hearing I was American, they said they would soon be performing near my hometown Santa Cruz in May. Funny world.

I ate a quick *biryani*, rice with meat and vegetables, a meal in one dish, at the hotel restaurant and then headed back out to the Kathakali performance C.A. Menon had directed me to. He had given me a print out of the story for that evening to read beforehand so I would understand. I met him at the entrance to the theater and he led me to a couple of chairs he had reserved. They began over an hour late.

Menon explained the long introduction to each character, and the purpose of the even longer drum competition, and then finally the story as it began. We realized it was a different story to the one I had prepared for so I was lost and as the hours passed I had to fight my eyes from closing. The performance ran until dawn, but after three hours Menon gave me a ride back to the hotel on his scooter.

I had a full and deeply satisfying day. I thought about how the attitude and energy that you put out into the world reflect what you get back from the world. I learned many lessons in outlook on life in Thrissur. I learned to actively and conscientiously send love out into the world in order to receive love. When I focused on fear and emitted that energy, I received fear in return, or acts motivated by fear. The world opened up to me when I opened to it. I was greeted with such care and generosity. People are naturally giving if we let them be.

8

**Ancestral dreams, limitless world,
dā dum dā, heart rhythm**

Two years before my trip, before I had ever considered visiting India, I had a profound dream, the kind of dream that stays with you always. I wrote it down at the time and looking back at it later I was amazed how prophetic it felt. The memory of the dream filled my mind the next morning as if I had just dreamt it, maybe I had had the same dream again or maybe watching the ancient dance tradition opened a little door in my mind.

> I was at a party in the evening, sitting among a group of people on the soft green earth of a lush bamboo grove. Little white lights twinkled here and there, strung up among the bamboo reeds. It wasn't dark, but it wasn't bright either. The light was distilled in green, surreal. I knew I was in India.
>
> My mother was there talking about Indian dance. She started singing. Then she began dancing with a young woman who I realized was my grandmother, although she didn't look like my grandmother. My mother sat down and my grandmother started to perform, singing and dancing–it was mesmerizing, intoxicatingly beautiful–real. She danced classically, gracefully, telling

a story with her movements. She wasn't young, but she wasn't old.

She danced into the bamboo forest out of our view, a few people followed, uncontrollably drawn to her like wisps of clouds collecting. I must have followed as well, but I don't remember walking. She and I were suddenly alone in a serene private glen surrounded by tall bamboo. Then I was lying on the grass next to her, crying. It was the first time my grandmother had showed any expression of her Indian heritage. I was crying tears of happiness for her new freedom.

She gave me one earring and a blouse she had had since she was a young woman living in India. She was ready to pass it on now.

I knew in the dream that this woman represented an ancestor as well as my grandmother, and I knew I had taken on her burden, a burden that had bound her, and now she was free. There is a thread, a connection between the generations that is not genetic, but ancestral. Our ancestors' pasts live through us, their karma is our karma, and we may relieve their past for them or we might relive their past in our own lives.

My female ancestors had been in India for generations and generations. They lived different cultural realities, some as part of the British Raj, some as high caste Indians, and some as a societal Other, a reality the family doesn't recount or remember. Mostly they were of mixed caste, mixed blood, of different religions, and from different parts of the country. They lived in between culturally identified definitions. In my grandmother's case she lived in transit alongside the newly built railroads as my great grandfather oversaw their construction.

I felt my ancestors were always "other" in India. *Other.*

Their souls inhabited several realities simultaneously, weaving roots above the earth upon which they lived. I joined that family tree rooted to an earth nourished by many countries.

I checked out of the hotel, thanking the manager for being generous with his assistance during my stay, and arrived at the train station to take the noon train south to Arunmula. I was told I couldn't buy a ticket because there was no train at noon. I looked behind the clerk to the printed schedule on the wall and pointed out that there was a noon train. He looked and shook his head yes/no in that particular Indian expression and said, "yes madam, you want the train at noon, of course." And he sold me a ticket.

The third class compartment on the train had open windows, hard wooden benches and open doorways to the outside. The compartment was crowded; I had to maneuver skillfully to get a seat as soon as someone got up to get off at a local stop. The view was unimpeded by glass, the scents of the earth, of life, told a story as we passed.

I traveled a few hours to the tiny town of Arunmula. I realized it wasn't far from the "hugging mama's" ashram and wondered if I could squeeze in a visit. Mata Amritanandamayai, known as Amma, shows her abundant love and compassion for all through not only charity organizations throughout the world but also through embracing everyone and anyone who comes to her in a hug. She was not at her ashram at that time and I had to wait until I was back in New York to be in her presence and receive her healing hug.

I arrived at the town's train station and found an auto to take me to the Cultural Arts Centre. The Centre was a cluster of buildings around the main road; its heart was one main building with offices, a few classrooms, and a few rooms for students. Fanning out from that building, were several houses solely used for student boarding, with kitchens and dining areas, and several thatched structures that served as classrooms for yoga, dance, and Kalaripayattu (Kalari for short).

Kalari is a deadly Keralan martial art taught in a regimented system. Only after eight years or so do you begin to learn how the exercises you have been studying are actual aggressive or defensive movements. To call the training intense is an understatement. The full training includes an understanding of the body, through the study of Ayurveda, and the mind through the study of meditation. Ritual is important and the spiritual is invoked through a short prayer and offering at the beginning and end of class. I just experienced a tiny taste of what a true study of the art entails.

I was given my schedule of private classes and shown to my own little room in a house I shared with four other international students. I settled in, walked around a little to explore, and headed to dinner.

Our meals were presented in a traditional South Indian way on a banana leaf–a base of vibrant green topped with a mountain of Keralan rice (non-sticky, red, large puffy grain) crowned with a crunchy *papadum* and surrounded by vegetables of all colors and tastes. I didn't know the names of most of the dishes, every meal was different. *Thoran*–a dry dish with green beans, coconut and spices. A carrot or beet salad. A coconut green leafy dish. *Kalan* with yams and yellow plantains in a thick yogurt sauce. Pinkish orange potatoes and spicy yellow cabbage with black mustard seeds. *Sambar*–a thin tamarind and potato stew and *dal* were staples at all meals. And sometimes we were treated to *payasam* for dessert (vermicelli pudding with cardamom and cashews). I was ecstatic to eat so many vegetables and fresh salad, the raw vegetables I was supposed to be eating every day.

The meal involved all senses: touching with the hand, mixing the foods together in different combinations with the rice, smelling the varying aromas, seeing the colors jumping next to each other and off the vibrant green backdrop, tasting sweet, sour, salty, and bitter, and hearing the birds and lizards surrounding us in the open patio. A rooster would sometimes crow while scratching and pecking its way through the garden. Indoor and outdoor melded under a palm-thatched roof.

The next morning, I went to the Sivananda style yoga class, one hour of *asanas* in a palapa, a simple open thatched-roof structure. After breakfast I headed to my first formal class. In a small room in the main building, with no furniture other than a simple desk and two chairs, I was introduced to Hindi.

My teacher was a married woman, younger than me, from Mumbai. Her parents matched her with a man who was from this small town. She obviously missed the big city and her family. She taught Hindi at the local elementary school to kindergartners, which is how she taught me—with infinite patience, like I was five years old. She had the most beautiful, lilting, soft voice. I recorded how she spoke so I could practice sounding like her. I loved the language. I loved the idea of having a better understanding of yogic terms. Even though they are in Sanskrit I found a great similarity in the languages, one modern, one ancient.

I studied everyday but eventually hit a wall, my brain seemed incapable of absorbing any more vocabulary. At that moment I felt old. My brain felt dry. Our hour together usually flew by as I was so concentrated and completely focused on the task at hand, immersed in another linguistic world. I was invariably startled when the next student knocked on the door—only then would I remember where I was.

Bharatnatyam class was held in another, smaller palapa with some kind of black rubbery material serving as a floor. Trees, shrubs, and garbage surrounded us on three sides. During dance class sometimes the wafting smoke of the burning garbage would be an excuse for a short break depending on the direction of the wind. If we weren't both choking I had to keep dancing.

My teacher was a young single woman living with her parents again after studying elsewhere for several years. She didn't want a local match but instead wanted to live somewhere a little more exciting than this small village, somewhere she could continue to dance. During our "smoke breaks" we'd talk about life and love. I'd sit on the floor and nurse my hurting feet; she'd sit on her little wood stool. As soon as the smoke passed or began wafting in another direction, she'd bang her stick on the stool and command, "Get up!"

Her teaching style was strict, she beat her wood stick against the little stool to keep time and keep me in line. She sounded like a drill sergeant. She would make fun of her adult students for hardly being able to make it through the basic exercises while her child students could go straight through. She kept a stern expression and sharp voice, calling out each exercise, chastising when I didn't remember what the next one was. But then I would make her laugh and she transformed back into a girl.

I loved the movements and practiced for hours every day. I tried incorporating the eye movements I learned with the legs, arms, and hands. I memorized all the *mudras*, which she tested me on everyday. While this dance form was quite difficult, it felt natural at the same time.

She taught movement through sound. I learned what steps her sound effects translated into not only by the sound itself but also by the order, her singsong melody, and staccato or legato emphasis. She used all these to emphasize right or left leg, the direction of the step, the speed, and repetition of the footwork, all this while concentrating on the arms. Sometimes she just marked time while I had to remember on my own what came next in the choreography.

Da dā dum	Ball flat flat–right left right
Dā dum dā	Ball flat flat–left right left
Dā kha ta kee dum	Heel flat ball flat flat–right left right left right
Dā dum	Flat flat–left right
Dā kha ta kee dā	Heel flat ball flat flat–left right left right left
Da dā…	Flat flat–right left…

The sound of the rhythm like a heartbeat, footsteps falling on a path, words of a story unfolding.

I loved the little room with windows on two sides that was all mine. The mosquito net over the bed kept it hot at night and only at the end of the program did I realize there really weren't any mosquitoes and I could have slept without it the whole time. We had a cold shower but they did provide an electric coil and a bucket if we wanted to heat the water to boiling. Putting a metal coil plugged into an electrical outlet into water went against all things I had been taught as a child. It was like a large plastic electric teakettle. I warily tried it a few times and survived, but after hours of sweating in class and out in the 90-degree weather, cold showers were welcome.

In between my classes I would study, eat, or sleep. Ravenous before every meal, I would arrive a bit early in anticipation. The others would trickle in and we would share our lives for this brief time. Ana, a Spanish woman who lived in London, shared with me some traumatizing love stories of abuse and low self-worth. She had escaped from her physically abusive husband, fled to India and begun the path of changing her life in order to break the pattern of abuse. She was studying Ayurveda and yoga. We talked about how the yogic path helps to enhance self-love, balance, and peace within.

Talking about the spiritual and philosophical aspects of yoga inspired me. Helping someone energized me. Ana said she thought I was a healer. I didn't react to her statement at the time. But it made me happy to see the change in someone. The dark cloud lifted, a lightness and a smile shone through.

Later that night, alone in my room, thinking about being a healer affected me deeply. At times I feel I have some gift that should be trained or channeled or mentored. It is something I don't know what to do with and leads me to see different paths for my life. I have thought about finding someone to guide me to help me figure out how to use this or to show me what it is. I think about the responsibility that goes along with healing and what I'm capable of handling. I'm scared to develop it and at the same time scared to let it disappear, like I would be throwing something important away, a gift given to me, squandered.

After a week, fatigue was beginning to creep in. I hadn't slept well with all the new information taking over my brain and my body, not to mention the constant nocturnal crying of the puppy living across the street. One morning I fell back asleep after my alarm went off. I dreamt I was doing a kung fu demonstration for some kids outside. This old guy and I were really going at it. A crowd formed, awed by our skill and aggressiveness. It was like a movie.

That evening I called the Singapore Air travel office to finalize changing my ticket. They had to research something so I was told to call back. I wanted to make plans, to figure out what I could do after the program ended.

It's difficult to explain the physical anguish I felt at the thought of leaving India. I literally became ill at the prospect. I felt like I would be killing a part of myself or I'd knowingly throw myself into despair. It was the paradox of India that while much of my experience was difficult, I wouldn't have wanted to be anywhere else. I just knew I couldn't leave.

India was a ceaseless string of lessons in contradiction, hypocrisy, and ambiguity. The coexistence of opposites was a given and I began to learn to accept that coexistence within myself as well. Human beings seem to be infinitely complicated creatures who are infinitely attempting to deny their complexities. If peace is the goal then acceptance seems to be the only solution.

While I roamed somewhat randomly, I felt at home. While I felt unable to move freely, I felt at home. I wondered what on earth I was doing half way around the world, by myself, with no purpose, while at the same time not questioning my natural place there. Life is what it is, why attempt to author its path?

Maybe when we focus on what we think are our limits, our boundaries, we begin to try to put those same boundaries on our understanding of the world. The universe is immeasurable yet we insist on inventing systems to create parameters we can understand, parameters that mirror those we feel we must embody. We focus on you and me, them and us, my space and your space, the difference between your body and my body, two separate individuals of separate flesh and blood and bone that resemble one another but are not the same.

At the same time we are two beings of the same divine stuff, a small part of a whole that is one.

Both realities are true because reality is our understanding of things. An understanding grounded, as it should be, in our humanness. Humans have limitations.

I called my mother for some support and she understood how I felt about leaving India. She encouraged me to look for some kind of work to try to stay.

That night I had a dream that I was at some kind of program–like I was. It was Friday–as it was. I was sitting around watching TV and thought, "why am I not going to New York? It's only a train ride away. I can visit friends!" I ran to my room to pack and accidentally walked right on top of someone's bead project on the hall floor. I said I would help her make another ceremonial beaded banner. I tried to call a friend on my cell phone but realized I was calling from India. Then I was already on my way back to the train station in New York when I ran into someone from the Centre and we decided to share a rickshaw rather than take the train back to the Centre.

Memories converged. Images soaked up and blurred together. The scattering beads, the sound of each bead ricocheting in slow motion on the hard floor, stays with me still. Why? On an empty concrete floor someone had laid out bead by bead some kind of religious banner to be sewn together. I slipped on the beads and they scattered everywhere, the design destroyed, all that time futile. I stopped in a timeless moment of regret and wonder while at the same time kept running to the door, apologizing, and promising to make up the work when I returned. It was like nearly completing a puzzle, only to have it taken apart, and being left in uncertainty–will I have enough energy to start all over again?

In the morning, I did yoga by myself in my room and felt balanced and strong. I was fatigued but now in a good way from satisfying exertion. After Hindi, instead of studying, I took a break and walked to the next town over. Kozhencherry was a typical little town. It had a beautiful church and there was a big Christian Fair going on with tons of people milling around craft booths, food vendors, and performing musicians. I started getting the stares again; I was enjoying a little break from that at the Centre.

I bought a box of assorted Indian sweets to share with everyone at tea time. They were well appreciated. I checked email in the main building but there was nothing.

I decided to visit an astrologer, not an uncommon activity in India. Astrologers help one understand life changes and decisions; they are consulted in most major events, especially in marital arrangements. I walked to his little office, crammed full of books, papers, and dust and was greeted with a smile. After clearing a chair for me to sit, this elderly gentleman immediately asked for my birth details and went to work. He created my astrological chart and explained all the points. It was quite interesting and actually reflected how I had seen my life up to that point. Love was not on the chart apparently so I asked. He responded that marriage was imminent. I think his response was culturally skewed; a single 30-year-old woman is a sad affair in India, a situation that must be rectified as soon as possible.

I walked back to the Centre in the afternoon when the world was tinged in tangerine; I felt like I was walking in a painting or underwater. I spent the evening thinking over my life and writing in my journal.

Feb 26 — I don't know my direction I guess. I'm strong enough not to get depressed right now but I still feel lost. I'm just very afraid that while everything is lined up for my achievement I'll make decisions that end up like the last 10 years and I'll have wasted opportunities and again be nowhere. I have to work on believing in my values, on knowing that I'm on the right path, that I'm contributing meaningfully, and am successful on all levels including financial.

If I am to be recognized for my hard work in this decade then I am failing — I feel I haven't put any hard work into getting to a place to be recognized. That's where my blues are coming from.

Dance has always been my joy. I started ballet in elementary school, continued with modern, jazz, a little tap, and belly dance until college, where I was exposed to West African dance, Afro-Caribbean dance, Salsa, and Flamenco, the latter I continued to study for years. Dance is my connection to the Divine. It is a scary form of freedom and expression because of the vulnerabilities it exposes.

While dance was my joy I was always too afraid to admit to my dream of becoming a professional dancer. I was afraid of failure, of success, of rejection, of letting anyone in, letting anyone know my hopes and dreams. Summer dance camp was my freedom, a profound happiness I rarely felt and that's all I wanted to do–dance every day, all day, in the sun. But I gave up on myself–or I suppose I never believed in myself in the first place. I allowed my fears to shape my life.

The days went by so quickly. I was given a compliment in dance class on my last day. A woman touring the Centre watched a while and clapped at the end of my little performance. She was so impressed at what I had learned in only two weeks. My teacher agreed that I was doing well. We finished class with some new challenging steps, just for fun. We laughed a lot. I would miss her class.

There was so much to learn. I worked hard—studying, practicing, trying—I got as much out of my time there as I could. It was great to stop traveling, to not have to think about meals, transportation, safety, loneliness.

I finally was successful in extending my plane ticket and securing a volunteer position in Bangalore through a contact. I had the next month worked out at least. I was a little sad to leave the Centre, but it was expensive and I had to move on and figure out how to earn a little money in order to stay in India. I would especially miss the food.

I thought I had managed to gain weight from scarfing down all the delicious food, but self-image is an interesting thing. After only two weeks of daily dance, yoga, sweating, and healthy food I must have lost between 5 and 10 pounds. Heaviness is not always physical. Physically I felt stronger and more exhausted, like there was more of me. I felt larger. Emotionally I felt heavier, I wore loneliness like a dense mantle, a thick layer between my heart and the rest of me.

9

***

ETA unknown, location TBD, locks and keys, Ooty disruption

I chatted away with another student from the Centre, laughing and sharing stories as we rode the train to Kochi. Although only a small accomplishment, I felt monumentally excited being able to read the train station names in Hindi. I planned to spend a few days in the capital of Kerala before taking a train back to Coimbatore to meet up with my old friend Madalena. She wanted to take me to Ooty. We had made a very loose plan.

My trusty guide book recommended the Kashi Garden Art Café for a good cup of coffee and I set off on a quest as soon as I had dropped my bags at a hotel. I took my journal. I stopped at an ATM to stock up on cash but an error message said, "Invalid user." I started to panic. How was that possible? I barely had any cash on me. But enough for coffee–priorities. I continued on my way.

Mar 4 — I found heaven. Unsweetened delicious creamy cold latte and chocolate cake. Of course there are mostly foreigners here. It's so comforting to hear some old American 60s music right now, sometimes a little bit of the familiar is huge. A lump came to my throat. And a slight knot in my stomach as I try to relax, write my thoughts, and think — but it's hard with the tension from my choices and the limited time and figuring out how to get things sorted.

*My money situation is so tight — and how many days could I
hang out with Madalena and her young friends? Although I'd be
more than happy to go out with locals and have fun.*

During the whirlwind tour with the Institute I had little time to
explore Kochi; I knew I wanted to return to this culturally rich city; I
was intrigued by its history and diversity. The city layout was planned,
the older areas had their cobblestone streets and straight order, the
new areas were winding and less obvious. I got lost looking for an old
palace. I asked everyone I passed and followed many pointed fingers,
winding through neighborhoods, until I finally arrived at a somewhat
dilapidated old building.

The entrance fee was nominal, the palace unassuming, but inside
were gorgeous mural paintings, so detailed and active. Wall after wall
told an epic story. There was little explanation, especially in English.
Many of the walls had been damaged but the sections that remained
told a story with a warrior monkey, Hanuman, I'm sure, which led
me to believe the epic was the Ramayana, an ancient poem revered by
Hindus. There was hardly anyone there and apparently little need for
security. I had the luxury to stand inches away and stare uninterrupted
at the intricacies of the art.

I meandered back to my hotel and met the owner. He offered me
a newspaper and shared some local history and politics with me, filling
me in on what made the city tick. I had already discovered the city was
made up of various sections that felt quite different from each other in
the local population and types of businesses. Tourists mostly appeared
relegated to the more historical old town.

I excused myself, went back to my room, and took a cold shower.
I had a rash and probably a slight fever. Prickly, itchy, hot. A few others
at the Centre had the same symptoms. One tried a doctor and a slew
of treatments, another just stopped complaining and ignored it. They

both got over it. I decided to wait it out. Most likely it was from the constant sweating.

I headed back out in the evening for dinner and a stroll. I went to a restaurant by the beach and enjoyed their fresh caught fish. A little cat, smelling my delicious meal, jumped into my lap. I gently pushed her down, she tried again, and then finally just jumped right onto my table! Three little kittens were curled up together underneath the table next to me, after her third unsuccessful attempt momma left me and lay under a chair, one kitten left the bundle to nestle in for dinner. The workers stepped aside, respecting their space as all a part of their little eco-system. They all lived in the neighborhood together.

I strolled along the beach filled with locals and tourists. Families played together in the gently rising tide. As the sun began to sink into the ocean, the sky filled with crimson, salmon, burnt orange, lemon, light mint green, dark royal blue, and lilacs lighting up a shock of clouds expanding up from the horizon, spreading its wings over and above me, reflecting down into the quietly rolling ocean. Chinese fishing nets sat quietly, abandoned for the evening, overlooking it all.

Kochi was a small town, people remembered me with a friendly nod or a brief conversation. I saw familiar faces from the day, from a few shops, from the palace. The historic part of town did seem fairly abandoned by locals except for those that worked in the tourist industry.

I tried another ATM and my card worked. It had been a glitch unrelated to me; I exhaled a huge sigh of relief. I slept deeply that night.

After breakfast, I walked through the historic cobblestone streets to the water's edge. I joined many other strollers enjoying the rolling movement of the sea in the sunshine. I stopped at an ice-cream vendor and bought a deliciously sweet florescent mango popsicle. I couldn't eat it as fast as it melted and much of it ended up dripping all over my hands and arms. I found some stone steps leading into the water and leaned down just to wash my hands when a little wave crashed up and soaked me to the waist. I succeeded in both removing the fluorescent stickiness from my arms and providing much entertainment for the many onlookers, especially the children who pointed and laughed.

I would have dived right in and gone for a swim if it were first, socially acceptable, and second, not totally polluted. The water actually felt great. I sat on the stone wall at the edge of the sea drying off in the hot sun.

In the mid-afternoon heat I retired to my room and started reading a book of essays I had bought by Arundhati Roy, the Indian writer and activist. It took me into another world.

Mar 5 — Wish I had someone to discuss the world with — but it's nice for my brain to exercise itself through reading, although I get emotional and have to stop myself before I cry from the horror of it all, the pain, suffering, violence, inhumanity we are capable of inflicting upon each other. Will there ever be a leader of any nation who truly attempts to inspire beauty, love, and peace? Truly? The hypocrisy of what is done in the name of each of those is sad. Heartbreaking. How do people become so awful? And some so awesome? Does breaking a cycle seem more heartwrenching than continuing it? Too much anger in the world. I don't think it's just lack of education. Even without knowing anything about another people, culture, experience — if you have compassion — I don't see how hatred, fear, and anger can grow.

The revered Buddhist monk Thich Nhat Hanh says, "Love, compassion, joy, and equanimity are the very nature of an enlightened person. They are the four aspects of true love within ourselves and within everyone and everything."[13] An enlightened person exudes true love. True love is divine, it is not from the ego, it is not from the heart. It is a state of being. Being love. Can practicing love lead to enlightenment?

How do you practice true love?

This Buddhist concept is reflected in the yogic concept of the Four Locks and Four Keys (Book 1 Sutra 33). The four locks represent four kinds of people: the happy, the unhappy, the virtuous, and the wicked (or those behaving wickedly). To approach these people while retaining your own peace you use the four keys. Approaching the happy with friendliness, the unhappy with compassion, delight for the virtuous, and disregard for the wicked.

The parallel between the two concepts is quite clear. Friendliness and love are often interpreted as the same. The word compassion is used in both philosophies. Joy and delight are also synonymous. Equanimity is evenness, remaining steady and unattached, as in the behavior of disregard.

The parallel is striking to me and deep. Both philosophies focus on inner peace and in achieving it in similar ways. In this case the practice is the same. Striving for this peace is showing love for yourself. Using the keys is showing love for others. In this way we are living in love, within ourselves and through action with others. We retain our own peace and hopefully bring peacefulness to those we interact with in this conscientious way. Living in love encourages enlightenment. It is a path of wisdom.

Swami Satchidananda says, "Whether you are interested in reaching *Samadhi* or plan to ignore Yoga entirely, I would advise you to remember at least this one Sutra."[14] If the purpose of yoga is to cultivate inner peace, then this is one of the most effective practices. Success in this practice leaves you more open to folding into other practices with ease. This practice is at the same time both a kind of foundation and a manifestation of the end result.

Like many practices that are not progressive, it is rather a conglomeration of coexistent, or cyclical, or ever-present experiences. I think of yoga as more circular than linear. It is a whole that we practice pieces of, some further toward the center, some at the far reaches of its expanse, all interconnected and equally valuable as a part of the whole. Practicing each piece can perhaps lead to the true experience of the whole all at once, as one.

It rained through the night. The next morning felt fresh. I discovered I suddenly had hot water and took a satisfying, steamy shower. I imagined green ooze seeping out of me as the hot water opened my pores, releasing weeks of oil, sweat, dirt, and whatever was causing the rash... but no. Tea tree oil was helping.

I walked back to the Kashi Art Café, I couldn't stay away–omelets, french toast, freshly roasted coffee beans. They played Indian music in the mornings which set a pleasant rhythm to my day. The earth smelled alive. A giant teddy bear cloud was silhouetted in silver against the sun.

After weeks of trying to connect with my friend Anil, one of the teachers from the Institute who introduced me to yoga dance through his choreographed piece at our graduation, he finally responded to my email and we arranged a place to meet. He had been traveling for business and had a meeting in Kochi. I found the restaurant he had recommended. Anil was waiting; my whole body smiled to see a friendly face and to be hugged. While thin and unassuming, Anil brightened a room with his broad smile and warmth. He had deep eyes that looked right through me.

We had a lovely lunch and chatted about all the things that had happened since the teacher training at the Institute. It seemed so far away. He updated me that Madalena had just moved to Ooty from the Institute. Swami Krishnananda wasn't very pleased. I told him that I continued to have problems reaching her mobile. He had the same number I did and couldn't help.

He told me about his business which took him all over South India and I told him about my adventures. He treated for lunch and carried my bag to the train station. I waited while he went to buy the ticket to Coimbatore and he stayed with me on the platform until the train left. It felt so good to have some help, to have something be easy, to be relaxed.

The Coimbatore train station was close to the Institute and an auto delivered me in no time. The cool marble steps under my feet felt so grounding as I made my way back to my old room. It felt like being home, it stayed the same while I felt a little older, a little more confident, and stronger. Dinner had been made for me and I sat at the table with Swami Krishnananda, Swami Arthyananda, and Raudra catching up and enjoying the meal not only for its deliciousness but because I could be just me. A meal at home is like no other. We were all excited to see each other again. Raudra thought I must have dropped five kilos. I thought his hair looked a little fluffier. Life happens. We laughed.

In the evening, in our pajamas, us girls acted like we were having a slumber party. We each brought our plastic bathroom bucket to the lounge, filled them with hot water, and Swami Arthyananda poured in a mixture of aromatherapy oils. We smooshed together on the big black slippery couch, each with our bucket of relaxation, toes wiggling happily in the warm liquid, giggling.

Their sweetness felt like a big mama hug.

Madalena had left no message at the Institute, except that she had already gone ahead to Ooty. Our plan had been to go together, but she went to meet up with her boyfriend. Maheshwar was from Ooty, his family from the tribal population there. He was pierced and tattooed and sang in a rock band. He rode around on an antique motorcycle that was forever breaking down. He had a degree in journalism but dreamt of being a pilot. I tried Madalena's mobile phone numerous times to no avail and figured Ooty was a small town. I'd find her.

I left a place of comfort and peace and embarked upon my second trip along the hairpin turns, back and forth, up the steep mountain, from sweaty heat to clear, crisp air. My fellow busmates each layered on more and more clothing as we lurched higher and higher. Green became richer as the valley expanded below us, the horizon reached farther and farther into the hazy distance. Local monkeys sat lackadaisically, looking on with little curiosity as we drove by in our metal contraption, nonchalantly noticing us wide-eyed creatures inside rubbing our eyes.

I loved the feeling of nature fighting back against modernity as the goats effortlessly tore advertisement posters from buildings, chewed them disinterestedly, and disposed of the remnants back into the earth leaving only a scar of torn paper where the polluting message had been.

I called a few Paying Guest houses–commonly called PGs–from the bus station and took an auto to my small, cold, damp room at the YWCA with a freezing draft that wafted in from under the door. I didn't realize how cold it was until that night when I had to sleep with two wool blankets, two pairs of pants, three shirts, socks, and a scarf wrapped around my head.

In colonial times the British would come to the lush hill station of Ooty in the summer to cool down and relax. It was more than cool at this time of year–it was freezing. I wore almost every piece of clothing I owned: yoga pants and tank top under full *salwar kamise* under a long sleeved shirt and the only sweater I had, over which I wrapped a thin shawl and *dupata* which I tied around my neck like a scarf.

I wandered the town, which had apparently lost much of its charm with the increase in tourism. I stopped in front of a private Anglo-Indian all-girls school that reminded me of my imagined memories of my grandmother's convent school in South India. I tried to picture her childhood.

I found an Internet shop and emailed Madalena again. I called her mobile again to find that it still wasn't working. I walked out of the shop and asked God to send Madalena to me. I walked aimlessly through the streets. I rounded a corner and nearly brushed up against a cute African guy. We made eye contact and then kept walking in opposite directions.

He turned around, catching up with me and stuttered out, "Where are you from?"

"The US. How about you?"

"I'm Sudanese, I'm studying here."

"Oh, what are you studying?"

"Engineering. Are you here on holiday? With friends? Where are you staying?"

"Wait, you're Sudanese and a student. You look familiar."

"I do?!" He was shocked.

"I think you know Maheshwar."

He froze in the middle of his "pick up a foreign girl" routine. His puffed chest deflated slightly. "Ya! Mahesh is one of my best friends," he informed me.

I explained, "I saw you dancing in a video Madalena shot of a party, here in Ooty."

"You're friends with Madalena? She's like my little sister!"

"I'm supposed to be meeting her here; do you know where they are?"

"Wait, I'll call."

He called both their numbers and had as little luck as I. Then he called their friends and a search party was formed. He suggested we get something to eat while we waited for information to come in. He took me to a little café with a bunch of locals and sat in a booth. He was obviously a regular as everyone nodded their hellos.

We sat across from each other and finally introduced ourselves, he was Omar. It felt like a date, I let it be a date and had fun. We talked about our families and how it felt being so far from home. He made me laugh and tried hard to be gentlemanly, ordering for me, opening doors for me, offering to help. He invited me to a house party later that night.

Omar picked me up on his bike and took me to a house filled with African and other international students. They had a DJ and we danced to American hip hop. It felt amazing to dance until all the men one by one tried hitting on me. I sat through endless drunken sob stories of loneliness, feeling unwelcome in this foreign land until Omar saved me and dragged me back onto the dancefloor. Omar dropped me back at my PG and we made a date to sightsee the next day; he offered to drive me around on his bike.

I was excited and hardly slept. I felt like a crushing teenager. I waited outside the lobby in the morning. The appointed time came and went. I waited longer. I asked inside if there were any messages for me. After an hour I gave up and took myself to the Botanical Gardens.

He had pressed my buttons of insecurity and pride. I actually felt like crying; maybe I had hoped he would be the shoulder I needed to lean on, the little bit of support I was looking for on this lonely road. I felt blocked from truly enjoying the beauty around me. And then at every turn it seemed some boy was trying to talk to me. I resorted to my successful Spanish ploy–I responded only in Spanish until they became bewildered and gave up. I just wanted a little peace.

I found an Internet café to connect to home. I opened an email from my friend's mother-in-law who I knew from their wedding. She invited me to stay with them in Bangalore. I called to work out the details. We chatted cheerfully about New York and my friend. I felt happy, I had a home to go to. The pieces were starting to come together.

I went to a restaurant for dinner and as I was ordering the server put his hand on mine. I pulled away quickly and he walked away awkwardly. If I were an Indian girl he wouldn't have attempted something so inappropriate and disrespectful. Something had changed in my energy in Ooty. My sensuality had been expressed in dancing and somehow it seemed to emanate from me. I was suddenly treated as an "American girl"–loose. I ate quickly and left.

I sat at Coffee Day, it was welcoming, modern, and warm unlike my freezing room. I missed having a friend to share with; not meeting up with Madalena was a big disappointment. Sipping a latte, eating cake, and listening to Indian MTV, I ran into a couple of Omar's friends that I had met at the house party, Victoria, an Indian girl from Bangalore, and her Egyptian boyfriend. They invited me to share a hookah with them and I told them my story from that morning. They were shocked that I had been stood up and while Victoria and I went outside for her to chain-smoke, her boyfriend called Omar, who said he was coming immediately and felt terrible.

A little while later he showed up, apologized, and gave me a note he said he had written that morning, an apology note he had meant to drop off at my PG explaining why, at the last minute, he couldn't meet. I thought it was funny that he thought I was that naïve. He had obviously just scribbled the note before coming into Coffee Day. So young.

He dropped me home. We made plans for him to give me the promised tour the next morning. I did really want to see the surrounding forest and sites, and I have always been a softy for giving second chances.

I sat enjoying the sunshine on a patio at the YWCA, not realizing I was preparing to be stood up for the second day in a row. Not being in a particularly talkative mood, I was somewhat dismayed when a man sat nearby and introduced himself. He was a blond, solid looking German and had just arrived in India, ending up in Ooty for some reason he couldn't explain.

We sat in silence for a while. He asked if I was Christian, I said no and jokingly asked if he was on a quest for Christians. He didn't laugh. Instead, he began a story of his search for spiritual people and environments to help him get over the deep depression he had fallen into. India was, in his mind, his last chance. He was successful professionally and had, through his influence and profession in the medical field, just saved his uncle's life. Surrounded by praise and gratitude from his family he felt nothing at all, just despair. He fled.

He began to cry. Really cry. We sat in the sun.

My mind went back to my own past depression. I searched for what I had needed to get through moments like this. I started talking about my experience with yoga, how I had gained steadiness of mind. But I knew he couldn't hear or see clearly. He thought about going to an ashram in Rishikesh for a while, desperate for a magical cure. I could only say that I had survived, struggled, gotten through the worst, grown, and now sat a recovering depressive in front of him. "It will be ok. You will be ok. It will get better."

The German's wife's emails were his lifeline. But he was so consumed with guilt and self-hatred for being depressed around his loved ones that he ran away. He was unable to face them, which only deepened the hole he had fallen into. I related how changing locations can be a tool. I thought it had been for me. But basically, at the root, it doesn't matter where you are. Depression is in your own head, and your mind follows you everywhere.

He was running from himself. He knew that. He was trying to get out of his head by searching to get into his soul. Where better to do that than India?

His energy scared me a little. He was a black hole I was afraid to be sucked into considering my own past. Added to that, as I sat in the sun I realized I had indeed been stood up for the second day in a row. So the German and I went to lunch. We talked about the world to distract each other. I encouraged him to go to the Botanical Garden since he loved trees. Motivation. Keeping one foot in front of the other. We parted.

I stopped at the bus station and booked a seat on a private bus direct to Bangalore the next morning. I checked email and was relieved to find a message from the Subud Organization where I wanted to volunteer. The woman who runs it gave me her number and was waiting for my call. She also suggested I could possibly stay with another American volunteer who was working there.

I was no longer motivated to explore and enjoy Ooty and went back to my room to begin packing. My equilibrium was off kilter. I struggled mentally between knowing this was a casual thing of no consequence and admitting I felt rejected. Where was my yogic training? I had allowed myself desire, indulged in hope and romanticism–only to be disappointed and pained. My mind–a flurry of distraction–imbalanced and chaotic. A twisted feeling in my gut interspersed with moments of compassion and quiet. I felt gratitude for this experience mixed with sadness, sadness from judging my own inability to stay calm and unaffected. I was fighting depression.

I dragged myself out to get a bite to eat. I took the back roads to avoid possibly running into anyone. On a side street upstairs from an Internet shop was Willy's. This cozy international student hangout was filled with pods of studiers commiserating over french fries and slurping caffeine. I sat facing the balcony, watching the rain stream down and intermittent bolts of lighting crash across the sky. I couldn't risk getting my clothes wet as they wouldn't dry in my heaterless room overnight and I didn't want to travel with wet clothes.

I chose a magazine from the stack in the corner and waited out the rain. Engrossed in an article I heard, "Sitting and reading?" I looked up to see Omar, dripping wet from head to toe, averting his eyes in shame. His story reminded me that he was only 23 and I felt like an older sister. I listened to how he missed his final exam that morning and failed his class. He spent the day angry and frustrated and now was ashamed to even stand in front of me. He apologized. Of course my heart went out to him. I held his hand and made him laugh. We parted on friendly terms with a hug and more apologies. I felt I had worked through my anger, sadness, and hurt feelings. I had gotten over it and moved on. I was of course overly optimistic.

Disappointment is really our own doing. It is attachment to a created expectation, our judgment of how another should think, feel, and act. They let us down, but really we are letting ourselves down by allowing our peace to be so disturbed by our own mental creations.

The Dalai Lama explains, "Though strong emotions, like those of romantic love or righteous hatred, may feel profoundly compelling, their pleasure is fleeting. From a Buddhist point of view, it is far better not to be in the grip of such emotions in the first place."[15] I had felt content and centered, stable and strong when romantic notions were far from my mind. Lucia was impressed by my asexuality–that was her perception, but there was a grain of truth in my energy, which was only mildly cluttered with distractions of that sort. As opposed to my current discombobulated self.

It was a choice I struggled with. Wanting to find a romantic partner, make a family, be "distracted"–or focusing only on the love of the Divine, forgo material concerns, and be content. I felt I could go either way. But I wasn't ready to choose. Does is have to be either or? I tend to shy away from extremes.

The next morning at an early breakfast, I was packed and ready to go when the German walked into the dining room as forlorn as the day before. The night was bad. Alone in his room. *Alone*. He didn't know what to do, so he announced that he would join me on the bus to Bangalore. In 15 minutes. Chasing peace. I said of course I didn't mind if he joined me. He ran to pack.

10

First impressions, yoga is, vampires, Catholic priests, radiant smiles

I began to realize that from the moment I entered India, people had asked for my help in one way or another. People were drawn to tell me their story, to ask my advice, or to just have me listen. I think I began to exude a quality of acceptance and love that some people were seeking. Or maybe most people don't take the time to listen to anyone and show true concern. I kept a little distance from the German but shared the journey. It was hard being around someone so depressed.

We had to switch buses in Mysore, half way, because of A/C problems. I realized that I had left my yoga mat on the first bus. I ran up to tell the driver, not sure how he could solve the problem. He smacked his palm against his forehead and shook his head. So dramatic. I said, "It's ok, it was nothing valuable." I slunk back to my seat. I spent the next hour visualizing the freedom of carrying one less thing, of learning to let go of attachments, of understanding the true value of material objects. On our way into the metropolis that is Bangalore, we pulled up to a congested stop light–coincidentally right next to the old bus! "Luggage, luggage" was shouted down the aisle. Other passengers were gesturing to me, waving me up to the front of the bus. I ran up the aisle and the driver of the old bus was passing my yoga mat through the driver's window. I was so happy, I cried. I guess I really was a little attached, as much as I was trying to cultivate detachment. And I was so moved that the driver had genuinely cared, remembered, and found a way to help. What a miracle, I said, "Only in India."

I parted with the German at the bus station. He was going to immediately get a train to Delhi and keep moving. I was sad for him. I did what I could. I couldn't offer more.

Although my friend's mother-in-law, Bheema Bhachan, had given me explicit directions, getting to their home turned into an ordeal, especially once the sun went down. I found the correct bus at the station and we were off. Lights glittered and the city felt filled with energy and life. It started to pour with rain; traffic was bad and I was relying on the driver to tell me when to get off. When he told me we had arrived at my stop, I peered out the doorway into only darkness and rain. There was no stop. No shops. Nothing. I decided to stay on the bus until I found shelter and a phone. I had to pay an extra fare to stay on the bus as they turned around, I was at the end of the route.

I saw a sign for an STD (which stands for Standard Trunk Dialing), stepped out into the rain and ducked into a tiny shop to use the pay phone. On the phone with Bheema trying to figure out where the city bus that she had instructed me to take had actually delivered me, an auto driver sheltering from the rain overheard our conversation and got on the phone with her. He said he knew exactly where she lived and would take me there for a flat fee. I agreed.

It ended up being so close I could have walked if it were daylight and not pouring rain. He completely took advantage of my ignorance. That was just the first of many negative experiences with Bangalore's auto rickshaw drivers. I heard a story later that summer that illustrates the blatant flaunting of their mafia-like power. At a major intersection between two busy three-lane boulevards in the commercial heart of the city, an auto ran the red light and was pulled over by a police officer. Immediately every auto in the city converged on the intersection, blocking traffic for hours. And on top of that, they beat up the police officer who had dared to write the ticket.

The Bhachan's had moved back to India after living in Queens, New York for 30 years. They were readjusting. They bought a condo in a new building that was still being completed around them. It was about a 30-minute drive from the center of Bangalore on Whitefield Road, where all the technology companies had opened shop. Every major tech name was represented in a giant tech park surrounded by construction in every direction. Their building was one of many modern concrete creations springing up from dust. It was only partially filled, mostly by young couples from all over India working in IT. Bheema became the matriarch of the building, her husband the head of the homeowners association. They had constant visitors from the building and Bheema organized all the social events.

She was happy to have a guest from home and talked my ear off. She fed me well and I slept heavily in my comfortable room. It was nice to be taken care of. I led Bheema in yoga on the roof under the bright blue sky and we meditated together.

Bheema introduced me to her neighbor Amisha from the coastal city of Mangalore who wore a big smile and tight curly hair in a ring around her face. Amisha was educated, had a great job, married, found love with her husband, had a son she adored, and was full of life. We liked each other right away. She had definite ideas about what it is to be an Indian woman, what she wanted, and how to balance family and work. We'd get so caught up in a conversation I'd forget where I was–which was a funny feeling on the bus. I would be chatting away loudly and uninhibitedly until I caught sight of all the eyes staring at me as if I were an alien. We'd lower our voices. Amisha volunteered to direct me to the Mithra Foundation on her way to work the next day.

The Mithra Foundation is a co-educational grammar school and vocational training center for local women located in the slums of Bangalore. It is an organization of Susila Dharma, the international branch of Subud. Most students attended free of charge, while some paid roughly one dollar a month in tuition if they could afford it. Uniforms were required but the school often paid for those as well. Mithra had a difficult time making ends meet. The vocational training was for garment factory work, tailoring, and teaching. They also supported micro enterprises and local women's issues in the surrounding impoverished neighborhoods.

A passionate, opinionated, and determined middle-aged couple, Joe and Bella, ran Mithra. They were a force to be reckoned with; small in stature but big in personality. They single handedly created and sustained the foundation and its programs. While we differed on our ideas of what yoga is, they were happy to have me there helping. We created a four-week intensive course for the teacher trainees to attend. I would teach every day and give them a comprehensive basic understanding of yoga culminating in an exam and certification.

In India, yoga is often taught to children as mandatory physical fitness, as a sport complete with national competitions. I found that young adults had little interest in yoga because of their history with it as children, as a forced activity, as competitive. Joe gave me a tour of the school. We walked around the classrooms and as we entered each room the children would jump up and stand at attention and he would call on a few to perform a yoga pose for me or to tell me what they were studying.

I have been involved with Subud since birth, through my parents, and I wanted to support this project. I saw the people they were helping. If I could increase these women's chances of getting placement as teachers or increase their pay with more skills, or if their experience of yoga with me in any way improved their lives, I was happy to offer myself.

I was also introduced to Cassandra, an 18-year-old American girl from Maryland. She burst out an exuberant "hey!" She was naturally beautiful and had mastered blending in with her long dark hair and tailored *salwar kamise*. She wondered how I had found this volunteer opportunity and wanted to hear all about my travels. She seemed thrilled to talk to someone from home and explained what she was doing at Mithra. I quickly realized her cute dimples could mask a keen mind.

She explained, "While I was researching and organizing my own volunteer experience, I noticed a lack of clear and comprehensive information about the projects and the expectations of each position. I'm taking a year off before going to Columbia University to volunteer and create an online network of Subud organizations in need of volunteers. I want to make it easier for others to confidently volunteer–to know where they are going, what exactly they will be doing, and what kind of support will be available."

I thought how valuable it would be if our government somehow supported all 18-year-olds in completing a year of service before fully entering the workforce or going to college. The understanding, respect, and compassion learned from exposure to the myriad ways people live, nationally or internationally, and the difficult issues they face would be a significant way to enter adulthood and an invaluable way to enrich our society.

When I returned to the Bhachans', Bheema grilled me on every detail of my day. I could only get up to use the bathroom when the doorbell rang and I escaped. Then it was back to rambling stories for hours. Bheema sat so close to me we were touching and she rarely stopped for a breath. I felt I was representing my friend, her daughter-in-law, so I sat dutifully.

My first yoga class was a logistical challenge. I had to take a bus to an auto and then walk. There were twice as many students as I was told there would be and they didn't appear to be too excited. And one was pregnant. There weren't enough mats and we had to move the desks and chairs to the back of the little room before we could begin. I wasn't sure how much they really understood my English.

But as class progressed they started to have a little bit of fun. The poses made them giggle; they had fits of nervous laughter in happy baby pose. Laying on their backs with bent knees, the soles of their feet raised toward the ceiling, they held onto their feet with their knees bending in towards their arm pits resulting in their pelvic regions being opened and exposed. Their *kamise* tops fell away leaving only two layers of protection. Some kept trying to adjust, others embraced the oddity. They weren't used to moving their bodies that way. I hoped through the classes they might become a little more aware and comfortable with their bodies apart from the cultural restrictions and sexual implications outside in society.

These students were so different from my usual students back home. Understanding their perspective, their needs, and their interest level, coupled with our communication limitations was challenging. A challenge I accepted, however intimidating.

After class I was told I could take the school bus to the city bus stop rather than having to walk or take an auto. We all piled in among the small children. Taking the bus with the kids was fun; they provided much sweet entertainment. They were so little and beautiful, full of vibrant energy.

I started going to bed early since I was back on a schedule–6am yoga with Bheema, teaching, then organizing my next move. I finally reached Madalena who said she was getting some people together to rent a house. I told her to keep me in mind and let me know the plans. Rain cooled the air as lightning shocked the sky. I lay in bed watching the storm and my thoughts were invaded by Omar. Silly distraction.

Distraction seems to be a function of the human experience, commonly called the "monkey mind"–thoughts always jumping here and there. Distraction can consume us, sucking away our ability to be present. It feeds unhealthy thoughts and feelings that fueled by imagination can lead to anger, sadness, confusion, and a lack of peace. Meditation is a way to focus, to calm the mind, and in turn, calm the self. It almost seems to counter our natural human tendencies. In meditation, are we attempting to transcend humanness?

On the path of Ashtanga Yoga (the eight-limbed path outlined in the Yoga Sutras–Book 2 Sutra 29) the final three limbs describe the levels of meditation. The first level is *dharana*–concentration. Before we are capable of meditation we must attain the ability to concentrate, to bring the mind into one-pointedness. In most meditation workshops, they don't teach meditation, they teach various methods to develop concentration. Meditation is beyond method, it is beyond trying, it is inactive.

The second level is *dhyana*–meditation is achieved when one is so absorbed in the object of concentration that the object no longer exists. If the mind is active, then the state of awareness beyond the mind is unreachable.

Fully detaching from the consciousness of the self, of body and mind, is *samadhi*, the final level. All the other limbs of yoga support the attempt to attain *samadhi*.

Most of us struggle with *dharana*, allowing the multitude of possible distractions to capture our attention and block the ability to concentrate or to break our concentration once achieved. The mind is an incredible thing, tangible and intangible simultaneously, controllable and uncontrollable, imaginative and thoughtless, insatiable and tired, quantifiable and mysterious, defined and amorphous. Swami Bhoomananda tells us where to focus:

> But there is a way of treating the mind. There is a way
> of generating peace and relief, lightness and freedom.
> The way is to make the mind interact with the Soul,
> the Subject or the Self. As the interactions with the
> plural world give rise to afflictions and tension, so will
> the contemplation on the one and uniform Soul generate peace, poise, freedom.[16]

Freedom from the distractions of the world. Stilling the mind, releasing it, allows the experience of the soul to develop more clearly. Contemplating this, rather than the distractions naturally pervading our minds, brings peace. The world won't disappear. Our interaction with the world goes on, hopefully with joy and wonder. What can disappear are the stresses and angst that we generate in reaction to the world.

We are back to the difficulty of simplicity. Sitting, surrendering, open and quiet feels unattainably difficult and therefore the results seem unreachable. Being wholly alone with the Self, the soul, imbues one with fear. We fear the unknown. We fear the pain we hide inside. We fear losing control. Without control, the world invades and we are unable to cope with the experiences openly. We close ourselves. True peace is then unattainable. To temper the fear we can start small, just dip a toe into the pool of serenity.

"So, even if a fractional percentage of the spatial mind you are able to develop and retain, that will be more than sufficient to remain afloat in your world,"[17] Swami Bhoomandana assures. The attempt at meditation alone has great benefits. Even tiny progressions are progressions indeed. Enough to stay afloat. You may have just a splinter of peace to hold onto at first, then it grows into a branch, then maybe into a whole raft to ride the waves, and maybe it will take root and grow into a strong, stable tree on a patch of earth in the middle of the sea.

Yogas citta vrtti nirodhah is the definition of yoga. Patanjali begins in Book 1 Sutra 2 with the goal. Yoga is the ceasing of the disturbances of the mindstuff, to liberate the mind through recognition of the Self, which is always free. We aren't liberating the Self, we are liberating the mind, the body, and the heart to experience our true Self. Free of disturbances. Free from the filters and programming accumulated over lifetimes. *Free.*

To see truly and clearly. That is yoga.

We liberate the mind from distraction, the body from illness, and the heart from its incapacity to love truly. True love is disassociated from the machinations of the mind and the sensations of the body. When we are truly free we experience only our divine Self. Yoga is the

practice of understanding our true Self, seeing the filters and disturbances, knowing how they affect us, and trying to let go of them.

MG (Mahatma Gandhi) Road was "downtown." Clothing stores,
music shops, restaurants, coffee shops, and bars lined the road within
walking distance to a big western-style mall with a multiplex, Marks &
Spencer, Body Shop, Baskin Robbins, and other recognizable national
and international chains. A short walk in the opposite direction lay Cubbon Park–a beautiful, big park with bamboo forests and rose gardens.

Located in an outdoor plaza, Barista was the most popular coffee
place. At tables under umbrellas, hidden among tropical plants, music
pumped and beautiful people, models, students, and young professionals sipped their cappuccinos for hours. I sat at a shaded table and wrote
in my journal.

Next to me were 12 guys crowded together, covered in colored
powder singing Holi songs. The guys were competing with Enrique
Iglesias whose song boomed out over the speakers.

During the spring celebration of Holi, Indians celebrate the triumph of good over evil and the individual's ability to accept all that life
has to throw at them. It is an acceptance of the world as it is and a belief and faith in goodness, in overcoming, in surviving. They symbolize
this by throwing colored powder on each other, smearing it all over
each other's faces and hair, squirting colored water from water guns,
and wearing white for the canvas.

Amisha "powdered" me in the morning with green and explained
the symbolism–each color represented something different like pain
(red) or growth (green). It's a time of joy, freedom, and vivacity. Holi
is a celebration of life.

Being a part of a community, staying in a home, was so comforting. Bheema gave me a few of her old *salwar kamise* to dress more

traditionally for my class and offered to take me shopping in their car, with a driver. Posh. I felt a great surge of positive energy in Bangalore. All around the city banners flew with messages of city pride, "City of Empowerment," "City of Progress," "City of a Thousand Lakes," and "City of Tomorrow."

I spent the whole of the next day at Mithra working with Cassandra on the huge project she had created and promised to complete. She looked overwhelmed and unhappy and in need of help. Bella told us about the room she was arranging for us in a boarding house for priests. It was only 100 rupees a night, had an attached bath, and access to the Internet. A little odd but a great deal.

Bella, Cassandra, and I decided to do *latihan* together. It had been a while since I had been in a group, however small, or even around other Subud members. Subud was created around the *latihan kejiwaan*, a spiritual practice spontaneously received by an Indonesian man, Bapak Muhammad Subuh Sumohadiwidjojo, in the 1920s. One night while contemplating death, he unexpectedly received inner guidance from God that led to a greater understanding of himself and of other people. Later he received how to share with others this openness so that everyone could receive this Divine guidance on their own. *Latihan* is a direct experience of the Divine that manifests in each person in a personal way. The path is surrender to the Divine. The final yogic observance, *isvarapranidhana*, reflects the same practice of surrender.

While *latihan* is an individual practice, it can be more powerful when practiced in a group. The group also provides emotional support and community. *Latihan* means "exercise" or "training." It is a spiritual exercise. Generally you receive whatever is right for you to receive. There is also a practice called "testing" where you ask a specific question and receive specific guidance around that question. That guidance manifests in innumerable and personal ways.

That day I felt my heart aching. Why?

Often in spiritual practice the heart and mind enter the equation and influence true receiving. In yoga there are many practices to remove that influence; meditation is one. Meditation is an exercise in removing the mind or allowing it to be so still that it forgets itself, leaving nothing of ourselves but the inner divine in conjunction with the outer divine and the realization that there is no separation between the two. This realization is not a mental realization. As we are mental creatures, this understanding is difficult to attain.

To me, spiritual practice is the journey to discovering the influence, the nature, the being of the outer person and body we were born into in this world on our inner Self, our soul. It's not an escape from our humanity, or our outer self, it's an understanding of that self. It's a love and acceptance of that person and our ability to love and accept others' outer selves knowing we are all one. Maybe this is nearly impossible, but that's why it is called practice. The attempt itself is a beautiful and rewarding way to live.

But I return to the more usually experienced reality of distraction and delusion, of *maya*. *Maya* is the illusion of the material world, the delusions we create based on this misconception of reality. *Maya* is distraction from the truth caused by only seeing illusion. It's where we mostly exist. It's where this book exists. It's where I continually fall, knees weak from the struggle. I laugh at my foolish clinging to the beautiful unreal, so beautifully elucidated in the Katha Upanishad:

> The foolish rush out into the world,
> Reaching for all that they see,
> Getting caught again and again
> In the snares of death.
> The wise cease looking for the real
> In the direction of the unreal.[18]

I returned to the Bhachan's, distracted by my receiving. I listened blankly to the evening's stories, ate dinner silently, glazed over as we watched television, and excused myself to bed.

I woke up from odd dreams, wondering what on earth was going on in my head. I dreamt I was in Flamenco class and was told we had a performance that night. I hadn't practiced and frantically tried to remember the choreography. Then I was eating a pumpkin yogurt and found an eyeball in it. I ran around trying to find a digital camera to borrow to report it when I ran into my recent ex-boyfriend. He told me he was already getting married.

I decided to get out of my head, to stop all these crazy thoughts, and do *latihan* alone in my room. But I received that I needed to get pregnant and I was back in my head again. I thought or decided the receiving was meant metaphorically like I needed to grow and give birth to a project. But with all the reproductive issues I was having in my body I also thought it could have been meant literally. I wasn't going to go get pregnant. I didn't really know what to do with this feeling.

My body knew at 27 that it was time to have a child. This was before my cysts and endometriosis. I ignored the urges. I was single and depressed and not exactly financially viable. After surgery I again had urges, feelings, and yearnings and my doctor told me my best shot at pregnancy was at that very moment. Life just wasn't working out that way.

Was something in me dying? Was this my last chance? Did I go to India to find that chance? Did I think a drastic shift in my reality would create a drastic shift in my body? What were all these messages trying to tell me? What was I supposed to do?

A month before I left for India I felt this urgency. I couldn't escape my body, I couldn't ignore the reality. The sunshine of Santa Cruz was no match for my gloom. I was in a dark place inside.

Nov 30 — The sun is so intense. It's distracting.

I'm exhausted, it's been a rough few weeks, I've been feeling reproductively ill. Unhappy. Tired. Uncomfortable. Pressure. Depleted. My dreams are about anger.

Scary vampire dream last night — I was hanging out with a couple of guys at a loft in NY. I decided to leave but got a really bad feeling that something was going to happen while I walked to the train, so I asked one guy to come with me. I really liked him. I joked, "Unless you're the bad thing." We were outside leaning against a wall making out. He turned into a vampire. Instead of biting me, he wanted me to change myself by getting really angry, concentrating, and through the anger, my fangs would grow. I pretended to try. I was scared. I heard a train coming, leapt down the stairs, and just squeezed through the train doors. I woke up and still felt his presence. I had to turn my light on and read. I fought the urge to fall asleep because I wanted to go back to him. It felt so real.

Dec 1 — I feel like my whole body is filled with blood. My heart is weak. My muscles are weak. So much pain last night, even after two Tylenol and a Vicodin. Freezing cold. Couldn't sleep until 3:30am from the pain. I'm so sick. It's my one fear in going to India — what if I need an emergency hysterectomy? That scares me.
My body quivers.

While blood flows through practically every part of our bodies, it is frightening to taste it, spitting iron, erupting from the inside out. Not flowing, out of place, existing somewhere it shouldn't. Fear from the unexpected, the unknown. Why was my body doing this? Why didn't anyone know why my body was doing this?

I woke up from my vampire dream with major chest pain. My heart must have been working overtime, beating fast. I felt so out of control–unable to control my body, my thoughts, my emotions. Far from my yoga practice, I couldn't still my mind. I couldn't detach, I was languishing in my preoccupation.

I kept having the feeling that I was going to die. I sat quietly, went deep inside, and asked God about my endometriosis. I received that the major causes were my own anger, stubbornness, internalizing, and life stagnation. It was literally hurting me, causing a disease. It was time to move; time to put myself out there and try–no one else could do that for me. I needed to feel like I did something worthwhile with my life.

What inside me was dying?

What was I supposed to do about it? How would going to India make a difference? Was who I used to be dying so who I would become could emerge? Would India change me that much?

———————

I moved into the Catholic Priests' center with Cassandra. Bella brought us to the narrow three story building, one of many in a row of residential buildings, introduced us, and made sure we settled in comfortably to our new accommodations. She had arranged everything so we were in a quiet, safe neighborhood, cared for by priests, and only a bus ride away from Mithra.

We shared a tiny room with two metal-frame twin beds and a little attached bath with no shower. I became adept at bucket baths. Downstairs was a kitchen with a refrigerator, filtered water, and a stove and we were allowed access to a computer and the Internet. We were in heaven. We had keys and came and went as we pleased. We found a nearby supermarket, bought an Indian cookbook and experimented. We hand washed our clothes in a bucket in the bathroom and hung them up on the clotheslines on the roof.

One night when it was particularly hot we dragged our mattresses up to the roof, hung mosquito nets over the clotheslines, tucking them under the mattresses, and slept in our little tents under the stars. We wished we had figured that out sooner. The air was sweet, the stars laughed, the palm tree swayed protectively above us as an eagle circled curiously.

Cassandra and I were immediate sisters; we had an indelible connection. We shared an excitement about the world, a love of dance, and the experience of growing up in Subud.

Cassandra planned to travel around India after she spent her half year documenting particular programs through the international Subud organization, trying to get a handle on creating her network. She was fiercely intelligent and independent. She began performing Flamenco at 16, confident despite being a beginner. She had a glow, an earnestness to do good. She was humble and real.

Once she met me at Barista wearing a somewhat fitted *salwar kamise* and a shiny *bindi*, her long brown hair flowing in the breeze as she walked over, nearly in slow motion. The men around me literally dropped their jaws, stammering at how beautiful and Punjabi she looked. It was right out of a Bollywood movie. In her modesty and sweetness, she blushed when I told her their reaction.

The city began to feel a little overwhelming away from the Bhachans' house. Bheema had been so welcoming—she provided a safe, comfortable home, cooked for me, sent out my laundry, introduced me to her friends, told me how to get where I needed to go, and offered guidance and advice. I focused on getting to know the area around my new home and figuring out the bus system. I needed a map and a job. I checked email and found that Anil was planning a visit to Bangalore and Madalena would finally be arriving.

Early Saturday morning, I took the bus out to Whitefield to teach a yoga class on the roof of Bheema's building. Although I had gone to bed early I was still tired as I sat on the long ride to the edge of town. I was happy to give what I could to Bheema.

I felt satisfied with my class at Mithra, the women were smiling before and after class. I had so much fun creating my classes each week. I wanted to show them everything but had to limit myself for the time we had together. After a few requests to "reduce their tummies" I added more focus on abdominal work. I truly hoped they would see a difference–not just in their abdomens but in overall greater strength and posture and a comfort with their own bodies.

I bought a book for the one woman who was pregnant. I didn't feel safe letting her do the regular practice but she watched and listened and I helped her with questions from the book.

At the end of class one day, Joe came in and announced he wanted them to "perform" yoga at the Subud congress later that summer. He told them if they weren't doing well in class he would give them a thrashing. I had to laugh at this very different perspective on yoga than what I had been teaching.

At the Center, I chatted with the Fathers about politics, the US, movies. They seemed a little bored in their isolated world. Father Saul was a scholar from Kerala. He was working on translating his PhD thesis from his native language, Malayalam, into English. I was not wholly clear on the complexities of his argument, but it examined the chasm that exists between Jesus' truths and the misinterpretations and untruths of the Church. The Church was not created by Jesus and its creation was not his intention. True Christianity should follow Jesus' teachings, not the teachings of the Church. This was the radical priest's project while he carried out his responsibility managing this small center, alone. It was a quiet place to work and focus. He rarely had guests, just a few times a year for conferences, and then the dormitory upstairs would fill with young priests. He was in his fifties and I believe felt a fatherly role toward Cassandra and me.

Over the months I had met countless foreigners who suffered the dreaded and seemingly inescapable stomach problem, but I had never been affected. I think the probiotics I took were invaluable. But I finally fell to the inevitable and had a slight stomach issue. I felt weak and hardly slept. I took a day off from teaching. Father Saul offered to get me whatever I needed. He brought me plain rice and papaya. I mostly needed rest. By the next day I was already feeling better.

I walked to the bus stop, took the bus downtown, and walked to Brigade Road, one of the main streets lined with music, clothing, and technology stores. I went to the Hutch shop and purchased a mobile phone and minutes. I decided not to push it and took an auto back home. The driver said he knew where my road was when I got in but then asked five times for clarification and still managed to get lost. Fed up, I got out and walked the rest of the way.

I emailed everyone my new mobile number and hoped that with my free incoming calls I could finally hear some familiar voices from home. I ate hard boiled eggs and retired to my room, finally alone for a few nights to get some real sleep. Cassandra had gone on a trip with friends for the weekend.

No TV to watch, no book to read, no friend to talk to, no music to listen to; I was lonely and restless. A train screamed by to pull me out of my self-pity. I finished unpacking and organizing instead and dove into thoughts about what I was going to accomplish in India. My need to accomplish something, to produce something reared its head again. Maybe the purpose of this trip was to learn to let go of that need, to enjoy and fully experience every moment with no attachment to or expectation of a particular outcome. To allow the year I spent there to just be the year I spent there. To practice being present. *Present.*

Yoga is the practice of being present, of being aware and observant of what is happening on all levels of the self in the present. This awareness and observation are what allow us to develop in our practice. Being sensitive to each disturbance, finding its root, digging the weed up to leave the tree of the true Self the freedom to grow into our awareness unimpeded, this is the practice.

I felt better enough to teach class then felt exhausted immediately after. Curd rice and papaya were a great help. I started sweating, I didn't know if that was a good thing or a bad thing. Father Saul was getting worried. Getting up early in the mornings was difficult but I wanted to keep teaching. I went to bed at 8pm with the newspaper for company.

After teaching the next day, I felt stronger and stopped at Coffee Day rather than going straight home. The young energy, good music, and hot tea rejuvenated me. I started to feel alive again. I people watched and wrote in my journal.

> Mar 22 — I had to do a double take at a man who walked by — he looked just like my ex. Amazing how feelings, perspectives, experiences of the same thing can be so different between the two involved. We humans have it rough. So much interpretation, thinking, decisions, moral choices/dilemmas, constant mind disturbances. And mind disturbances leading to heart disturbances and then to "soul searching." You finally come to a point of ease and then go through it all over again. Ah, to be a lion! But then, what of the experience of God?
>
> I feel backwards. I am actively developing my spiritual life — but not my material life that I thought/think should come first. Am I on the path to becoming a monk — spiritual life only? But I still want to be a parent — which is definitely grounded in the material world.

I thought of the Hindu concept of the stages of life: from child/student, to householder/parent, to retired wisdom seeker, to spiritual renunciate. From learning as a child to working as a young woman to giving as a mature adult is how I pictured the structure of my life to form. But I have come to realize that I will always be a student and I am a teacher before I am wise. I may one day earn enough to raise a family comfortably, but I may lose the desire or physical ability to do so by the time the opportunity comes. The prescribed stages of life have become convoluted.

In my twenties, this traditional structure propelled my depression, now I am comfortable letting go of any expectations of how my life "should" be. These stages were of course also constructed for men not women. Women were meant to support the man's evolution. The world has changed, especially for women in regards to the structure of the family, earning a living, and having a spiritual practice and relationship to the Divine. Women now can experience all aspects of life in relation to her Self, not in relation to a man. She supports her own evolution.

So what is the new structure? Experiencing the stages of student, teacher, parent, child, partner, worker and spiritual practitioner all simultaneously and ongoing throughout our lives?

So in this ever-changing societal structure where gender roles are challenged and experimented with, the traditional idea of how life goes, its prescribed timeline, no longer applies. The options are expansive. This makes most people uncomfortable and they instead cling to tradition. Challenge is accompanied by fear. It's harder, it's more work, and it takes a level of detachment, creativity, and self-awareness, as well as an ability to live in the present. It is swimming in the unknown. Why swim upstream? Why create conflict while you are trying to create peace?

I practiced yoga on the roof early because by 9am it was already too hot. My back had started hurting again; I thought it must be the endometriosis. I had tried pretending I didn't have it, I didn't think about it and instead focused on how healthy I was. Pretending could only take me so far.

Walking became my time to think and my time to meditate. I was in no hurry, and it certainly saved money, to walk from place to place. I observed the vast differences between neighborhoods on a socio-economic level–clean, tree lined streets, shiny foreign cars parked in gated driveways–garbage strewn gutters outside single room cement structures, half naked children playing in the dirt. I watched women bent over, hand sweeping the sides of the roads. I watched women walk a step behind their husbands, silent. I listened to groups of women chatting and smiling, walking home with bags of groceries. I waited at stop lights as a sea of yellow and black autos flowed past like a swarm of bees, followed by motorcycles, some with a child at the front, a father driving, a mother sitting sideways and holding another child at the back, and private cars, some blasting music as the driver spoke loudly into a mobile.

At that point I had become comfortable on the street on my own and had accumulated more appropriate outfits thanks to shopping at Fab India and receiving gifts from Bheema. One of the old *salwar kamise* she had given me was pink and made me feel like a puff of cotton candy, but I appreciated the gift and wore it nonetheless.

I had a list of items to purchase downtown; I had stretched my two month provisions into three, but now my clothes were tattered, my flip flops less flip and more flop, and I was squeezing out every last drop from my face cream, shampoo, and toothpaste. Running out of supplies made me face the decision of how much longer I was going to stay. I felt an intense, nearly physical aversion to going back to California. I could see possibly moving on to somewhere else, but I wasn't ready to go back. I would wait and pray and see what opportunities came along.

That night I went to bed longing to see a movie, to see some art, creativity, beauty. I needed to dance to truly feel like me. I needed to find a balance if I was going to stay. I needed to get back to my own yoga practice.

I need. I need. I need. I felt lost, directionless, and purposeless–I dove into *maya* and swam in circles. I was focusing on what should be and not what was.

Living in the present is undesirable when the present is difficult. We don't always want to challenge ourselves when life already presents

us with challenges. The easier, although only momentarily rewarding choice is to live in fantasy, in the past, or in desires for the future.
Desires.

Like a drug, fantasy provides a high that when confronted with
reality leads to a lower low. The pendulum of ups and downs exacer-
bates, elongates to an oval with a tight arc that whips you sharply back
and forth.

I tried to focus on what was wonderful in the present, what was
fulfilling and balancing–teaching. I loved teaching and I loved my students. I looked forward to each class but especially to the moment at
the end when I said *namaste* to all the students and they smiled back at
me with radiance. That afternoon at the bus stop one woman said she
really felt a calm that day in class. At first it was hard but now she was
getting into it and starting to feel the benefits of the poses. That she
got the aspects beyond the physical gave me joy. I introduced *yoga nidra,* a guided meditation while in corpse pose to let go of awareness of
the body and let go of connections to the thoughts, resulting in "yogic
sleep." Cassandra described feeling separate from her body, as though
she had fallen asleep but knew she hadn't.

By then, the children at the school recognized me and would sa-
lute me saying, "Good afternoon, miss." It was so cute–their energy
was a smile. Eyes smiling–open, pure love. I saw a hope and joy in their
eyes, a true happiness as they giggled on the bus with their friends on
the way home.

Maybe some of them would have a chance at a healthy, stable life.
We drove past garbage heaps littered with other children from the
neighborhood, children who weren't lucky enough to go to school,
combing through the refuse for any usable items. Some street children
chased the bus yelling and laughing. We passed others carrying trays
of small stones on their heads to their mothers who were working at a
construction site, their bare chests puffed out, their eyes empty as they
stood and watched us go by.

11

MG dazzle, clubs, *moksa*, Oh, that Bollywood hair!

I finally got a hold of Madalena to find out she was in fact in Mumbai and not Bangalore and would be arriving in a week or so. I learned not to rely on Madalena's sense of time.

When I met Victoria in Ooty at Omar's party she had given me her number and made me promise to call her when I arrived in Bangalore so she could take me out dancing. Victoria was a tiny girl with a huge personality, who made you feel like she was your best friend, and would do anything for you–she sucked me in with her laughing eyes. She walked like a queen, talked like an expert, and smoked like a train engine on fire. I later came to realize she was also a great deceiver. She'd laugh and come up with some convoluted story when caught in a lie.

She was in love with the Egyptian I had met her with in Ooty, but wasn't sure he was being faithful to her. He had confessed to me that he had a girlfriend back in Egypt. The way they acted I assumed he and Victoria had been together a long time, but in Bangalore I found out they had only been together a week. She had many boyfriends who hurt her but she still believed in love. It was hard to tell what she really thought since, I came to realize, her story changed every time I talked to her.

I met up with Victoria at the Coffee Day on MG Road where the lights dazzled like a mini Las Vegas, excited to have a guide to Bangalore nightlife. She brought a date, Ajit. I brought Cassandra and her Austrian boyfriend Sharif who had just arrived. Victoria took us to a hidden club, down an inconspicuous corridor and into a basement, where she knew the DJ and could get us all in for free. Sharif didn't like to dance, so he and Ajit sat at a table talking while we girls danced in a tight circle in the middle of the dark room, avoiding stray male hands.

I found out later that the club Victoria took us to had once been a "gentlemen's club." I'm not sure what that means in India but it certainly meant some of the men there were used to women performing as sexual objects for their pleasure in some way. They stood out quite clearly considering most of the patrons were under 25 and these men were over 50 and by themselves.

One such "gentleman" who was inebriated, roved the dance floor staring at women's bodies as if he had never seen one before. He was standing near our little group for a while, Victoria warned us to be wary. He walked behind me and squeezed my butt. I turned with fury in my eyes and he stumbled backward immediately apologizing for his hand as if it weren't connected to his body. He wandered away.

After about 10 minutes, he reappeared, with his hand accompanying him. He started to walk behind Cassandra and managed to also grab her butt. I filled myself with a sense of anger, tightened my fist, and screamed at him. Then I physically pushed him off the dance floor. He kept apologizing as if he couldn't help it. I nearly had to be held back; he flinched like I was going to punch him. A bunch of men shooed him off good humouredly, laughing at his drunkenness as if it were all just a good-natured joke. He disappeared.

Really I wasn't so offended but I felt I had to play a part in order to establish my position in society. I was not a loose American girl, I was a woman to be respected and treated like other respectable Indian women–meaning hands off. I acted the part not for him as an individual but for all others watching.

In India everyone notices and discusses what goes on around

them. Wherever I stayed I attempted to make a respectable impression to ward off any negative behavior. This is what I felt I had to do and I had very little trouble. Maybe related to my efforts, maybe not.

I looked over at Ajit and mocked their bored looks, crossing my arms and hunching my shoulders. His eyes shone and in slow motion, a smile crept onto his lips. It grew bigger. Then he laughed. Suddenly I was alone in the room with him. His smile stopped my heart.

A cigarette was passed my way (a sign of friendship) and I came back to reality. I talked myself out of the experience, of the connection, of how he stopped my breath. I'm not a smoker and had smoked a few, he was much younger than me, and we knew nothing about each other. At the end of the night, we went our separate ways.

Victoria promised to take us somewhere better the next time. Cassandra was in her element and relieved to finally have some fun away from her focus on work and living with nuns and priests. I realized I needed to buy some culturally appropriate clothes to go dancing–jeans.

The next morning Cassandra, Sharif, and I went to group *latihan*. Sharif went upstairs to practice with the men (men and women practice separately) and Cassandra and I joined the women. It was powerful being in a room full of female energy, practicing together. Open, loud, free. Then someone's mobile phone rang and instead of ignoring it or turning off her phone she answered it loudly saying, "Hello? Hello?" over and over. I laughed (so India) and then regained quiet when she finally gave up.

After practice, we all met up in a common room. Bella introduced me to an older woman, Indira, who had long practiced yoga. Her calm, steady, and sweet energy attracted me like a moth to her inner flame. I loved just being in her presence. She told me about the Bihar School of Yoga and offered to take me to their ashram. I enthusiastically accepted. I had been searching for somewhere to focus my practice, to give me direction again.

On the bus, Cassandra sat with me rather than Sharif. They looked uncomfortable and weren't really talking to each other. Cassandra thought we should stop for tea. It felt like they didn't want to be alone with each other. We got off the bus in Frazer Town, a quiet little neighborhood comprised of a cluster of diverse restaurants; there was a Muslim restaurant that actually sold beef hamburgers and kebabs, a park, a Coffee Day, and a huge mosque. It was the neighborhood right next to ours.

We walked into the cool air conditioning of Coffee Day, ordered our teas and found a table.

"So, what are you going to do after India?" I asked Sharif.

"Well Cassie and I are going to go to Indonesia together," he explained.

"Oh, right. I wasn't sure." I looked at Cassandra quizzically. She had said their plans were up in the air.

"I want to spend a little time at Auroville before we go as well," he continued.

"That's a great idea; it's so interesting," I encouraged. "You've got to get Cassandra out of here–she's hardly traveled at all. She is at the nunnery or working and that's it. Nose to the grindstone. I usually have to drag her out just to get a coffee."

"I want to take advantage of being here. As soon as I go home I'll be starting a job with my father. The day I graduated from college he expected me to suit up. I begged for a month off to travel. I guess this is my last fun for awhile. Cassie is going to be amazing at university."

"She's a smart cookie," I added with a smile. Cassandra blushed and sat quietly. "Let's make something from our new cookbook. I'm told you're a good cook, Sharif–let's see."

"I can't claim to do more than boil an egg. You've been misinformed," he countered.

"Wishful thinking. You'll have to entertain us while we cook then." Sharif liked the assignment.

Cassandra and I discovered a bright happy supermarket; the elation we felt at the sight of fresh produce, spices, refrigerators filled with eggs and cheese, aisles and aisles of unknown varieties of lentils and rice may have involved some jumping up and down. They even sold Nutella! We stocked up and walked back to Benson Town along a few blocks of a residential street behind which were the railroad tracks, then up and over the railroad tracks on the pedestrian bridge, through a small commercial area, and past a few streets more to our building.

I left Cassandra and Sharif to unload the groceries and stepped out again to do a few chores. I stopped by a STD and called California. I missed voices from home. Sometimes I felt in such another world I would forget myself. Hearing a familiar voice brought me back into my understanding of myself, to the eyes I usually see through, to a rootedness in me. I could identify with who I was in this unfamiliar world again.

I checked email and researched plane tickets to renew my visa in June. London was the cheapest option. I stared at the computer screen wondering where to even start looking for an opportunity that could keep me in India. I thought about teaching English pronunciation to call center workers, about teaching yoga at dance studios, about applying for some kind of grant, about leading a tour of South India, whatever came to mind.

I thought about what I was going to teach during the next week. I had created a whole lesson plan to slowly introduce all aspects of yoga practice, to teach something new every day, to foster in my students a feeling of comfort, trust, and confidence in their practice, as well as an understanding of yoga. I noticed a few students not practicing whatever pose we were on if I wasn't looking and then jumping into it when I turned back to face them. It made me laugh, these teachers acting like the students they would soon be teaching themselves. Of course this progam was ascribed to them–they weren't there by choice. But a few were really enthusiastic and that was wonderfully fulfilling.

We spent our Saturday night creating a feast and experimenting with new flavors and ingredients. Cassandra and I cooked while Sharif and Sujit entertained. Sujit was a lanky young man from Kerala with thick black hair; he was sharing the dormitory with Sharif while he attended a computer course in Bangalore. He was wide-eyed at big city life, meeting foreigners, and talking to girls; he was excited to explore this new unsheltered life and was trying to shed his natural awkwardness. He helped by cranking the music on the computer. He and Sharif told jokes and stories. We invited the Fathers but they left to eat at the quiet Catholic Center commissary as usual.

I woke up to back pain and wondering what my purpose in India was. My stomach churned at the thought of leaving on my scheduled flight in a few days. It was a possibility still, although I was doing everything to try to stay. I would be watching money float down a drain as I gave up the ticket. I tried to focus on faith.

I did laundry and worked on a handout for class. Father Amal knocked on our door and asked if I had time to help him. Father Amal was the other priest we lived with, a young and passionate Tamilian embroiled in a Catholic mess. He was working on a letter to the Archdiocese to explain a series of situations that had culminated in him receiving death threats, fleeing his home, and seeking refuge in this quiet, isolated building in the middle of a huge city. The trouble began when Father Amal distributed Church monies to those affected by the tsunami in his village. Not being an accountant he had given funds to needy fishermen without keeping detailed records. Hard feelings among some disgruntled locals ensued, and in his support, the Church sent him out of the volatile climate temporarily to a Catholic school in another city until the situation could be sorted out.

As an administrator at the school, he discovered a ring of corruption involving the local mafia and a particular teacher and her family who controlled not only the appointment and dismissal of teaching staff, but also school funds. His forthright nature led him to expose his findings, putting himself in danger. He thwarted an attempt on his life by confronting the aggressor with love. The man broke down in tears and said his family had been threatened, he felt like he had no choice, but in the end he couldn't do it.

Through further investigations Father Amal began to see the extent of the Church's involvement in the school's misappropriation of funds; it went higher up the ranks than he had imagined.

He was writing this letter in English to send to various Church bodies in the hopes of not only clearing his own name from the tsunami funds misunderstanding, but to also cleaning up the Church from what he had discovered at the school, and ultimately to restoring faith in the community. He wanted others to have the same strong faith in the Church that he had. I was helping him translate his complicated story into a coherent English narrative.

That night my mother called on my mobile and we talked for hours. She's always there when I'm feeling a little lost. She encouraged me to start writing about my time in India as a travel memoir rather than just journal entries. I took the next day off, rested, and walked downtown. I took more secluded streets on my walk all the way to MG Road. I imagined I was going in the right direction and just trusted that I was, winding my way forward. I didn't keep track of how long it took. I needed to breath, to have space around me, to let my direction and my thoughts meander until some clarity was found. My brain was muddled with big decisions. It wasn't easy but it was possible to find nearly empty streets.

I ran into the back of Commercial Street, a busy shopping area with streets and streets packed with little stores, wove my way out, strolled past the Parade Grounds, and finally ended at MG Road. First I stopped in at the famous five-story bookstore, Gangaram's, that appears to have existed for hundreds of years. Every floor is crammed with stacks and stacks of books and dust. I was thwarted in my quest to buy a new journal, they had just closed, and ended up a few steps over at buzzing Barista as the sun faded into orange and purple.

I didn't have the glint and glow of youth anymore–that vibration from an inner energy source, an excitement left from childhood. Did I look like the two old guys across from me? I started to feel old surrounded by the young. More than anything I felt alone surrounded by groups of friends shining with laughter and admiration for each other. Commraderie, support, enthusiasm.

I brought out my notebook to work on some kind of budget and it flopped open to the plane ticket I had stuffed inside. My departure date was a few days away. I stared at it. A piece of paper held so much power over my life. It had forced a decision and remained as a symbol of jumping without a parachute. I had decided not to leave. But I didn't know what I was going to do to earn money stay. I had two more weeks of the yoga program and then a six week long dance course I had enrolled in, afterwhich was just an emptiness of unknown possibilities.

I thought about the dream I woke up from that morning. I dreamt I was on a bus driving on a road that began to turn into sand. The bus tried to continue on. Struggling through the shifting earth unsuccessfully we finally decided to try to turn around; the bus drove up on a steep bank and flipped over. Everyone was fine but we were in the middle of nowhere. I stood on the sand heavy around my feet, looking into a barren void; I was stranded and lost.

Moving forward may be a struggle but turning back is not the solution. You can never go back–if you try, you end up even more lost than before.

What is the connection between feeling lost and feeling free? Sometimes I felt as if I was nowhere. I felt separate from my location, my body, the earth, like my place was pointless but not in a negative way. Like everything was really unimportant and wherever I was didn't matter.

I was free. But lost.

At the same time I was trying to get somewhere, I just didn't know where. And maybe in not knowing my direction the path turned to sand and disappeared and there no longer was a direction. I was no one, nowhere, with nothing.

Having a lack of attachments, total self-reliance, no responsibilities, nothing binding you to anything or to anyone, being alone with your self—alone—is that freedom? Or is that being lost? If you are aware of your inner Self, of your connection with the Divine, then being alone shouldn't feel so alone.

Being lost then is not feeling the true Self, not feeling God.

I was feeling lost in purpose and therefore unsure of who I was. My fundamental purpose, I believe, is to love. I felt blocked. I was feeling very alone, isolated even from myself. Loving myself had been a long and trying struggle, a struggle that had diminished over the years, yet remained present on some level.

Being able to truly love is to find your Self, find God, and find freedom. Finding the kind of love that is free even from the heart is a divine love, an inner love. True freedom is being found in God, in the divine oneness of all. In yoga this liberation is called *moksa*. Swami Bhoomananda expounds on this concept:

> *Moksa* is a clarity, a freedom that you need from whatever troubles you have now. If there is no trouble, you don't need *moksa*. If there is no torment, you don't want any freedom. But generally the world and the life in it are such that everyone who lives will have tension, stress and strain…. Stress and strain—actually this is what we mean by bondage. I always say that all interactions with the world objects are interactions externally; but in the ultimate effect or outcome level, they become subjective—mental, intellectual and emotional. Whenever you interact with the world, the interaction may be external and object based. But the resultant of the interactions is always in your mind. These resultants become a bothering element for you.[19]

There is a freedom in accepting who you are with all your imperfections. Once you let go of the self-judgment you can get to know yourself and understand how and why you behave the way you do. You can begin to understand how stress affects you, why you react in ways that tighten the bondage of stress around you.

Approaching this self-study with calmness reveals the workings of the mind, the roots of our reactions, and the tethers that chain us to the realities of the world around us. *Svadhyaya*, self-study, is one of the observances of Ashtanga yoga. It is an important step in freeing the Self from the mind, in separating the knowledge of the Self from the knowledge of the mind. Feeling that separation of the Self and the mind allows a level of objectivity and detachment from thoughts that do not represent our true being, our Self, but represent a reaction rooted in bondage.

We all live in bondage in this life. We are mostly consumed by what is unimportant, by what is immediate, by distraction. We fluctuate into moments of *moksa*, of freedom, like waves rolling up and down.

My goal is to roll gently on a calm sea accepting the rises and falls.

Free from judgment, expectation, from the mind's machinations, the heart's fluctuations. Free to let one's Self be. Free to let go. In letting go maybe I can feel, for just a moment, true freedom before forgetting and holding on again.

I sat at Barista lost in these thoughts, writing in my journal. I looked up for a moment at the crowd of young professional Indians listening to Justin Timberlake, sipping their blended iced coffee drinks, to see Ajit walking over to my table with that same big smile.

"Hi! You're here by yourself?" he asked.

"Just me and my journal. You?"

"I was here with friends, they're just leaving. Can I join you?"

"Of course," I beamed. "Do you usually just walk up to someone and ask to sit down?"

"Yes, if I want to. I'm a refrigerator, I make everyone cool," he responded.

"Huh?"

He had to explain his metaphor. "My heart generates coolness to everyone around me so they aren't scary anymore. I don't fear anyone and no one fears me."

"Oh." I smiled, still somewhat confused, being a literal American.

He slouched into a chair, lit a cigarette, then leaned forward for intense discussion. We talked for hours, oblivious to the rest of the world. I got lost in his eyes, they were gentle and direct but with a glint of roguishness lurking deep within. I couldn't stop smiling.

Ajit was sweetness personified but he would never want to be characterized that way. He preferred to be seen as a bad guy. He smoked and drank, though he was drunk after only half a Kingfisher. But his home was always open to friends in need, he fed whomever was around, he lent his bike out constantly, and when he had it he gave a ride to anyone who asked.

He was easy going and funny–in Hindi he was apparently exceedingly entertaining, in English he was a little more reserved. We were instant friends, we saw into each other's eyes and beyond, we were real with each other. Neither of us were good at small talk or cared for pretention. And he had the most beautiful dark, floppy, perfect Bollywood hair. Oh, that Bollywood hair!

Through a convoluted journey of unexpected encounters I found the person who would fill a space in my heart.

12

Piercing, rebels, clothes make the woman, negative thoughts

Father Amal told me a story about why women wear nose rings. He explained, "In a time long ago when there were separate kingdoms, it was common practice for the king to send his men into the land to find the most beautiful women to be his mistresses. In order to protect themselves from this fate, women mutilated their faces with big nose rings to become undesirable to the king, leaving them in peace."

Father Saul then argued, "Actually women pierced their noses to look more beautiful and desirable because they would want to be chosen to be the king's mistress–it was a good life."

Father Amal insisted it was enslavement. They had a lively debate.

Is being the king's mistress enslavement or a safer, healthier life? Or both? Women have been forced to make such choices for centuries. Compromising their selfhood and their freedom for safety and financial support, in order to save their own lives and to save their families from poverty. It isn't much of a choice.

Beauty or mutilation? Sexual availability or unavailability? Drug abuser or worldly hippy chick? Socially defiant or a poser? I've encountered all those reactive labels in the West. I pierced my nose in college. I was not attempting to become more or less attractive, socially acceptable or unacceptable, to play a role or create a persona. I didn't want to be found by the king; neither was I trying to hide.

It was Halloween; I was living in Los Angeles and went to Venice Beach with an Indian-American friend who instructed me that I should have it done on the left. She gave me the impression this had to do with caste or social standing in India. The shop was also a tattoo parlor. My piercer was a huge, muscle bound, tattooed, pierced tree of a man who made me feel steady and quiet. We went into a sterile room; he swabbed my nostril and pierced it with a giant needle that he left sticking out as he went to get the ring. I closed my eyes. My friend stared at me and laughed. He inserted the ring after making sure for the third time that I really wanted that large of a ring instead of a tiny stud like most people. He was talented, not one drop of blood was shed. I was so excited and went nearly cross-eyed looking down at my large silver ring. I felt like it had been missing from my body.

I was drawn to the piercing, to the ring, to something I couldn't explain. I had suddenly noticed its absence. I sighed in relief at its presence, a part of me that had been missing was reattached. I relaxed.

I researched the history of piercing in India and found that the practice had been around since the 16th century. A nose piercing is usually in the left nostril because in Ayurvedic medicine the left side is the female side and is associated with reproductive organs; it can make menstruation and childbirth easier.

Were my reproductive organs trying to tell me something at 21? Several years later I removed the ring, the hole rapidly closed and I was left missing something for another several years. Maybe it is coincidental that during that time my reproductive issues began, my depression increased, and I found ovarian cysts and a disease plaguing my reproductive organs. I know of course that is a huge oversimplification. I re-pierced my nose.

I had an interesting dialogue with Father Saul about the Church. He believed there was no God in Catholicism, there was only "The Church."

"I'm living in the house of heretics!" I said.

Father Saul laughed. He explained that after Jesus died, St. Paul created "The Church," the creation of which in many ways actually went against Jesus' teachings. For the first 300 years Christianity was made up of groups praying and discussing–no priests, no hierarchies.

"Jesus was a revolutionary. I want to emulate him. The Church focuses too much on sin, especially sexual guilt and sin. Jesus' life is more important than the moment of his death. His death is what defines Catholicism. Rather it should be his life that defines us."

He wanted to be a rebel like Jesus.

Father Amal, while critical of the Church, was still passionate and accepting of the structure as necessary. He countered with arguments of how the institution could do more good as an organization than as a scattering of disconnected individuals.

Father Saul preferred to focus on Jesus' life and teachings and sense of sharing and equality. He was exploring an Indian interpretation and perspective of the Bible. Like Paramahansa Yogananda, Father Saul also believed that Jesus spent time in India and learned from and shared ideas with ancient sages and monks. I wondered how you could separate out Jesus' true ideas from the layers and layers of cultural and linguistic interpretations, as well as from political agendas that muddled his original teachings?

Father Amal connected with the Church in childhood when his primarily Christian fishing village was brutally attacked by Hindus. He watched people he knew lose their homes to flames, see their boats battered apart, watch their families beaten, and mourn the loss of lives. The Church's help was the one bright light in the aftermath. They picked the village back up, put out the flames, rebuilt, and re-enlivened the community. He decided then and there he wanted to be a priest to help others. To bring back hope and life.

Father Amal turned on the computer and turned up the volume on his favorite Tamilian songs. He joined in at the top of his lungs, belting the words out passionately.

I went to Barista to write and again ran into Ajit. This time not alone, he introduced me to his friends Saif and Sameera and invited me to join them. We drank coffee and people watched, chatting and joking. It felt like college until they found out I was 30 and started calling me "ma'am" as a joke to make me feel old. They helped with ideas about working, suggesting that tons of young Indians would come to my yoga class just because I'm western. I could rent some space and with just 10 students earn enough to pay my own way here. But of course it wouldn't cover my bills from home. We talked for hours about clubs, culture, relationships, jobs in the US, sacrificing for your parents, and the unacceptability of intercaste marriage.

Saif was Muslim. Sameera was Hindu. Their parents were unaware of their romantic relationship though they had been seeing each other for years and were secretly, informally engaged. Publicly they were only friends, which was tolerable while they were in college. As soon as they graduated they would become marriageable, and friendships between men and women would no longer be acceptable.

With all these public rules how do relationships actually work here? Unmarried people do have sex. Many men try to meet foreign women for this purpose. If you are Indian and sleep around you can become part of the "wrong crowd," not a good person. But if there is an intention of love, friendship and loyalty, then it seems more acceptable. Although as a woman you also run the risk of becoming unsuitable for marriage, which means you will end up with no place in society and a disgrace for your family. Romance is a serious situation.

They explained how relationships are a minefield of negotiations, contradictions, secrets and promises, and a separation of the private and public. Everything is dependent on parental acceptance. If you fall in love and want to marry, you must find a way to dupe your parents into believing they arranged the match and that you are accepting it out of respect for them. If you are in love with an unacceptable match then you either end the relationship and marry suitably or you defy your parents, disgrace the family, and are disowned and removed from the most important structure of Indian society. This is, of course, highly simplified and traditionalist but other manifestations of the love match scenario seem uncommon.

These strict rules create intense melodramas, which are perfect inspirations for Bollywood films. This is one of the attractions, as well as befuddling aspects, of Indian society–everything is intense. Coming from a fairly apathetic culture that seems to prefer television to real life, these very real, life-changing interactions between people are exciting, scary, and inspiring. Maybe one of the reasons privileged westerners flock to India is this realness, this intensity, this "in your face" way of experiencing life.

It seemed to me as if this new generation of Indians were trying to enact an American soap opera on speed. Another example of paradox and extremes. Extreme conservatism and traditionalism paired with extreme westernization.

Saif, Sameera, and I parted new friends and Ajit walked me to the auto stand. He settled the price with the driver for me and waved goodbye as I rumbled off in a puff of exhaust.

The next morning, arriving to teach, before we even made it into the classroom, my students launched into an argument on why class should be canceled the next day. It was Ugadi–Karnataka New Year. I let them convince me; I had been invited to a celebration myself.

Then I asked where the mats were for class and no one knew. I tried the office, everything was locked and no one was around. I had made handouts for the next class but decided to give my lecture on the eight-limbed path instead. We pushed the school desks and chairs back into the middle of the room and everyone found a seat. I wrote out the limbs on the chalk board and went through each one. I found some examples of the concepts that seemed to make sense for them and even made them laugh. The room was filled with good energy. I asked them to think about each *yama* and *niyama* in their own lives as their homework.

The next afternoon, I arrived at the Bhachan's and Bheema helped me get ready for the Ugadi celebration. She leant me a sky blue *sari* with tiny embroidered white flowers on the edges; it was as light as a cloud. I felt beautiful. We went downstairs to the open courtyard where tables had been set up. Bheema was in charge as usual; she had organized the whole event and was now directing everyone in what to do. The food started to arrive in pots and containers. It smelled incredible. I had saved my appetite and now was about to faint from starvation.

Once everyone had congregated we had a short *puja* where different people chanted or said a few words to give thanks and pay respect to the Divine. There were prayers and some offerings of food and flowers to bring the spiritual into the event. It made the event meaningful and special.

Traditionally at meals, women serve the men first and only eat later when the men have finished. But this crew of professional young married couples, both equally educated and working, did not approve of this gender-biased tradition. We mixed it up, split the group in half, and both men and women served the first batch, then we switched and the other half served the servers.

I could hardly wait to try all the aromatic dishes. I was seated on the ground with a banana leaf in front of me. Mounds of food were spooned onto it in a circle around the center of rice. Every family had made their own contribution from their home state in India, so it was an eclectic mix of southern and northern food, all home cooked. I ate too much, of course.

Then the men disappeared, the ladies sat around in a circle and each sang a song. I sang a yogic chant, not knowing any Bollywood or traditional songs the others were singing. We drank tea, played games, and delighted in the sweetness of *barfi* a dessert made from milk, sugar, cardamom and other flavors like almonds or pistachios, boiled down to a chewy soft mass. These were made with carrots and ghee, rich and addictive.

I was sent home with bundles of food. I couldn't imagine being hungry again–I was bursting. The bus schedules were off and it took three buses and several hours to get home. I slept hard and late into Saturday morning. I did laundry, went food shopping, emailed, and cleaned my room. I had finally bought my writing journal and started some work on ideas for a book. It was a productive and satisfying day. In the evening I met up with my now usual crew–Ajit, Saif, and Sameera. We decided to go dancing.

Spinn was a club within walking distance from MG Road, around a corner and down an unassuming side street. We walked through a seemingly random door along a tall white wall where a large bouncer appeared guarding the entrance; he selected who was allowed inside into the small vestibule that led out into a hidden open courtyard with tables and chairs. Through the courtyard was another white door, with a porthole window, leading into the club. White leather upholstered couches lined one side of the lounge; a long sleek bar in front of a wall of mirrors filled the other side; windows opened to the courtyard; a balcony provided a view of the courtyard outside as well as the dance floor inside. It wasn't as large as the fancier clubs, but it was my favorite.

Sameera was in a dance company. They performed Bollywood style and some hip hop, western dance numbers, providing entertainment mostly at corporate functions. She was paid, had her own scooter, and was a full time student as well. Her parents weren't too pleased, as performing can be seen as an improper activity for a girl, but they allowed it while she was still a student. We had great fun dancing together and sharing moves.

Ajit never stopped moving, free in his dancing, he sang and hollered and smiled, him with his Bollywood hair. Ajit's energy was infectious, he radiated good vibes, we fed each other's joy, egged each other on and made each other laugh and feel free. We vibrated on the same wave length amplifying our individual selves into something bigger and better. We lived wholly in the moment. I tried to convince myself my feelings toward him were like those toward a little brother. But at moments, his eyes could seduce me. We were both dripping with sweat by the end of the night, our clothes drenched like we had walked through a downpour.

Outside we saw a girl rolling up her skin tight red pants under a burka before getting on the back of a motorcycle. I remembered her from inside the club, she had been drinking and dancing freely with different guys. On the street everyone was watching her and someone teased, "*as-salaamu aleykum*." She responded with a defiant smile, "*wa aleykum as-salaam*," lowered the burka over her head to complete the head-to-toe coverage, and drove off.

Clothes make the woman. There always seemed to be an observation and judgement about what a woman wore, how she wore it, and where she wore it. I was still in *salwar kamise* even in clubs, while Indian women were in tight western tops and jeans. I received many strange looks for that incongruity.

At other times and in other situations, I wasn't traditional enough in certain areas of the city, for my class, or for riding on the bus. There seemed to be a division in worlds. Of course for me the looks weren't meaningful–I wasn't concerned with being judged–but I did want to be respectful and blend in. For Indian women a decision to wear something out of place was extremely meaningful, it would not only effect how they, as an individual, were treated and judged but it would also extend to their family. What they wore reflected their place in society, their worth, their respectibility. It meant everything.

I spent the next day organizing and re-prioritizing. I planned out the remaining curriculum for my students. After the course ended, I had to find a new place to live. I went to Attakkalari to register for the dance program and talked to the Director. I proposed teaching community yoga classes, which he was interested in but only after the dance program was finished in June.

I tried creating opportunities. I was focusing on positive thinking and forward momentum. I wanted to prioritize studying dance and teaching yoga. I extended my positive energy from envisioning the life I wanted to lead in India to envisioning life around me in general in a positive light.

There is a yogic practice for awareness and control of the thoughts called *pratipaksha bhavana*. It is awareness of when the thoughts are negative, toward oneself, toward another, or in general, and then actively transforming those negative thoughts into positive ones. I find I do that when I am with other people, but my candid thoughts, as seen in my journals, could use work. That internal dialogue is the most difficult to change; we are changing the essence of who we are–in how we view the world and ourselves in the world.

Negative thoughts are an insidious poison that sometimes lead to great depression. In the past I incessantly insisted on my dislike for myself. Then, I disliked how I focused on the negative. The cycle was never ending. I could be so positive about anyone else, even optimistic about the world at times, but the virus of self-hate spread. Starting within was the only way to achieve some kind of peace. The virus had already infiltrated every cell so I needed to go into battle at every level. One level was to change my pattern of thinking. How could I truly love other human beings if I couldn't love myself?

Looking back into my past I remember times when I was filled with rage at the world and toward myself. I suffered through some very dark years. I periodically look through old journals to remind myself how I fell so deep and how far I've come since then.

September 2002

I spent the day mentally writing my will. Who would I give things to? What do I have that is meaningful? Then, how would I kill myself? Leaving a body is a messy detail. But that takes too much thought; then I wouldn't be letting go. I think people in my capoeira group now think I'm a freak. Sometimes I am such a grumpy, anti-social bitch. I can't even perform normalcy anymore. It's hard when everyday is a struggle to figure out why I'm still alive. That my pain came back this month doesn't help. I'm trying so hard not to be stressed out, to spare my body. I exercise, eat right. And still. Another thing for me to be angry about—at my body, at the world, at the toxins I live in, at a world that doesn't care about women's health but then chastises us when we can't get pregnant. Everything is always our fault and yet we don't run the world or make decisions that affect all humans. But we still accept the blame. It really sucks to be a woman. Constant de-humanization. Slow torture, hidden, almost imperceptible when we spend most of our lives teaching ourselves that insults are really compliments, objectification is really appreciation. It's like I've jumped out of the matrix and can only see a horrific, disgusting, evil-filled world of hate and anger and violence. Physical, emotional, psychic violence. Soul-mutilating violence. Or maybe I'm just seeing myself.

In my darkest hour, an old college friend told me about affirmations. The idea of affirmations has come back into my life many times over the years from many different directions. They have been difficult for me to remain dedicated to because it takes strength to truly believe your words. The point is that with repetition the belief or reality will come, will unfold within you and without.

I was fighting my own progress by re-affirming the negative throughout the day after affirming the positive in the morning. Every thought was tinged with negativity; my entire outlook was depressed; my self-worth had been devalued. I was without the strength to change. I needed something utterly positive to destroy the virus.

Step 1: Detect the nature of the virus. Step 2: Defuse its impact. Step 3: Bring the self back into health. 1-2-3. Sounds simple. I had already spent my life analyzing my symptoms, analyzing the causes and allowing myself the comfort and ease of surrender. I had some external means of momentarily defusing the heaviness, but they never lasted. I had to find some internal means.

Without knowing, I had already begun the journey with yoga. Monday nights for an hour and a half I listened and absorbed a different message than the one I had been telling myself for decades. Words are powerful. Whether we want to take them in or not, they creep into the mind and can be reflected quietly in our own thoughts and actions. I magnetically attracted all the negativity around me and let it in. The antidote was to let in some positivity. The hardest part was letting go of the tight grip I had on my acceptance of the negative.

I looked to faith. Faith that the more I changed each negative thought, however much I believed in it, the less true it would become until eventually I would no longer believe or be attached to those thoughts. Faith is not something a depressed person has much of. Where does that strength come from? Dig deep. *Deep.*

On the tour of South India, I read another Louise Hay book, *You Can Heal Your Life*, in which she offers steps to heal ailments when they are detected.

1. Look up the mental cause. See if this could be true for you. If not, sit quietly and ask yourself, "What could be the thoughts in me that created this?"

2. Repeat to yourself, "I am willing to release the pattern in my consciousness that has created this condition."

3. Repeat the new thought pattern to yourself several times.

4. Assume that you are already in the process of healing.[20]

I surrounded myself with activities that promoted inner strength.

Yoga and dance. I hoped to absorb their positivity without having to do much work, work for which I didn't have the strength. It was an outward practice of loving thought and loving action when I was incapable of an inner practice. It kept me alive.

Later, after I had relieved my body of the heavy burden of endometrial tissue and cysts and intensified my yoga practice, I was finally able to actually work on myself, to truly engage in the battle for my health. Actively changing my thought process was an important step, and still is.

13

Under a watchful moon, a funny bunch, love goes and comes

Ajit and I messaged every night. It made life lighter. He was a happy distraction of fluttering butterflies. Running up to the roof to talk to him at night, so as not to disturb Cassandra, I'd sit on the dirty cement ground next to the solar water heater and the clotheslines under looming palm trees and a watchful quiet moon.

"I was just dialing your number," he answered.

"I beat you to it," I laughed.

"Did you find out about the yoga job?" he asked.

"Not yet, we'll see. I'm not sure what I'm going to do."

"You're going to stay though, right?"

"I don't know yet."

"I can help you, just tell me." He insisted.

"Thanks."

"Then you're staying."

I laughed, "Since you've decided for me, I guess so."

"Good."

We told each other everything everyday. I couldn't sleep until we messaged good night. My friend. Considerate, thougthtful, generous. Ajit's personality mirrored a list I had made of my ideal companion. Our cultural incompatibility did not provide as clear a reflection. I was an older, more educated, non-Hindu, non-Indian woman–I violated every requirement of a marriageable woman, and Ajit would never go against his parents.

It seems beyond complicated and nearly impossible to find our vision of happiness in a partnership. When some factors meld two people together, others fracture them apart. If we do find compatibility in the moment then in time, things change. Then people grow apart. And then people unnecessarily rely on each other, rely on expectations, and are crushed by disappointment. What's it all about?

My heart felt weak, I was faint, my back was hurting again, and I was sweating uncontrollably–I felt my disease. I collapsed back into bed after a simple errand, and tried to read, but couldn't concentrate; I couldn't still my mind. With no music, television, company, food, I started to feel restless and decided to walk to Coffee Day to get some hot tea.

Saif and Ajit joined me even though I was cranky. I noticed strange things coming out of my mouth. I wasn't very present. I commented on something being better than something else–I was making an unfair judgement–and Saif said that nothing is better than anything else. I stopped dead in my thoughts. That's what I usually said. Where was my head?

Being tired–just plain tired–in my body led me to also feel weak in my mind. I spoke without attention or care. Sometimes it's the most natural, easy thing in the world to care, to be caring, to speak with care. But at other times it's the most difficult, and recognizing the difficulty aroused fear in me. That fear lurked insidiously, waiting for any memory of depression or depressive thoughts to pounce, hoping to drag me down below the surface, to smother me in darkness. That didn't happen, but I feared it when I heard an echo of my past state in my behavior or thoughts. When others too easily influenced me, I became wary of my weakness.

I went to bed early and slept a long, deep sleep. I felt a million times better with a returning energy, strength, and peacefulness. I practiced *pranayama* and breathed in relaxation. I spoke with the Director again at Attakkalari and he mentioned the possibility of a job as a coordinator for dance education. He needed to research hiring me as a US citizen and said we would talk again and see what we could work out. I tried not to get too excited. It was exactly what I was looking for.

Attakkalari Centre for Movement Arts was a Contemporary Dance company and studio. The studio itself was a large, warehouse-like, open space connected to an office and a covered patio. They were in the middle of construction to expand; the patio was to be enclosed and turned into another studio space. Once a year they conducted a six-week intensive dance program to raise money and publicity and partly to find new talent to add to the company. The intensive program included classes in Contemporary, Contact, Bharatanatyam, Kathak, Capoeira, and Yoga.

I loved the feeling at the studio. Madalena and I had gone previously to pick up a class schedule and were immediately befriended by several dancers. It was a warm and open place with a vibrancy that attracted me.

I sat at Barista for two hours that night chatting with Saif, Ajit, Cassandra, and Sharif. Saif decided to be my Personal Advisor/Business Manager–Mitra, Inc.–we'd be famous in five years.

"International tours," Saif began.

"Books," added Ajit.

"We could open ashrams." Saif was getting more and more animated.

"How about an action figure you can bend into any *asana*," I suggested.

"And your own clothing line," Cassandra jumped in.

"You could have purple robed devotees following you around," Saif joked. We all laughed, taking the idea to sillier and sillier levels.

"This is the first time I've seen you motivated about business, Saif," I said.

"It's boring in school, I need a job, then I can get excited."

"But if you finish, then you could go for your MBA and really do something exciting."

Saif shrugged.

It seemed that the parent-child relationship was enmeshed in lies. Saif told his mother he had already graduated from college, when in reality he had stopped going to class and had basically been buying his way out of his exams. He thought he could continue and just buy his degree (not an unusual practice in India from what I had heard), but the head of the college was holding his degree hostage for a hefty ransom that he couldn't afford. So he got a job to try to make the money to pay for his diploma.

He had no recourse to remedy the situation, especially because no one in his family could find out that he had lied and said he had graduated the year before. He gave up on the situation and got a job at a call center. He also took over some of his late father's business but there were issues with his father's business partner which was complicating his ability to do more. As the eldest male, Saif was responsible for his family, which meant he had to appear to be what his mother wanted and expected him to be. In order to experience any of his desires outside of that expectation, he lied. This was normal. Truth is elastic.

In India, telling someone what he or she wants or expects to hear is of great value. When you ask for directions someone would rather give you completely wrong directions than not be able to "help" you at all. They don't say, "I don't know," but with a smile begin pointing in some direction (many times opposite to the verbal directions they are giving) and creating an imaginary route for you, all with the most sincere and good intentions.

There is a strong tensile pull between tradition and westernization. The youth pull away, struggling with themselves knowing that they are going against what their parents and society find acceptable, but then quickly snap back in the presence of authority. Bollywood culture is misleading. The lives portrayed on film are fantasy to most Indians. Smoking and drinking are considered immoral. Romance is not part of the normal marriage process. Wearing western clothing is barely permissible for youth, let alone for an adult.

Sure these are generalizations and change does occur, albeit in small ways. I watched a television talk show that depicted four Bollywood couples discussing their decision to co-habitate without being married, showing new thought and experimentation, a rebellion, a demand for individual freedom. Although one of the first questions was, "How did your parents react?" all of the couples had to assure the host that after initial reluctance their parents were accepting. They were proving India could be modern. All the couples worked in Mumbai in the Bollywood entertainment industry, and both the men and the women were individually successful and financially self-sufficient. The women were not in the position of needing marriage to secure their financial future. They had also decided to postpone parenthood in support of their careers. The ability to pay for their wedding themselves released them from the burden of a dowry, freed them from familial control, and afforded them greater freedom in their life choices.

I texted Ajit constantly, I was a SMS addict. Short Message Service–short and sweet, limited, intermittent communication. Or maybe I was addicted to Ajit. My mobile minutes slowly disappeared. I spent money to stay connected. I bought a pair of jeans for 700 rupees ($15) to be more modern, to fit into his world. I felt more energized. I bought green tea to drink at home and fresh vegetables to get healthier. My hair had been coming out in masses; I decided to think of it as purification rather than stress about the real reason.

It was Father Amal's last day with us. He had decided to go back to his village, face the problems head on, and work it out. He was done hiding. I was sad to see him go–he was lively and warm. I would miss his big smile as he crooned his favorite songs. He planned to write a book on his experiences and wanted to stay in touch to get my help. I was happy to help and thought editing could be a job avenue for me. I made tea for us both, sat and listened to his hopes for the future.

Cassandra, Sharif, and Sujit joined us and we all went out for a goodbye dinner at a restaurant downtown. The five of us squeezed into a booth, took photos, and shared laughter. Father Amal insisted on paying for the feast.

After dinner, walking on MG Road, a girl carrying long-stemmed red roses approached us. She was maybe 10 years old and brilliant. She laid two roses on Father Amal's folded arms and demanded 20 rupees. She had a long discussion and negotiation with him when he refused to take them. She first argued that he should give them to his girlfriend. He countered that he was a priest. She argued that if he was a priest then he should give the roses to us as his friends. They went back and forth with logical arguments. Ten minutes later he said she had wasted his valuable time and she should pay him 2 rupees per minute. She sheepishly held out her hand with 20 rupees in it and said quietly, "Here, sir and now you can give me 40 rupees for the flowers." We all broke out laughing.

Giving a few coins doesn't work for westerners as it does for Indians. Ajit always gave a few coins when asked and then the person would walk away. If I gave, they would poke my arm or tug on my clothes, putting an open hand in front of me asking for more. When I walked away, they followed behind insistently. When others on the street saw that I had given, they would join in until I had a crowd of beggars surrounding me. I never figured out how to react well and could never reconcile the head/heart separation. Some said not to support begging because it promotes or continues begging; some said not giving is cruel, these are individuals not a political cause. Ignoring a beggar felt like treating them as less than human. Giving money created a harassing mob scene that chased you away from what you were doing.

It was always heartwrenching.

The next morning, I woke up exhausted. My yoga practice felt off balance and weak. My body frustrated me. I was feeling blue. I started to notice how often I was having imaginary conversations with no one. Not a good sign. I missed being close with someone, holding hands, hugs. Everything was so transient. Wonderful but fleeting. Fulfilling then gone. Established then changed.

I texted Ajit that I was sad and he said he would meet me. Twenty minutes later we were sitting together at the Frazer Town Coffee Day on the patio, secluded under palm fronds.

"So you don't get lonely." He handed me a CD player.

"Thanks!" I was surprised.

"You don't need to say thank you to a friend. Never say thank you to me." My heart swelled with sweetness. He knew exactly what I needed.

"I'll take you to a shop tomorrow and you can buy music from home."

Ajit was always there with a solution when I had a problem. He offered so much of himself as a friend, not just to me, that was just his way–always giving. We sometimes forget how big the little things can be. He went out of his way to meet up with me when I needed someone to talk to, he would drop anything to spend time with me, and always with a big warm smile that would make me smile. He brought me music when I had silence.

After coffee he dropped me back to the center. I hung out with Cassandra and Sharif for a bit while we made dinner. They seemed preoccupied. I left them to be alone, lay in bed, and fell asleep listening to the radio on Ajit's CD player.

After school Cassandra and I rode the bus together; it sometimes seemed like the only time we had to talk, she was so occupied with finishing her obligation at Mithra and with Sharif. She told me how the night before Sharif had announced he planned to go to Auroville alone and from there would move on. I had overheard some of the conversation but left the room so they could talk. Cassandra said she was in too much shock to react so it wasn't much of a conversation. She looked as if Sharif had just broken up with her although that hadn't been decided; she wasn't ready to process this possibility. Adult decisions. Poor girl.

I had noticed that Cassandra wasn't herself around him. I didn't know why or when things had changed for them but clearly something had changed. I tried to help in some small way, to get them out to different parts of the city, to meet new people, people closer to their age, to have some fun. They appreciated the interference too much for a couple in love and eager to plan their future.

I tried to bring a cheerfulness to our little family, when in my heart I was saddened, not just for them, but for love in general. We were two Catholic Priests who had chosen love of God over a family, an innocent, sheltered boy enthralled to speak to girls for the first time, a young woman going through her first heartbreak, an Austrian man who had waited for his teenage love, traveled across the world to be with her only to encounter a cooler reality, and me. We were a funny bunch. But we were a family of sorts.

I was distracted thinking about my next chapter after Cassandra's departure. Constantly readjusting was wearing. I searched for a little stability. I hoped it would come through work. I had a meeting at Attakkalari that didn't go as I had hoped. I thought I could teach at the dance studio without too much worry over visas, paperwork, etc., but the Director would only entertain the thought if we went through all appropriate channels, which seemed nearly impossible. The only possibility was forming a collaboration with a US organization and creating a joint project with Attakkalari where I could be sponsored. This seemed quite difficult since I was already in India. I was disheartened and disappointed.

I met Ajit at Coffee Day and he brought his roommate Abhishek. Abhishek had a great laugh and friendly eyes. He was the mature one. He was more at peace with how life was going to go–the prescribed college degree (they were both studying to be pharmacists), getting a respectable job, getting married at his parent's choosing. He had fun and was making the most of his years of freedom without being beset with angst like his best friend Ajit.

"How are your classes going?" I asked over coffee under an umbrella on the patio.

"Always the same," Ajit sighed.

Abhishek laughed, "How would you know, *bhai*? I haven't seen you in class in a month."

"Always the same," Ajit grinned.

"You don't go to class?" I asked.

"Why? I don't understand it," he explained.

"Then why did you choose it?"

"I didn't."

"What do you want to do then?"

"I'd like to be a designer." He surprised me with his answer.

"Then why don't you?"

"How can I?"

"You just do it."

"It's not possible."

"Isn't your job now related to that?"

"I'm trying to do events, mostly fashion shows, but I can only do it here, for now. I can't do it in Gujurat. I don't want to do something I don't love. I want to do so many things." He exhaled and then changed the subject, "Let's go to the cinema."

"You're not going to be a pharmacist at this rate either," I challenged him.

"It doesn't matter. Abhishek will hire me." He put his arm around Abhishek's shoulder with a grin.

"Sure *bhai*, sure."

The future was not theirs to write. They could only joke about it. We talked about movies and their favorite Bollywood stars. Abhishek left to study. Ajit and I drove on his motorcycle to a big cineplex on the top floor of a massive modern shopping mall. We rode the escalator to the top and realized we had just missed every movie we wanted to see. This became a running joke with us over the months. For some reason or another we always just missed the film every time we tried to go. We decided to hit a club instead. Spark was more of a bar with a small square dance floor in between wood tables and chairs. It was the first time Ajit and I had gone out alone. We had a few beers, got tipsy, and danced.

The DJ played the Sean Paul song "Temperature" and Ajit sang to me. I thought of it as our song, and it made me smile. The chorus rang true–Ajit always wanted to give in my time of need, he was my hug in an isolated world, he kept me safe. Singing to me was as hot as he got on the dance floor. The nuns at my Catholic High School would have been happy with the 12-inch distance he maintained at all times, and certainly no touching.

I could have ridden around on his bike all night, my arms around him, the city moving past us removed, leaving us in our own world.

Talking to Ajit was like talking to myself; he was my mirror. We looked at the world in such a similar way, had the same sense of humor, and at the heart of it wanted the same kind of life. We had had the same problems in relationships, stemming from our similar perspective on what we expected a relationship to be, and criticized ourselves in the same way for how we made big life decisions. He even wanted to adopt children and for the same reasons I did.

I was trying hard not to like him too much but it was too easy, scarily easy. His smile killed me. His big heart and desire to love everyone embraced me in a soft bubble. I was addicted to the high I felt when in his presence.

I spent the next morning with Amisha, my friend from Bheema's building, shopping, having lunch and coffee. I enjoyed our more mature conversations. She talked about office politics, managing male co-workers as a woman, taking care of her elderly mother-in-law. She loved to tell stories that highlighted how smart and sweet her son was, her pride bubbling. I talked about my course and trying to find a place to live. Every place I had contacted wanted a long-term lease with more financial obligation than I was comfortable committing to without income. And I had to leave the country for awhile to renew my visa.

I admired Amisha, I liked her–I just didn't relate to her life situation. I felt in between these friends I had made. Beyond the college years but not in the world of a career and family. I was a traveler but trying to find solid ground. I felt apart.

For me solid ground has never meant "settling down," buying a house, living in one location for the rest of my life, sticking with one career, being what our cultural concept of "an adult" is. My solid ground is a balance and peace within myself, a steadiness in myself and in my life. I think I will feel rooted in some way with a life partner, someone who is grounded in who they are, someone I can rely on and lean on.

My tree will be rooted in love.

14

Perplexing love, riots, dinner parties, goodbye moon

Cassandra and I eagerly got ready to have dinner at Ajit and Abhishek's house. I borrowed her hair dryer, straightened my hair, and put on makeup for a change. Cassandra, Sharif, and I took an auto, giving the driver their address since we had no idea how to get there. It was a lot farther than we had expected. Bangalore is a sprawling city. I called Ajit several times so he could give directions to the driver who was also lost. We finally arrived at a bus stop where Ajit stood waiting for us.

He walked us down a few narrow dirt roads; the area was residential and appeared somewhat poor. They lived walking distance to the college, along with quite a few other students who lived in the neighborhood. We finally arrived at their mostly unfurnished yet clean two bedroom apartment, a typical student pad.

We sat on the balcony and met a bunch of their friends. One of them announced that he and his girlfriend were getting married. I gave him my congratulations. He thanked me and told us the wedding wasn't for another two years.

I said, "Oh, then I won't say congratulations."

"Why not?" He was confused.

"Well, it's so far away," I tried to explain. "Anything can happen."

I didn't know how to explain my confusion. In India, girlfriends aren't who you marry. And who you marry has nothing to do with love. I was confused about what I was giving congratulations for, love or marriage. Was he engaged to a woman he loved, or to a woman he called his girlfriend because their marriage had been arranged? If he was with his girlfriend for love then that gave no guarantee that a marriage would be acceptable or even that they wouldn't break up during the years they had to wait. I realized it was a terrible judgment, but I didn't see real love among these new friends I was making; they expressed momentary infatuations or just a desire to love and be loved.

Our two nervous hosts scuttled in and out of the kitchen, not wanting to completely abandon us on the balcony. I went into the kitchen offering to help but was waived off. Abhishek was nervous and dropped half the potatoes he had spent ages peeling and chopping. They slid onto the floor in a splat. We laughed, which I think made him less nervous. They debated over how much of what spices to throw in, the rice to *dal* ratio, and finally how many times the pressure cooker was supposed to release steam until the *khichdi* was ready. They had little to worry about, everything turned out delicious and a home cooked meal was quite a welcomed change.

After eating we went back out to the balcony where it was cooler. I leaned up against the railing. Ajit stood in the doorway and stared at me, his eyes became smoky in a lustful haze–the effect I had intended. That was the first expression of sexual attraction between us.

Cassandra showed off her Hindi skills and shone in the attention. Abhishek confessed to me later that was the beginning of a huge crush he had on her. I listened to conversations about school and parents as they flitted in and out of Hindi, forgetting we couldn't understand them, I really felt our age difference. I wasn't in my element surrounded by all that youth. I was in a different place in my life. I couldn't really engage and realized how much I missed having someone to talk to on a deep level.

I didn't want to revisit a kind of "college love," a crush, fun, no thoughts about the future or the meaning of anything, but somehow

I had surrounded myself with this energy. It was a form of masoch-
ism–indulging my feelings and thoughts of romance with Ajit. I was
addicted to the way he looked at me.

Ajit walked us to the main road and found an auto for us. He gave
the driver instructions and we were off. Cassandra chatted all the way
home–she had been awakened in some way. Sharif was quiet but happy
to have met some great guys and to learn a bit of Indian culture at
someone's home. While I fell into bed, Sharif asked Cassandra if they
could talk and they went up on the roof together.

I awoke to sniffles the next morning. Cassandra hadn't slept much
and was crying. "We broke up," she confided.

"I'm so sorry." I gave her a packet of tissues to replace the wadded
up mass on her bed.

"I know it's the best thing. I didn't think it would be this sad," she
sobbed.

I threw out my agenda of chores and told Cassandra we should get
out of the house. We walked downtown and Cassandra did a little shopping and picked up her custom *salwar kamise* from a tailor. We went
to a music shop and listened to CDs. We had coffee and talked about
everything but the events from the previous night. We bought some
sweets at a sweet shop. We ate at our favorite South Indian restaurant, a
popular family place, and tried a new kind of *dosa*. A dosa is a fermented
rice crepe with a savory filling. We had feasted there often and for only
a few dollars. Their *dosa* menu was extensive–paper thin giant *dosas*,
spiced *dosas*, plain *dosas* with cheese, potato, vegetables, chilis all served
with *sambar* and coconut chutney. *Dosas* were comfort food for us.

We went home and ate our sweets with tea. We shared with the Fathers and Sujit who rarely allowed themselves treats. When Sharif came
in Cassandra decided she needed to do laundry. I helped her hang her
clothes on the lines on the roof.

"I'm so happy I left the nuns and came here," she started.

"Me too! I don't know how you survived there with the 6pm curfew."

"My parents were happy about that," she laughed.

"I think I've been a bad influence."

"Probably," she grinned, "but I needed it."

"Well, I've loved having a friend, having you as a friend, and while your texting all night and constant calls from your parents at one in the morning drive me crazy, you are still an excellent roommate and an inspiration. I'm so glad you came into my life."

We teared up a bit and hugged.

"Thanks for today, I didn't know what to do with myself. I know you didn't get to copy your exams, I'll do it in the morning and bring it to class."

"You're an angel."

Cassandra really was an inspiration in sweetness and hard work. She had a strong integrity that's rare to find. I laid in bed starting to feel a sadness for Cassandra and Sharif, and so texted Ajit.

"Don't be sad. I can't stand it," he replied.

"I'm just sad for them."

"Love is confusing. Sameera's friend is always calling me. I told her I don't like her that way but she won't give up. Everytime I see Saif they are there."

"Oh. Is she nice?"

"Yes. But not as nice as you."

"Don't confuse me."

"??"

"You're flirting," I explained.

"With her?" he misunderstood. "Sometimes I can't help it. I'm a flirt."

"So you do like her?"

"I don't know. I don't want to fall in love right now."

"Well, I don't know about you either."

No response.

Several minutes pass.

I start to panic–did he understand what I said?

The phone rang. He was calling. What do I say?

"What do you mean you don't know about me?" His voice was serious.

"Nothing, I was just confused."

"About love?"

Should I say it? Why? There's no point. I don't want to get hurt. He's 24. He couldn't be with me even if he wanted to.

"Just kidding!" I blurt out.

"Why just kidding?"

"You've been flirting with me without meaning it–you're a flirt– you can't help it. Well–me too. I was just getting back at you. Did I confuse you?" I fake laughed.

"Ha. Ha. Ha. Funny. Yes."

I changed the subject, "I haven't found a hostel for next week. Do you know of any?"

"I can ask around. No problem. You can stay with me if you don't have anywhere to go."

"Really?"

"We have two rooms. No one would mind."

"Well, if I can't find anywhere it's good to know I won't be homeless."

"You could come anyway, you would save money."

"I don't want to cramp your style...with all your girlfriends," I teased.

"I don't have any girlfriends. I can't help it if girls like me."

"Ha. Ha. Ha. So modest."

"Yes. Wait, what is modest?" he asks.

I just laughed, "Not you."

"Abhishek will be happy you're coming."

"I'm coming?"

"Yes."

"I'll let you know," I correct him.

"Ok, I'll tell cook to buy more food next week and I'll borrow another mattress."

"We'll talk about it tomorrow at dinner."

"Can we bring anything?"

"Just your smiles."

"I can do that," he smiled through the phone.

I slept so deeply that even my dream was of myself sleeping. I was in a big double bed with a firm yet soft mattress, a down comforter, and fluffy pillow. I awoke to a message from Indira that she would pick me up in her car and take me to the Bihar ashram. I made sure to be ready and waiting.

The Bihar School of Yoga is one of countless styles or traditions of yoga. These traditions are systems generally created by an experienced swami out of yoga philosophy, science, and practice. The system follows the method that worked for the swami to achieve his or her own level of higher consciousness. They form a tradition from this perspective and impart their knowledge and experience to others. Most of these traditions share the same beating heart, pulsing life into different expressions. Different traditions resonate with different people, leading to an accessible philosophy that allows many paths in order to reach the same understanding.

Atma Darshan Yogashram was located on the outskirts of the city. Indira picked me up in her car (she had a driver) and we drove around the Ring Road which circles the entire city and was previously unknown to me. The city forever expanded in my continued exploration. The quiet little ashram was nestled in a residential neighborhood. It was a small compound, with a few buildings and a garden. We crossed the garden on a sparse stone pathway to the little office. After being introduced to the monks I wandered over to the meditation hall–open, serene, and cool. I sat alone on the cold stone floor while Indira visited with her friends. The energy was still, calming, and peaceful.

We left refreshed and centered. I thanked Indira for the introduction to this lovely place and hoped we could come back again. I needed somewhere like that to help root me again. While I was teaching yoga and about to start a dance program, I had a direction on the surface, but I felt spiritually lost.

Indira dropped me at Mithra and I met Cassandra before class. She had faithfully copied my final exams for me. My students were waiting in anticipation for their last day. We did some *pranayama* and then I handed out the exams. I pretended not to see them cheating–copying each other's answers. Joe wanted an exam, but I wanted them all to pass his requirements. I just wanted them to be interested and maybe excited about yoga. But most of all I wanted them to smile, to feel good about themselves, confident, and accomplished.

They gave me hugs and thanks at the end of class. One student invited me to her wedding. It was sweet and wonderful. I would miss teaching them. The children on the bus singsonged, "Hello, miss" as we all got on and waved and yelled from the windows as we all got off at the bus stop. I would miss their energy as well.

Cassandra and I stopped at the grocery store on the way home to buy food for our dinner party. I was getting nervous. Cassandra, Sharif, and I had decided to invite Ajit and Abhishek to our place for dinner after they had cooked dinner for us at their home. I had previously asked Father Saul if we could have a few friends over for dinner sometime and he had agreed. Cassandra and I opened a bottle of wine and started preparing the food. Sharif and Sujit, went through their playlists on the computer, picked some music, and began rocking out.

We started to notice some unusual noises outside, honking and banging, and Sujit checked the news on the local radio station. He reported back that there were rioters in the street. We were in our safe little cocoon and had no idea what was happening. Ajit called to say it was too unsafe for him and Abhishek to get to our house, but they would try. Several hours later, they ventured out and managed to make it safely while dodging troublemakers on the streets.

That afternoon, unseen tidal waves of violence crashed into the streets after the heart attack of the beloved Indian actor Raj Kumar. He died in a hospital after a prolonged illness, poor health, and finally a heart attack.

The city erupted, anger spewing from the earth through human voices and actions. Buses were burned, auto rickshaws destroyed, people trampled to death, businesses vandalized and looted. Those who failed to put a poster of Raj Kumar in their window had them immediately broken, as if insulting the mourners, challenging them, defying their heartbreak. Motorcyclists were pelted with stones.

We let the outside remain outside and Abhishek began his *roti*-making lesson. They admitted how nervous they were to cook for us at their house. We laughed; our own jitters calming with the wine. We honed our *roti* skills and began our delicious meal.

Father Saul appeared in the doorway and motioned for me to join him in the hall. He quietly and sternly asked when our guests would be leaving. His face red, his voice controlled. I was nervous like a misbehaving child. I said they could leave soon, but we were just now eating. I explained they were delayed by the riot and arrived much later than we had originally planned. He said we were putting him in a bad light by doing something inappropriate and the neighbors would judge him for it. I apologized and said I had no intention of that. He accepted my apology but said they had to leave. I was instructed to eat quickly.

So, with that, the evening was over. It was inappropriate for me to have invited men to our house in the evening. I learned my lesson. We finished quickly and Ajit and Abhishek ventured back out into the streets, letting us know later when they finally arrived home safely.

Underlying the apparent calm of everyday life was the lava of discontent, inequality, unhappiness, poverty, and lack of freedom ready to flow uninhibited. The balance was destroyed when the fulcrum–the people's god, Raj Kumar, was removed. Their hero, who had brought joy or some meaning or escape from their existence was gone. His death caused a furious storm that flooded the city causing people to flee for safety and shelter for days.

I tried to accept the cultural difference but I only saw insanity. I tried to respect this expression of mourning but I could only judge the senseless violence. Why kill each other as an expression of pain, only causing more pain to those sharing your pain? I was in turmoil. I know I don't understand the life experience that motivates the catharsis of chaos.

Sometimes we can be too far from peace to imagine there is any possible way to attain it. Sometimes life is too immediate to see the possibility of removing our attachment to it.

The life of a yogi is to prepare the self in times of stability to pass through times of disquiet with peace. It's a preventative care strategy. It's a long-term plan of dedicated, continuous work. The waves of life move and break unceasingly—whether we tumble under, get pummeled, get swept into unknown regions, or ride them with a smile is up to us. Staying afloat on the surface, not engaging, not fighting against the current, remaining only a witness to the tide is the practice of yoga. Swami Satchidananda expounds:

> If you want to be peaceful always, identify yourself as the ever-peaceful witness within. "I am that eternal witness. I am watching everything that's happening in the body and mind." That is the supreme way of maintaining your peace. If you can't get to the state of identifying yourself as that eternal witness, simply say, "I am not all these things. I'm not the mind, not the ego, not the senses, not the intelligence. I simply watch them. I am the seer, I just see. I am the knower, I just know."[21]

Remaining detached from emotional reactions, understanding that they are a function of the mind and the ego, brings a perspective and calm to one's experience. This is a difficult yogic practice but incredibly powerful. Understanding the difference between the ego self and the true Self is true wisdom. The ego self is created and affected by our interactions in the world, our emotional and psychological reactions to outward stimuli.

The true Self isn't affected by anything but exists within, from the place of the inner divine. It remains unchanged always. By practicing the perspective of a witness, remaining detached, we can begin to experience living from the awareness of the soul, our true Self, from a oneness with everything to see actions and reactions for what they truly are. Rooted in *maya*–delusion.

Understanding the energetic levels of our being puts truth in perspective. The physical, mental, and emotional layers are closer to the material and to delusion, while the immaterial layers impart wisdom and bliss. Practicing yoga is learning to discern the ego from our true Self, *maya* from truth.

Raj Kumar's funeral was held at a stadium to accommodate all the riotous mourners. One person was killed by the police, others were trampled. Software companies lost millions of dollars from shutting their doors. Cars were set on fire, rocks thrown through windows, hundreds of people were injured and a few killed among the mobs. For safety, I didn't leave the house. Everything was closed anyway. The buses were on strike. I couldn't get to Mithra to deliver the course completion certificates to Joe.

I felt claustrophobic, stuck inside, and sensitive to negativity from Father Saul even though Sujit assured me he was no longer angry. I needed to recharge my phone, get cash, and research hostels. I had a few phone numbers but no minutes left on my phone. I sat in bed and read.

In the morning I ventured out to the Hutch shop to refill my prepaid phone and change my plan to include free SMS to avoid using all my minutes texting. I called a friend in the US from an STD and felt energized with her support. It was so wonderful to be understood. I was still searching for my purpose in India. She brainstormed some ideas and encouraged me to have faith.

I finally texted Ajit back: "I'm fine. My phone ran out," I explained.

"I was worried."

"Don't worry about me."

"I do. You are alone."

"I called a friend and don't feel so alone anymore. She told me she loves me."

"I love you."

I wasn't sure how to respond. I re-read the words over and over.

"You are my friend," he continued. "You're not alone with me."

"Thank you."

"Don't say thank you," he responded.

"I forgot, sorry."

"You don't have to say sorry either."

"Ok! Ok! What do I say then?"

"Say you're staying."

"But I don't know why I'm here."

"You're here to meet all the people you have met. It's simple."

I pondered his idea of simplicity.

I made a list of everything I needed to organize and started making calls. First I called Madalena and asked her to meet for coffee. While I waited I called hostels and tried to secure an available room. I wasn't having much luck. Madalena arrived with a smile. We shared chocolate cake, and caught up on all the craziness. She and Maheshwar had fled back to Ooty for a couple of days and stayed with his mother. She confessed to me that they were actually living together now. A confession because neither of their parents knew or would approve. They were in love. She said she would have offered me a bed but it would be awkward with Mahesh.

The plan was to move in with Madalena and a group of her friends to a huge apartment. It was a bit far from the center of the city, but use of a motor scooter was thrown in to sweeten the deal. We were both too scared to drive in India so it wasn't much of a sweetener. I didn't know the others and was skeptical, as was she. We planned on checking it out together. Either way I still needed a room in the immediate future.

We parted with a hug and I walked to Cubbon Park to find some quiet and space; it seemed almost abandoned in this bustling city. I spent more and more time there the longer I lived in Bangalore. The park had separate areas, from vast grassy fields, to manicured rose gardens, to rough natural flower beds, to dense tree stands, and impressive clusters of giant bamboo. I would stand in peace in the towering bamboo forest and close my eyes amidst the cool rustle. The swooshing energy moved me as the bamboo swayed in all directions with amazing resilience. They talked in creaks and loud cracks that sounded like gunshots, pulse quickening, blood cooling, breath clean and deep. I was out of my head and moving to their dance.

I was nervous on the first day of the dance program and arrived too early, which allowed me time to clear my head and breathe in the sweet cool air of the early morning. Was I too old to even dream of joining the dance company? I was about to be confronted with reality. I sat on a bench in a nearby park and watched a group of older women in *saris* and sneakers doing their morning exercise.

The studio was in a neighborhood called Wilson Gardens, which did actually still have some gardens. I followed the flow of what the other dancers were doing, changed into sweatpants in the bathroom, left my bag at the back of the studio, and found a place to sit on the black spongy floor. I breathed through my nerves and stretched until the teacher arrived.

We started as usual with warming up and some technique, then onto a combination. The movements were foreign and challenging. I felt at home in the familiar context of a dance class. It felt good to sweat. My body hurt but felt alive.

I took two to three classes a day with a lunch break in the middle. In between classes we all sat in the covered patio on plastic chairs and chatted as we snacked and gulped water. We introduced ourselves. Some of the dancers were already in the company. We shared our dance backgrounds and found that most of us weren't from Bangalore. Most of the dancers were from other parts of India with diverse backgrounds but a common love for movement. They were filled with good energy. Dancing felt like home.

As the day ended it began to pour. The sky opened up and released a wall of water, not in drops but in waves. When we ventured out, the streets were flooded, knee deep in areas. Someone explained to me that since construction debris had filled in many of the once famous lakes of Bangalore and new buildings had been built right in the middle of the waterways that originally released rain accumulation out of the city, the water had nowhere to go. Officials were paid off and infrastructure was overlooked. Roads became lakes. Traffic stopped, life stopped.

I waded to the bus station and slowly made my way home through chaotic traffic. It took hours.

I was exhausted but couldn't resist meeting Ajit for coffee in the evening. The gang was there and we all decided to go dancing. I wanted to sit and chat but Ajit only wanted to dance, dance, dance. We shared moves and laughed. Ajit insisted on getting me home safely and we took an auto. We drove by Cubbon Park and I inhaled the smell of grass and earth. I loved that smell. So alive, fresh, and cool. I waited outside my building with him until Abhishek could come and pick him up on his bike. We sat on a little bench and talked.

"Have you ever been in love?" Ajit asked.

"Yes."

"What's it like?"

"That's a hard question. It's unique I think to each person–but I guess it's feeling truly like yourself with someone. You want to give,to share; you feel bigger somehow, your heart is bigger. Everything you do you think of them, they become a part of you. You want to know what they think and feel about everything. I don't know how to describe it really."

"I want to be in love."

"You will one day."

"No. I won't. Not like that. My Mom sent me a couple of photos for my match."

"Were they pretty?"

"You can't like someone from a picture. You have to know them, know you can talk to them, know they make you smile, know they have a good heart, know you can be happy just sitting next to each other looking at the moon."

He looked up at the moon and I blushed.

Abhishek arrived and as we were saying our goodbyes at 2am, Father Saul pulled up in a car. He looked at me with shock and walked right past us and into the building. I had caused another big cultural problem. I assumed I had incited his anger once again and felt terrible. Cassandra texted me at 6am to let her in the front door; she had gone out with Madalena and was only then getting home. I snuck her in as quietly as I could.

I went to dance class, had lunch, and collapsed in the afternoon. I helped Cassandra finish packing; it was her last day. Father Saul had been making himself scarce, increasing my anxiety and anticipation of a lecture. He reappeared to say goodbye to Cassandra and after some small talk I let him know I would be leaving the next day.

It was a sad ending for me. Cassandra was leaving. I would be leaving and again moving on to a new place, a new bed, a new chapter in my time here. I had a freedom, an independence, in this little room sharing with a friend. I didn't know what was next. I liked the Fathers. I had felt safe.

I made *masala chai* in the kitchen and packed up my food. Sujit said he was sad to see me go because I brought energy and happiness to this place. He wanted to make sure we stayed in touch. I assured him we would meet up for coffee.

I packed in the evening and walked up the stairs for the last time to the roof and almost cried. It was my peaceful spot, where I could breath. I said goodbye to my three palm trees and gazed up at the stars and the moon.

15

Living with the boys, free to move my body, melodrama

What's mine is yours," said Ajit. And he meant it. Instead of moving with Madalena into a situation that didn't feel right to either of us, she moved into her own studio in Frazer Town and I temporarily moved in with Ajit and Abhishek. Their place was a bit far but easily accessible by bus. It was welcoming, safe, and free. They shared one bedroom and gave me the other with my own little mattress on the floor. They had a cook who made simple but delicious *dal*, rice, *roti* and *sabzi*, a vegetable dish everyday for lunch and dinner. Their cleaning woman came every day and did my laundry along with theirs. I didn't know what she thought of me staying there.

Three other students lived across the hall with the only computer in the building. We watched DVDs together or the boys would play video games. Next door to them was "the TV guy"–that's how I knew him–he was the only one with a television. And finally Hrithik, Ajit's cousin brother, came back for the semester and the three of them shared the other bedroom so I could have my own room. They had a hot water shower and flushing Indian-style toilet, a kitchen but no refrigerator, ceiling fans but no air conditioning.

I read the newspaper everyday on their little balcony and listened to Bollywood hits on the radio. Everyone asked after Cassandra and was sad to hear she had left. She was a star.

Living with the boys, I met the characters in their lives who had previously only lived in stories. One day I met the infamous Sonali, Ajit's ex-girlfriend, who showed up unexpectedly and unwelcome. She wore blue contact lenses, tight western clothes, and a thick layer of makeup. Her voice dripped with sugar.

She was Ajit's first and only real girlfriend. She was secretly a model because her parents wouldn't approve–it would disgrace her family if they knew her profession. She did runway shows and print ads that they would never see. She used to be friends with Sameera who told me Sonali had managed to alienate all of her female friends through her manipulativeness and insincerity. Ajit told her over and over he didn't want to be with her. But they still managed to get back together and break up several times. She found ways to convince him.

One night she came over at 3am, banging on the door, and threatening to scream until they let her in. They felt compelled to or their landlord would complain to their parents that they were having relations with drunk women. This would shame the family. Ajit conceded. These real life soap operas offered entertainment and an unexpected education in certain aspects of Indian youth culture.

I imagined what I would say to Sonali if we were friends. Why would she let herself be treated so badly? Where was her pride? How could she still love someone who so clearly told her he didn't love her? Why would she call 12 times in one day to be ignored or told to stop calling? How could she continue to accept the rejection over and over? I couldn't figure her out. Low self-esteem? Maybe she thought she had found her match and once you are matched there are no other options and you have to take it for what it is.

Ajit asked my advice on how to get her to stop loving him. "I've tried being nice, I've tried being her friend, I've tried being mean and unlikable. I told her how I feel."

"I have no idea. I'm as confused about love as you–why it happens, how it lasts, where it goes. I'm clueless and definitely not qualified to give advice."

He handed me a bag of Haldiram's, a crunchy, oily, and spicy snack, satisfying like a bag of potato chips. There are many varieties with different ingredients, usually with some mixture of gram flour, nuts, lentils, puffed rice, spices, and salt. As I started to open it "American style," meaning I was pulling on the front and back of the bag to pull open the top of the bag from the seam, he took it back, tore off a corner with his teeth, chastised my method, and handed it back.

"I have opened a bag before in my life, you know. My method works just fine." I raised an eyebrow. We laughed.

"Sorry. Americans do things in funny ways."

"You're bossy!" I continued, "and don't say sorry to me."

He grinned.

"Do you think that would work with Sonali? Being bossy?"

I shook my head and shrugged my shoulders.

I went to bed and slept heavily. I had felt a cold coming on and hoped to prevent its manifestation. Sunday was a day off, I woke up at my leisure. I lay in bed and couldn't stop my mind from imagining kissing Ajit. I decided to get out of the house.

I sat at Infinitea, a European restaurant with an extensive tea selection, and enjoyed fresh salad and green tea to the sounds of eclectic world music. My body was a wreck after five days of back to back dance classes–bruised, sore, dehydrated, and tired. The Director said I was doing well in Contemporary Dance; the encouragement was a necessary jolt for my old body.

I was in a reflective mood as I wrote in my journal. More than three months had passed since I landed in India at Chennai airport. It seemed like a lifetime ago. Living in Bangalore felt so comfortable. I was no longer the only woman walking alone, there were women everywhere–students, call center workers, IT professionals, women in every industry at coffee shops, eating in restaurants, shopping, driving cars, going to movies, living in the world outside of the home.

Caught up in teaching, taking classes, hanging out with friends, looking for an apartment, I would forget I was really a transient. I would forget I was alone on a personal journey, that I was actually "other" there in India. Sometimes being "other" was unmistakable, but in Bangalore I felt accepted, I blended, I became a local.

Some days I let myself feel like a tourist again and enjoyed my role as observer. I would wander around the city exploring, eyes wide open with wonder and interest. I looked again through the eyes of a foreigner at a way of life that was so different from where I had come from.

In the oldest part of the city, Jayanagar, an upper middle class area with wide streets and sidewalks, colleges and malls, near the main long distance bus terminal where buses arrived and departed in a rumble of exhaust and shouts, there was a huge market. Streets and streets of old established shops piled on top of each other in a maze of cement buildings. Lining the sidewalks were products laid out elaborately on the ground one after another, the proprietors sitting among their goods. You could find mirrors, metal dishware, mangoes, plastic buckets, chicken parts, car parts, garlands of marigolds, soccer balls, sweets, *sari* fabric. Anything and everything you could possibly need or want was available to be haggled over and exchanged. Later in the summer when I began teaching a community yoga class I found rubber yoga mats there for my students.

Outside the market, on a dusty side of the road near the bus terminal, a thin elderly woman sat with a small pyramid of vermilion pomegranates laid out in front of her on a little cloth. I felt an unexpected flood of childhood memories of summers in California. I purchased two and couldn't wait to get home.

I peeled one open, the skin thicker than I had expected, dry exterior tough to tear. But the sparkling ruby jewels inside spurred me on. I plucked each jewel into a bowl, the process becoming meditative. The juice stained my fingers, the hard encasements pricked my skin. I proudly surveyed my little metal bowl full of inviting gems. I found a spoon and offered the treasure to Abhishek and Ajit as they played video games across the hall. And then I sat alone, quietly on the balcony, savoring each precious gift.

I was in my own world. Cassandra had left me with her copy of *Anna Karenina* and I sat alone reading. I didn't have much to talk about with the boys, they were mostly studying, complaining, partying, or watching movies. And they slipped back into Hindi much of the time, excluding me without realizing it. But I could always disappear into my room, close the door, read, write in my journal, or listen to music. I felt at home.

I spent most of my days at the dance studio and was happy to really immerse myself. It was so relaxing to be around people comfortable with their bodies, with wearing sweat pants and tank tops and sprawling on the ground. I could completely let go and be myself, I could sit how I wanted, wear what I wanted, and move my body how I wanted. I was free.

In Contemporary we rolled around on the ground endlessly. We rolled over each other, up onto each other, around each other, quickly, slowly, simply and through complicated leg swings, arm thrusts, and shoulder balances. We rolled in a ball and extended in one body line. We danced through levels of space from the ground to jumping through the air. We moved in contact with another body, leaning on or supporting each other, or chaotically through the room avoiding contact. We spun, walked, flew. We rolled and rolled. I was covered in bruises every day.

To move and create. Dance fulfills those needs for me. It originates from deep within, moves through the body, and outward into an expression, an energy, an action. My creativity has usually been the impetus behind the decisions and directions in my life that have felt true. The opposite also occurs; I notice my lack of creation and feeling of power through the lack of movement in my body. It is an obvious indicator of my will power's strength. In dance, balance and power come from the core, the center. It comes from a depth that touches the inner Self.

Through dance we match the vibrations of music or a beat within our bodies and become an extension of that rhythm. We embody the spirit of that rhythm and become other. Our expression of that other moves those who are participating as observers. We hope.

While we are immersed in movement, within the body there is interplay between the mind, our senses or emotions, and the divine energy within us. When all three are in harmony the performance is deeper, richer, more moving, and more powerful. It inspires. When the heart and mind are left behind and just the Divine controls the movement, it becomes something beyond the expression of dance. The body becomes a tool, a message, an expression of spirit. Reading or feeling the movement is a way to understand the Divine. The body is not removed when having a spiritual experience; the body is the medium.

The yogic idea that *samadhi* is experienced only through stillness, through essentially removing oneself from the awareness of the body, has challenged my previous ideas and understanding of the Divine through movement.

If the experience is only in the body that doesn't mean it isn't also transcendent. When the mind controls the movement in cerebral choreography there is still an element of the transcendent through dance's connection to the inner truth. Sometimes going through the motions can exercise a deeper part of us without our awareness. A dancer can also function as the inspirer of that connection in an audience member, while the dancer's movement is calculated, the effect of the body's movements may touch and move an inner experience in an observer.

Dance moves back and forth between these experiences, the body affected by the energy of the Divine and experiencing the Divine through the movement of the body. Many religious traditions include ecstatic movement, understanding the connection between our inner divine vibration and that vibration pulsating through the body expressed in dance.

Our bodies are vessels of the Divine, of the life force, of energy. Dance can also be a connection between the energetic layers of the self. We can explore each layer through movement and awareness of the energetic subtleties within and between each layer. Yoga describes a "subtle body" that overlaps our physical body and encompasses five layers called *koshas*. The *koshas* layer from the outer to the inner, from the body to the soul.

The *koshas* are:

o *Annamayakosha* (Physical) – Flesh and blood, the senses; movement connected to awareness; action and reaction.

o *Pranayamakosha* (Energy) – *Prana* and energy flows within and around the physical body connecting with the subtle body and our consciousness and mental movements.

o *Manamayakosha* (Mental) – The workings of the mind connecting to the heart; exposing the ego.

o *Vijnanamayakosha* (Wisdom) – Knowing the ego, differentiating between what is real and what is illusion; knowing the true Self.

o *Anandamayakosha* (Bliss) – Experience of oneness, of the Divine.

In yoga the idea is that as we refine and develop through the *koshas*, we become more and more removed from the physical body and better able to still our mind and its effects on the body, leaving the body in stillness. We move from awareness of the physical, to awareness of the energetic, to recognition of the mind, to knowing the Self, to experiencing bliss. From the physical, to the subtle, to beyond. In the Katha Upanishad it says:

>More powerful than the senses
>Are the desires that compel them,
>More powerful than the desires

Is the mind that formulates them,
More powerful than the mind
Is the awareness which organizes it,
And more powerful than the awareness is the Self.[22]

The physical body can reflect the subtle body and vice versa. What is happening with us energetically and mentally is visible even in our cellular structure, but more obviously in our body language, in our breath, in our posture, in how *prana* is moving or not moving in the body, in the light in our eyes. The body reflects it all. Understanding the *koshas* leads to an understanding of these connections, relationships, and signals, leading to a deeper understanding of the Self.

As the physical body is affected by the mind and the emotions, so too can it be affected by the bliss state. Being filled with the Divine doesn't need to be in utter stillness. The physical body need not be left in silence. The inner can be still while the outer moves. The body's reflection of the divine experience, of bliss, can unify the experience of being human along all its levels. Everything surrendered to the Divine. Breath, image, movement. The Divine can move all when we surrender completely. We dance.

I went to Madalena's place after class instead of going home. Madalena and I became a little oasis of understanding for each other. When it all became too remote, we could vent and comfort one another. We came from similar perspectives and supported each other in dealing with issues that were out of our cultural frame of reference. I could relax around her and speak with my own voice. In private I melted back into the full expression of me. I could drop the stiffness of propriety, the careful attention to body language, dress, and speech that I had adopted. There was a very real difference between my inside private home life and my outside public social life.

I convinced Madalena to join me the next day for Kathak class. I ignored my impending cold, the runny nose and exhaustion. I was feeling miserable on the bus but as soon as I walked in the door and Ajit's smile greeted me I felt energized and healthy. We hung out for a few hours playing with his little dog before I forced myself to bed to get some much needed rest.

Madalena made it to class as promised and was excited to do something new. I showed her around, where to change, and we stood next to each other in class.

Kathak is a North Indian classical dance style characterized by fast rhythmic footwork; this aspect is where I felt a connection to Flamenco. The body is more upright than it is in Bharatnatyam and there seems to be more focus on the feet during phrases of the dance rather than integrating simultaneous focus on all aspects of the movement. As in Flamenco, there are phrases where the footwork is highlighted, while most other movements are minimized to accent the feet. The rhythms become more complicated in their exchange with the musicians and tend to speed up to an impressive climax.

Madalena decided to sign up for the course. We chatted with some of the other students after class and a couple girls offered to take me to their local PG where some of the dancers were staying. They introduced me to the owner and we had such a great philosophical discussion. I missed those kinds of discussions more than I had known. The place was expensive but convenient to the dance school and very comfortable—western bath, hot water shower, soft mattress, hot meals. I planned to move in a few days when a bed became available.

I headed to Coffee Day. Anil had connected me with a yoga teacher living in Bangalore—Rakeesh. I arranged to meet him for coffee. I waited for an hour. I never really got used to Indian time; I knew to expect a different concept of punctuality but still never believed it as the minutes ticked by sometimes into hours. I was getting worried I would have to leave to get back to my next class before we met. Then I debated about just going straight home, my cold was definitely coming on and I thought rest may nip it in the bud.

Rakeesh finally made it. We had coffee, talked about yoga and briefly about how we became teachers. Like many Tamilians, he had moved to Bangalore for university and stayed to work. He wore his hair buzzed short after years of keeping it rebelliously long, sported thick rimmed glasses, smoked pot, philosophized, and climbed mountains. He had climbed in the Himalayas and taken a motorcycle tour through northern India. *Zen and the Art of Motorcycle Maintenance* changed his life. (I borrowed a copy from Maheshwar, also an avid motorcyclist, to read.) Rakeesh listened to heavy metal, drank beer, and wondered at the meaning of it all.

He was unmarried in his early thirties and looking for love. He was lonely. He was intense, intelligent, and completely present. We hit it off. I felt full having a meaningful conversation. It was a short meeting though, as I had to run back to class.

I made it through the day but collapsed as soon as I made it home. The cold had arrived in full force. I went straight to sleep and woke up miserable. I stayed in bed for three straight days, feverish, exhausted, and consistently getting worse. I was so frustrated I started crying. Ajit didn't know what to do with me. He loaded me onto his motorcycle, took me to a doctor, spoke for me, and waited with me until someone would see me. The doctor gave me antibiotics. Ajit bought juice and bottled water for me on the way home. I needed to call the PG to confirm my room but sleep seemed more important than anything at that moment.

The next morning, I was lying on my mattress reading, feverish and tired, when Ajit came in and said I had to leave right away. Abhishek started cleaning up my room, packing my things. Ajit's cousin's husband happened to be in town on business and was coming by to visit them. They were nervous and running around incomprehensibly. If a girl were discovered staying with them, it would be scandalous. And an American at that! How could they explain it?

As I was getting ready, the last person I would expect showed up. Ajit had inexplicably called Sonali and asked her to take care of me with the reasoning that her parents were out of town and she would be a good host. I couldn't argue at that moment; I had to leave. She was already there with an auto waiting outside and I was too sick to think clearly or quickly.

I called Ajit later and explained that I could have easily gone to stay with Madalena or moved into the PG, which had a room already available, or even stayed at a hotel. Sonali would have never entered my mind. Why did she enter his? He explained that he didn't want me to have to worry, he wanted to organize it all and take care of me since he was in the uncomfortable situation of having to kick me out. He felt terrible. I was family to him and he tried to do everything he could not to cause me any stress or trouble. He admitted it wasn't the best solution but it was all he could come up with in the five minutes he had to figure it all out.

Sonali treated me like a child. I could only laugh inside as this 20 year old attempted to mother me–a poor, lost, bewildered, sick, helpless foreigner.

We arrived at her parent's tiny cement block house. She carried my bag for me. She made me some Maggie noodles, which was all she knew how to cook. I lay on the day bed in the front room and let her talk at me incessantly while she did laundry in their washing machine that wasn't hooked up to running water. It shimmied across the room on the spin cycle. She went outside with a long hose and attached it to a waterspout, filling the machine. She then filled a big basin in the washroom for cold bucket showers. This was also where she washed dishes, crouched down on the floor, over the only drain in the house. When she was too lazy to go out to the outhouse she also squatted and peed there. But they had a television with cable, the washing machine, and an air conditioning unit in the bedroom.

Sonali instructed me on what to say in case her parents came back

unexpectedly. She invented a detailed story of how we met at a ficti-
tious call center at which they thought she worked, and I had come
from the US to provide training to her department. And just in case
they asked, I should assure them that she did not smoke.

Sonali lied out of respect for her parents; I tell the truth out of
respect for mine. Different mentalities.

I counted the minutes until I could leave. Sonali told me all about
her life as a model and showed me some photos, some of which included male suitors. She was sweet yet spoke badly of former friends.
She was a bit self-congratulatory and expressed how generous she was
in taking care of me. She served me. It was uncomfortable. I am far
from the helpless stray she was enjoying saving.

I "slept" in the other room under a dripping A/C unit that soaked
the mattress. As soon as the sun rose, I got dressed, called the PG, said
I was coming right over, and asked Sonali to get an auto for me. She
kept insisting I stay, that I shouldn't spend money. I felt sorry for her.
I thanked her and told her this was the best thing for me and anyway
the PG was expecting my imminent arrival.

She accompanied me to the PG to make sure I got there safely and
to check it all out for me. She charmed the owner with her big blue
contact-lensed eyes and finally left. An older couple owned the PG;
they had the original main house for women lodgers and a dormitory
built next door for men. Upstairs in the main house were three rooms
and a shared bathroom for women only. Living in the main house and
without my own key to the front door, my arrivals and departures were
noted by Uncle and Auntie who slept on the ground floor. The men
staying in the dormitory came and went as they pleased. Two meals a
day were provided, as well as laundry service. The neighborhood appeared middle class, with fine houses and cars, and quiet streets. I could
walk to the dance studio and come back for lunch to avoid eating out.

Still sick, I watched the classes I was missing to try not to fall too
behind. I found out other people were also sick–something was going

around. I felt weak and light headed walking. Right when I needed it the most my body was collapsing. It was my moment to shine and I could only sit on the side and watch.

I floated around to check email, call my mother, and pick up basic supplies I had run out of, as well as everything I could find to help my symptoms. I couldn't stand being sick anymore. I stopped at a juice shop on the way home from the dance studio. I began going there every day; they learned my drink and started making it as soon as they saw me coming: apple and mango. It was a little hole in the wall with shelves of fruit piled in pyramids over a simple counter lined with blenders, bowls, and giant metal strainers. Following others' example, I stood on the sidewalk, drank from a glass and then handed it back to them to wash. I didn't think about the cleanliness–it was pointless to do so. As long as none of the flies ended up in the blender, it was all okay.

I laid in bed again. My roommate wandered in and out of our room, in and out, in and out. I couldn't figure out what she was doing or why. A single room was opening up in a few days so I didn't bother finding out.

Some days life felt very foreign. I listened to and watched life experiences that were so different from my own. I found I couldn't put myself in others' shoes, I couldn't imagine where they were coming from. And I knew they couldn't imagine where I was coming from either.

I dreamt I found insects inside me (the virus) and doused myself inside and out with vinegar to drive them out.

Abhishek met me for tea and to see how I was feeling. Abhishek was my brother, my rock in a turbulent sea. Over coffee, he always provided sage advice or support and understanding with a warm smile and a joke. Our friendship was uncomplicated, comfortable, and even. He discussed relationships and human behavior with maturity beyond his 24 years. I felt a little less lonely in his company.

He tried to cheer me up by confessing the story of his first kiss.

They had lived across the street from each other and were childhood friends. She moved with her family to the US when she was still a child but came back when she was 18. Abhishek noticed a beautiful young woman at the house across the street but didn't recognize her. She finally cornered him, teasing him until, with great surprise, he realized who she was. They joyfully reminisced as if still children but felt awkward because they no longer were. She pursued him from that moment on. He finally succumbed to her romantic attempts and let her kiss him. Kissing "American style," according to him, meant she chewed his lips with her teeth leaving them huge and swollen.

When he went home his mother asked, "What happened?!"

"I walked into a wall," he mumbled walking away to avoid inspection and further questioning.

They continued meeting clandestinely and kissing. One day he returned home with sparkly lips.

"What's that on your lips?"

Dumbfounded, he had no answer for his mother. His sister finally figured out the secret when she saw his girlfriend putting on sparkly lip balm.

I started to feel a little better.

Abhishek dropped me home. Ajit and I flirted over SMS all night. It was so high school, complete with silliness, butterflies, and possibilities. I told him to stop flirting with me because I didn't want to be like any other girl. He decided to stop flirting all together; girlfriends were too complicated.

"Goodnight" ... "Goodnight" ... "Are you still there?" ... "Yes, why aren't you asleep?" ... "Neither are you, so go to sleep" ... "Sweet dreams" ... "Dream about me" ... "What?" ... "Nothing, good night" ... "Ha ha ha, going to sleep now" ... "Me too" ... "Good night then" ... "Are you still there?" ... "Shut up and go to sleep!" ... ":)"

I moved into my own room, unpacked, and decided to stay at the PG for a month. Rakeesh called and wanted to introduce me to his boss. She wanted to start a healing center with classes in yoga, dance, music, and meditation and needed a partner to manage it. I loved the idea of helping build such a place.

Rakeesh picked me up in his car and drove me to Rashma's house. He worked in the firm she shared with her husband. Rashma was an architect and had designed her house and office and won awards for a candle factory she designed in Kerala. She was an accomplished woman at 40-years-old and I planned to be as respectful as possible.

I wore a *salwar kamise*, no make-up, my hair tied back, and a demure countenance. Rashma on the other hand was stunning with her thick, black kohl-lined eyes, soft short hair, and natural smile. She wore jeans and a t-shirt, and was perplexed at this unexpected American woman sitting in her home looking so traditional. She joked with me and I let down my veneer of propriety and knew I could be myself.

Her home expressed her perfectly–the openness, abundance of light, incorporation of the outside with the inside through a balcony that flowed into the master bedroom while at the same time providing a separate space open to the sky. There was peacefulness in the clean transitions, intricate but apparently simple at the same time. I loved the design. Everything was in exactly the right place, connected yet still private, flowing. I felt like I was inside art.

We hit it off immediately. We inspired each other with our ideas about the center and generated a vibration of good energy, a wave slowly forming. We promised to meet again.

16

What is it to be a yogi, equality, dreams, reality?

What is it to be a yogi? The Mother's definition is: "Yogi–one who practices yoga; but especially, one who is already established in spiritual realization, one who has attained the goal of yoga."[23] I have shied away from the label of yogi or yogini that seems to be bantered around so lightly in the West because of this feeling that being a yogi is deeper than a surface intention alone. Doing some *asanas*, reading some books, trying to meditate, these things reveal an interest, maybe a desire, maybe a dedicated intention–does that make one a yogi? Is my life infused with a yogic perspective? According to The Mother, it is much deeper than just a practice; to be a yogi is to have fully accomplished surrender. *Surrender*.

> But for this one must give himself entirely, totally, exclusively, reserve nothing, keep nothing for himself and not keep back anything, not disperse anything also: the least little thing in your being which is not given to the Divine is a waste; it is the wasting of your joy, something that lessens your happiness by that much, and all that you don't give to the Divine is as though you were holding it in a way of the possibility of the Divine's giving Himself to you.[24]

If I am a yogi and everything I do is a practice of yoga, then my goal must be the goal of yoga–*samadhi*. My confusion lies in the simultaneous experience of being a yogi who both lives a material life while at the same time strives for a goal that is of a non-material life. I have difficulty with the idea of seeing these two experiences as dualistic opposing forces.

Swami Bhoomananda asserts, "The life of sensory delight is completely opposed to the life of Self-delight."[25] Should I deny all my senses, all joys experienced through interacting with this world of *maya* in order to experience the joy of the true Self? The joy of the Divine is far greater but I feel as if I am abandoning being human–as if being human were a bad thing. Was I not born human? Is human existence solely for realizing the Divine? Is the rest all just a game?

How can *samadhi* be my goal when I have not chosen to renounce the sensory world? I am not ready to be a renunciate, a monk. So, I am not a yogi. Or is my concept of *samadhi* confused? A friend told me that experiencing *samadhi* doesn't have to mean that your consciousness separates from this worldly, sensory existence. The experiences co-exist. To me *samadhi* seems like the ultimate detachment, disconnecting the plug from the mundane and existing beyond, in a level of reality of which you weren't previously aware. Consciousness expansion.

There appear to be two ways to approach the path, either full throttle or a gentle acceleration toward the goal. One is to completely throw your whole life into the pursuit, letting go of all material, worldly things, letting go of all attachments including family. The Mother says, "The other way is to go forward from where one is, seeking the Divine centrally and subordinating all else to that, but not putting everything else aside, rather seeking to transform gradually and progressively whatever is capable of such transformations."[26] According to The Mother, these two ways both result in an eventual and complete letting go of the material, the sensorial.

If I am in fact on this path then I am definitely taking the scenic route at a leisurely stroll.

I practice yogic principals but practice alone does not make me a yogi; there needs to be some level of mastery. I am far from attaining mastery over anything. I am far from renouncing. Do I even want all attachments to fall away or am I attached to attachments?

Even if I could release from all attachments of the material world I can never release from the attachment to my body. It is possible to perceive a detachment from the body through a removal of all reactions to the senses in deep meditation. Examples of this detachment taken to the extreme are stories of swamis whose bodies were eaten by ants without them even noticing, or who exist infinitely without food or water or even air, completely independent of the needs of the body to survive.

We have analytical brains that can override instinct and emotion. Controlling, stilling, calming the mind can lead to increased brain productivity even to the extent of finding previously invisible areas of brain functioning whose potential we are usually unable to grasp, to utilize, to understand. Magical powers. An entire section of Patanjali's *Yoga Sutras*, Book 3–Portion on Accomplishments, is devoted to describing the attainment of magical powers. We've heard the stories of levitation, stopping the heart, lying on a bed of nails. All these feats prove the existence of a power over the body, mind over matter.

But aren't we supposed to get out of our heads? *Isvarapranidhana*–surrender to the Divine? At what level of meditation do we cross from understanding and focusing the mind to becoming mindless? Is that really the most accurate way to put it? Can we ever be mindless if we can't be bodiless while alive?

We can only change our awareness, our experience of ourselves, and the relationship between our Self and our body, the mind being a part of the body. This level of detachment from the body is unattainable for nearly all of us. And happily, I have no interest in leaving the existence of being human. If that is the goal then, why am I on this path to transcendence?

I would say transcendence has many definitions and encompasses a multitude of experiences. It does seem as if the yogic path attempts to remove our understood experience of being human in order to live within our divinity alone. Should our divinity be our motivation rather than our being? Should my human actions, thoughts, and feelings be guided by the Divine rather than resisted as embodiments of humanness, an innately material concept?

The only remedy to the confusion is of course experience. At some point, you realize you are too in the mind, trying to understand, to codify, to philosophize about the meaning of it all. While thinking can be a joyful pursuit, it brings you no closer to the experience.

A friend argued that all this philosophy was only for men anyway because men don't experience life and death, the dying and regenerating of the life-giving womb, the suffering, the inseparableness from the cycles of life as women do in their daily lives and through the creation of human life within their bodies. Men need to think about it, learn about it, make decisions about it, while women live it. Are men just trying to catch up, using the mind to fill in the absence of sensorial awareness of life? Is this terribly unfair and grossly oversimplified? Obviously, but there is some truth to the feeling that in many religious contexts, a woman communing with the Divine at the highest level is not welcome, and sensorial awareness is devalued in comparison to intellectual awareness.

Women have been sent into the home to support the men's striving for divine connection, to support Adam's quest to regain the closeness to God that had been corrupted by Eve. Men became the intermediaries, able to reach across the sky and touch fingertip to fingertip with God. Women became earthbound, rooted to life cycles echoed in the Earth's own cycles of regeneration. The Divine and mundane separated. Rules established. Roles delineated. Fragmentation. Under patriarchy, the mind becomes dominant, diminishing the equality, depth, and importance of the body and the heart, to the point of nearly invalidating it.

The view of "progressing" to the more spiritual by way of the intellectual coincided with the rise of patriarchal religions and the view that the spiritual does not exist in the mundane. Women occupy realms that are more mundane in our bodily functions tying us to our reproductive organs, to blood, to bodily processes. However healthy our body is, we still bleed. However, in balance our mind is, we still bleed. However detached from the material we become, we still bleed. There is no separation from the body.

Pure Self–the Self as it is without layers, without the trappings of the body, without the body. To attain true purity we purify the body in order to remove awareness of the body, we purify the mind in order to remove awareness of the mind. We remove all awareness and just exist. That is pure Self. Or is that true purity? To be human is to be beautifully impure. Women's menstruation is considered impure in most religions. At the same time, bloodletting is commonly considered purification and is practiced integrally in many religious ceremonies. Why are women excluded? Menstruation is something pure coming from inside the body. It's not a waste product of the body; it is the fertile womb lining that has gone unused and so sheds to begin the creation of a new layer. It is a refreshing process.

On my path, I have felt a desire to reconcile my body with others' concepts of spiritual practice. This desire is a reaction to judgment and exclusion. It feels as if I am being accused of being a woman, belittled, judged as not as important, forced to be obedient to men's rules of acceptability and regulations around spiritual practice in order to be considered respectful.

I invoke the complex powers of destruction, retribution, and rebirth wreaked by the goddess Kali–destroyer and creator. Kali is naked, without shame as shame is a cultural construction. Her hair is wild and natural, her inner being free and unencumbered by outside expectations or judgments. Blood flows from her mouth like honey, sweet destruction. Blood. Kali is unpredictable because she follows no rules.

She is free from *maya*. She flies in the face of convention to massacre our grip on the unreal.

The chaos she inflicts makes us question what it all means. Reality is chaos when we don't understand what reality is. Everything we hold onto is insignificant. Death is not real. Therefore, fear of death is pointless. Ultimately, understanding and surrendering to Kali liberates us from this cycle of *samsara*–birth and death. She is the destroyer of duality, of the illusion of separation, of *maya*. By destroying our delusion, we are liberated in the knowledge of oneness, the experience of oneness.

I am no one other than everyone. There is no gender.

My anger about gender and sex definitions is rooted in *maya*, in the desire to live in the material world in a particular way. I am attached to my body. My ego and pride rebuffs attempts by society to confine and define my presence in the world. I struggle with this paradox. I want to be above all the anger, to see it all as unreal while at the same time I also want to change hurtful, demeaning, and dehumanizing cultural norms. The Mother asserts:

> The best that can be done for the progress of the present human race is to treat both sexes on a footing of perfect equality, to give them the same education and training and to teach them to find, through a constant contact with a divine Reality that is above all sexual differentiation, the source of all possibilities and harmonies.[27]

While our bodies are different, our souls are sexless. Our beings are undifferentiated. That should be remembered in our material and spiritual pursuits. There should be no subordination of one's exploration of the Divine to another's.

That is equality–an equal right to pursue liberation from these pursuits.

My body creaked and cracked, my ribs felt bruised. Reality was hitting me hard. I wasn't out of shape but everything hurt. I ordered tea and enough sweets for an army at KC Das; the sparkling glass case was filled with too many temptations. I enjoyed every bite as I waited for Madalena to join me so we could catch up with each other's lives. She and Mahesh had been sick as well. We all still had a cough; the whole city seemed to have a cold. I complained about blisters, she complained about love. She supported my dance dreams and I supported her new dream to study Indian textiles and to design clothes.

She walked me to Barista to meet Ajit and left for the yoga course she had started. Ajit and I decided to see a movie and walked to the mall. From the dusty hot street, we entered a glass oasis of cool air. We traveled up the four escalators to the top of the building to find that we had just missed every movie. Another failed attempt, we decided to never try to see a movie again, and walked back to Barista.

Ajit brought me a mug of tea and we sat shaded by an umbrella in the afternoon heat. He told me all about his family, growing up in Gujarat, missing his older sisters. One lived in the US and the other in Singapore.

"I'm the only son," Ajit explained.

"Your sisters made good marriages, right?"

"Yes, but I am still the son. They left."

"So, you have to stay in Gujarat?"

"My Dad works in New York actually. He goes back and forth."

"So you could possibly work there with him."

"I could. Maybe."

"I'll be in New York," I smiled.

"I know," he said.

"You could marry an American."

"Are you proposing?" he grinned.

"Ha. Ha. Ha." I articulated each syllable.

He laughed, "My oldest sister would really like you."

"We're the same age anyway," I teased.

"Ha. Ha. Ha." He mimicked me and lit a cigarette.

"I could show you the city. You'd love it. The people, energy, fashion, dancing. Food from around the world. You could stay with me," I offered.

"You'd take care of me?"

"Of course. But I would probably have to support us, so you'd have to cook and clean."

"And take care of the kids," he added.

"Exactly."

He took a drag. "I want to stay home and be a Dad. I would love that. And I'm a great cook."

"I think it would suit you. You're not much of a career person."

"I would be if I was doing what I want to do. My degree... I can't do it. I can't get myself to do it. I'll end up working for my Dad or Uncle anyway. It doesn't matter. I don't want this to end." He looked into my eyes.

Saif's voice boomed, "Hey *yaar*, what's up?"

The mood was broken.

Saif waved over his friends and they all crowded around our table. Sonali showed up and asked Ajit to help her with something. I didn't have energy for this scene so I went home.

The night was filled with dream after dream as I tossed and turned. In one, I was in a town in California–it was strange, different, people were weird. Then I was with a friend and we heard about some riot being planned, violent and non-violent, with yoga people leading it. The town was taken over. There was still physical beauty but we talked about how much had been eroded over a short period of time. I didn't know what any of that was supposed to mean.

I woke up to the smell of smoke in my room like someone was smoking a pack of cigarettes right next to me. Nowhere else in the house smelled of smoke. It aggravated my cough. My back hurt. And suddenly my head hurt as I read a text from Ajit saying he was with Sonali.

I messaged Ajit all morning trying to understand what happened. Did they get back together? He went back and forth trying to explain and wanting me to understand but then pushing me away saying, he just wasn't a good guy. He didn't know what he was doing and neither did I. I tried not to care. I had no right to have an opinion; I was just his friend after all.

I went out to Coffee Day to clear my head and ordered an iced latte. The barista said they didn't have iced latte. Confused, I asked if they had ice. He responded, "Yes." "And you have espresso?" "Yes." "And milk?" "Yes." He was bewildered by my odd questions. So I ordered a hot latte and a glass of ice. He obliged. I poured the hot coffee over the ice, handed him back the mug and returned to my table happy.

A coffee and chocolate croissant were band-aids for my heart. I had no energy, no will to do anything. I wondered why I allowed myself to be masochistic, to set myself up for hurt. Why did Ajit affect me so deeply? Why couldn't we choose who we fall in love with? I felt hopeless, sad, tired.

I closed my eyes and went to a happy place–summer in Santa Cruz at a reggae concert dancing barefoot in the sunshine on warm grass surrounded by irie vibes. I felt my joy in dancing and knew I shouldn't have skipped class. I was making the kinds of decisions I had when I was depressed, feeding the dark, rather than nourishing the light.

I felt the squandering of my potential–so many obstacles mentally and physically rising up within me. Why? Was it time to let go of old dreams? Was it a test? I was experiencing a falling back. A struggle to clamber over rocks I had already scaled. Revisiting my pitfalls, my fear. *Fear*.

Was I learned enough to climb back up with new skill, faster with fewer scrapes and bruises? Should I have learned the lesson that this endeavor to fulfill my dream was futile? Or was this a chance to get past my own fears that had held me back before? Whether from internal or external forces, I always encountered a binding of my body, my potential, my ability to freely act.

I woke up at 4am sweating. I had a dream that I had a penis. I was in a plane with someone, we ran out of gas and landed. I peed into a container, it was supposed to keep the engine clean and running or something. Then I was peeing against a wall in a bathroom. I had to laugh at my dreams.

Maybe these were inspired by the freedom men have in India to pee wherever they want, to be men, to just be. Body freedom is not allowed for women. The body is triple layer covered, still, allowed only to follow behind, an appendage to a man. Although there is incredible variety in color and a small amount in style, a woman is relegated to a uniform of *salwar kamise* for the unmarried and *sari* for the married. Bodily functions and realities for women are not for public viewing or awareness. A woman is private. Men can pee in public. Men are actors, creators, instigators, strong, forceful, dominant–phallic.

I wanted to create. I wanted to stand tall with no preconditions, no obstacles, no qualifiers, no hesitancy. I wanted to be seen for my actions, my creations, my thoughts, and my true Self. I wanted to express myself freely.

I went back to sleep and dreamt I was hiking on a dirt trail on a wooded mountainside where you could look down on a coastline. I came upon a view of a little star-shaped island in the middle of a tiny turquoise blue lake far below. It was called Paradise Island. There were miniature buffalo. I was saying to the man I was with how they should be looked after or at least noticed to make sure they were preserved. He was uninterested. I couldn't understand why people didn't care. They were amazing, these tiny buffalo.

My time in India was characterized by incredibly vivid dreams, on subjects both wild and mundane. I worked out anxiety, imagined the past, lived in a film, and explored desires and exhaustion. Too many dreams to recount. I have always been an active dreamer. I tried to be more diligent about writing down my dreams for clues into my internal experience of India and this period in my life. I indulged in self-analysis and the luxury of time to over-think everything.

Swami Bhoomananda warns, "Some people suffer from excessive thinking, improper thinking."[28] Thinking is related to suffering. By indulging in the machinations of the mind, the distractions and delusions created by thought, we are straying further from peace, from inner truth and connection. The point of yoga is to end these distractions, to release us from the bondage of delusion. I suffer from excessive thinking, but it's not an affliction I would do away with at this point in my life. There is a balance to be achieved. My imbalance in the past manifested as depression, which is improper thinking. I always skate a thin line between the proper and improper, bouncing back and forth from health to imbalance, peace to disturbance.

It's dangerous to be too in the mind while neglecting the whole self. But as humans, we have an amazing intellectual capacity and ability to control the mind. Exploring the mind enriches our understanding of life.

Dreams are one way that exploration is expressed. The unconscious or subconscious mind seeps into the conscious mind. We experience true honesty with ourselves. Sometimes dreams can be cathartic, purging, and healing. They can be a link to the past or a link to the future or an insight into the present. Or they can be absolute junk–the junk that accumulates in the mind–a dream can be taking out the garbage. Sometimes it feels as if the Divine is giving us guidance or our inner divine, unhindered in its connection to the greater, can more clearly communicate with our mind. We are defenseless against our own Self in the dream state.

I lay in bed pondering it all when Madalena texted that Leela, our friend from the training in Coimbatore, was in town visiting from Chennai. She had invited us to dinner. I was happy for the distraction. We reunited at a swanky hotel and caught up on how her studio was doing, how the training had helped her teaching, and how she was adjusting to focusing more on the yogic path. She poured another glass of wine and shared stories from some recent travels. I realized too late it was past my curfew at the PG and Madalena suggested a slumber party.

I checked my phone and found a bunch of texts from Ajit. He wanted to talk. He knew I was upset and he was angry with himself for hurting me. I was angry with myself for being hurt and told him he could be with Sonali if he wanted; it wasn't any of my business. He insisted on seeing me. I told him to meet me at the hotel bar.

"I didn't get back together with her," he explained.

"Why did you say you were with her?" I was confused.

"She needed to talk. I owed it to her. We worked it out. She said she was going to try to get over me."

"Oh, I'm sorry."

"Why? You told me to be with her so I thought... I don't know; I was upset. I didn't know what to say. I was mad you wanted me to be with her or thought I would get back together with her."

"I just want you to do what you want to do," I said unsteadily.

"But you're my friend. You're my best friend. I don't want to do anything to hurt you."

"But we're just friends."

"You're my friend that I love. There is only you."

We walked out into the parking lot to meet up with the others when it started to rain. We laughed and let ourselves get soaked. We came to an unspoken understanding that our hearts belonged to each other even though there was no future in us.

I stayed with Madalena. In the morning, we hunched over her

laptop and watched videos she had taken of our yoga course and tour and some of her adventures without me. Seeing videos from on the road around India, I realized I missed being "in India." Bangalore was a strange sensation, remote from my previous experiences. I decided to take some mini trips; I didn't want to stop seeing India or exploring new places.

I stopped by the PG to change and pick up my dance clothes. I was interrogated by Uncle as to my whereabouts and said I stayed with a girlfriend. I said we lost track of time at dinner and I didn't want to disturb him by coming back too late. He seemed satisfied with my answer.

In between classes, I checked email and opened responses to the resume I had posted online. I made a plan to research the companies and set up some meetings. I needed a plan of action for sorting everything out to stay. Make it happen. Visa? Teach yoga? Dance? Editing job?

Ajit and Abhishek invited me to a movie. I jumped.

Sometimes we need a break from all the deep thinking or the not-so-deep-but-disturbing thinking. Sometimes a little fun distraction can clear the mind, rebalance the emotional energies, and leave us better able to focus. *36 China Town*, based on the American comedy, *Once Upon a Crime*, with the addition of some melodrama, a kidnapped child, and song and dance numbers was a real B movie for pure entertainment's sake.

The audience consisted mostly of young people who spiced up the film with sound effects of their own. When two of the characters crept into a scary, dark mansion, someone in the audience baaahed like a sheep. Everyone laughed. When one of the characters shockingly came face to face with the eyes of a killer, a guy screamed like a little girl. During romantic scenes of longing looks, someone added their own silly dialogue or kissing noises. It provided a whole other level to the film. It was laughter and light. *Light.*

The next day in Contact we explored free expression–free style, moving however felt right, and expressing our individuality through our own movements. I was having a hard time relating to some of the choreography so with the movement vocabulary I had learned I really enjoyed the freedom. We practiced improvising encounters. I missed touching and being touched.

I hoped the Director would invite me to stay on and study with the company but it was completely up to him. I wanted someone to recognize my potential and push me, invite me, support me, but art doesn't usually follow that pattern. I never had the guts to champion myself.

I lay in bed after dinner; I was too tired to go anywhere, too tired to read; it was too hot to sleep. My mind wandered to my heart. I imagined my romance from afar, sitting at a movie theater, watching a Bollywood movie–I fell instantly and unexpectedly for an unlikely hero, our love was impossible, we tried to ignore it, but song and dance (clubbing) provided us outlets to express the truth, tension increased through desire but no physical contact, our emotions were heightened, our sensitivity like a trigger, we tried to forget each other but were incapable of untangling our lives or being apart, we knew in the end there would be inevitable heartbreak. Even when you know the plot of a formula movie, you are still engrossed in every minute, your emotions ride the roller coaster of the characters, you long for the happy ending, and it is deeply satisfying on some level that reminds us we are human.

I was worn down by all the emotional and physical activity, plus trying to find a job and an affordable place to live; I tried to stay energized. I ate plums and dark chocolate, indulging a craving. I dreamt about cheese and pasta and salad and soda. I was becoming addicted to sugar and thought it must provide an aid in alleviating dehydration, a constant problem.

Existing constantly in an unfamiliar and stressful lifestyle challenges our concept of priorities and needs. What do we really need? I was inundated with cravings and convoluted thoughts of home. I was breaking down my concept of self from a cultural perspective and slowly re-informing myself around what constituted my sense of home. Home is a calm stability. Feeling a lack of stability, I gravitated toward things that gave me at least a fleeting sense of calm, such as chocolate cake and coffee.

My greater sense of understanding my true Self, my self at home, was through dance. Dance had always been a constant in my life that connected my awareness to that inner stable core. As my body was unable to keep up with my need to experience this–I felt betrayed–even this constant in my life was challenged with obstacles. I was back to the same uphill struggle that I always chose, the same road to where? Was I being challenged to let go of everything? In reaction to that challenge, I was holding on even tighter.

My overactive brain took control filling me with reminders of the habitual desires, past patterns, and crutches I fell back on when unable to cope with the challenges of life. But I was now aware; I could step outside myself and observe and process my behaviors. And even if I wasn't aware, it was somehow happening unconsciously. The smaller challenges here were surmountable.

While I saw shimmers of depression like hazy waves of a mirage, it was just a mirage. I was falling back into old patterns but as a new person so those old patterns didn't take root as they had before. I was proving to myself I could handle difficulties and obstacles in a more balanced way.

I had dreams of home and wondered if it meant I was ready to go back. I dreamt I was staying with an old friend in San Francisco but we got into a fight when I told her she was being self-absorbed. My mother was supposed to pick me up to take me to get a ticket at the airport but she was late as usual so I rollerbladed there. Some old guy on the sidewalk tried giving me tips on technique. I was flying down the hills like a master, which was surprising because I'm a terrible roller-blader. I got back to my friend's apartment, finished packing, didn't say goodbye, and left. I knew she felt bad but I couldn't even talk to her.

My dreams of home were about my disappointment in myself, in others, and in my continued feeling of only having myself to rely on. I think my friend either represented my own internal struggle with self-absorption, a part of me I can't even talk to right now, or she could have symbolized my feeling of abandonment by my friends (even though I'm the one who left the country). I again had to do everything myself and for myself. This was a life pattern that developed as a child and I only recently had been able to break free and allow others to help me. Even to ask for help. *Help.*

My negative feelings and fears were churned up, my mind a turbulent sea of insecurities and weaknesses. Maybe this was a time in my life where I was able to withstand the internal processing and purging of residual issues with my parents and childhood that formed negative patterns based on insecurities and low self-esteem. Now that I was stronger and able to understand my reactions as just that–reactions–without falling into the turmoil, I could withstand the crashing waves like a rock, still standing, maybe a little eroded but still solid at the core.

My father gave up on friendship completely and my mother is a social butterfly. I flit between the two extremes and somewhere in the middle am disappointed by both. I wondered at my own expectations and my level of engagement in the world and in relationships. My pattern had been to make new friends wherever I went and then either I or they would move and I would feel a loss. I always loved meeting new people but at that point it was tinged with a sadness and loneliness for old friends and knowing these new friendships would most likely be temporary.

I felt disconnected from my old friends and was hit with a hard realization that I wasn't the best friend. I was scattered and shifting and often distant. I expected friends to be like family–always there no matter how much you neglect them. But mostly they aren't and it was my responsibility to nurture the friendship. I guess I didn't expect to be needy and to really be so alone. I had made this choice after all. I had created the distance. What right did I have to ask for help?

It's true all these desires and expectations lead to distraction, inner turbulence, and a falling away from the serenity of the path. But I have chosen this bumpy trail, chosen to participate in friendships, in coupling and the hope of procreation, which inevitably leads to detours and rocky obstacles to clamber over or skirt around, hoping I don't stray so far that I completely lose sight of my Self.

I went out for coffee with Abhishek. I needed some air, I needed the energy of people, of the world, of a friend. Abhishek listened to my angst, counseled me with his wise words, and then tried to make me laugh.

Abhishek described to me how he and his friends would stand around a tea stall and watch women go by. He concentrated, turned around in his chair, turned back, and was wearing his "leering look." I burst out laughing. I thought he should be an actor. He did various looks for me: love, anger, desire, sadness. I wanted to take a picture of each one to create a poster just like the one I had of a Kathakali performer displaying nine different attitudes through intense complicated facial manipulations.

After that whenever I saw a man leering at me I just pictured Abhishek and laughed instead of feeling uncomfortable or getting angry.

It was all an act, a performance through understood markers of an emotion conveying a kind of reality within reality. On stage we understand the differentiation, but in life we are unable to see beyond the performance. We only see our own reaction, not what is really happening.

How much of life do we perform and how much do we sincerely feel? Are we aware when we are performing? Do we perform the role we feel we are given to the point of forgetting it is an ascribed role? All societal relationships are constructed and upheld with communality. In India, tradition is generally highly valued. In times of upheaval it is natural to go back to what is familiar; traditionalism strengthens in times of uncertainty.

17

**"Dreams from clouds," love is complicated,
"Where's the party, *yaar?*"**

Back in Coimbatore I had bought a pair of amazing patchwork, embroidered, beaded pants. They weren't cheap, but they were fabulous. I had been carrying them around carefully folded in a plastic bag in my suitcase since January. The night to unleash them had arrived. Madalena said they were all dressing up for Maheshwar's birthday and she was treating everyone to a fancy dinner. The only problem was I didn't have any shoes other than my falling-apart flip flops and my dirty, torn K-Swiss tennis shoes.

I was meeting Rakeesh (it was his birthday as well) and asked if he wouldn't mind spending a little time shoe shopping. He reluctantly agreed and I took him to lunch at my favorite place near MG Road. The restaurant looked like a cave with strange mud-like wall formations. Waiting for a table was not uncommon. They served mostly North Indian food, deliciously prepared, like *bhaigan bharta* and *bhindi masala*, but they also offered some South Indian dishes like curd rice and lemon rice. I always ordered too much, wanting to taste everything.

We stopped into a couple of shoe stores and I found an inexpensive pair of simple black heels. We then ducked into Coffee Day as the heavens opened up and sat looking out at the pouring rain for hours, drinking coffee, discussing philosophy and life choices.

Ajit met up with us. He and Rakeesh were from different worlds and at different phases in their lives. Ajit was forever in school and unsure of his future, balancing his parents' wishes with his own. He was privileged to not have to make difficult decisions at the moment; he was light. Rakeesh was independent, educated, and a professional. He knew what he enjoyed and he knew where his turmoil lay–it was within rather than with his outer life. He was heavy. Their meeting was awkward.

I was suddenly nervous. I said goodbye to Rakeesh and knew somehow I was on a date with Ajit. Our first real date. He had shaved, styled his hair, and wore slacks and a dress shirt. He dried off the seat of his bike and we set off for the restaurant.

After getting lost for a while, going back and forth on Airport Road while on the phone with Madalena who was on the back of Mahesh's bike, we finally found each other and the restaurant. We entered a big open courtyard with a tiled fountain surrounded by dark wood tables, lush green plants, and a bar. There was a balcony all around with more tables that looked down into the courtyard. We went upstairs and found the rest of the guests. The décor was beautiful, the food aromatic and reminiscent of the Persian cuisine I often ate when I lived in West Los Angeles.

The US, France, Mexico, and India were represented at this international table. We ate, laughed, traded stories, and thought we'd draft some summit resolutions; then ate, drank, and ate some more. Madalena had arranged a cake with candles and we all sang Happy Birthday and hoped Mahesh's wish would come true. Madalena and I promised each other we'd come back but somehow never managed to.

After 10pm I couldn't return to the PG so Ajit offered me my old room. Driving back to Ajit's house on the back of his motorcycle was calming and open, literally open to the world. I breathed in the peaceful clean air, the smell of rain, the smell of life, my arms around Ajit, my cheek resting on his back.

He exuded a sweetness I couldn't stay away from.

We flirted by phone only separated by a thin wall. "You looked beautiful tonight," he started.

"So did you."

"I'm blushing."

"Hahaha. What are you doing?"

"Laying here thinking about you."

"What are you thinking?" I asked.

"How perfect your lips are."

"I'm blushing." I beamed.

"Good."

"Now all I can think about are your lips." I rubbed my finger on my lips.

"Should we introduce them?" he joked.

"Yes."

No response.

"Hello?"

"Really?" he asked. "You had some wine, I think you're tipsy."

"I'm not. If you want to kiss me, come in here and kiss me."

No response.

Finally he knocked softly on my door, came in, and lay next to me on the floor. We lay in silence unable to continue the flirting in person. I thought he had come to make good on his desire to kiss me but we looked at each other and realized we needed to figure some things out before we took a step we couldn't go back from. Neither of us wanted something casual. We stayed up until 2am talking about love as the thunder rumbled outside and the rain splattered against the roof.

Love is complicated. Putting the concept of love and marriage together was difficult for Ajit. He had never been in love. His parents were already trying to arrange his marriage and he kept putting them off. He wanted to feel true love before he had to marry. He wanted to explore who he was and what he wanted in life before that script was handed to him with his bride. That script entailed giving up his dreams, working for his father, and providing for a family he wasn't ready to have.

I knew he loved me and wanted to have a future with me but we both knew that was a cultural impossibility. For him, love had nothing to do with the future. At the same time, he didn't want to disrespect me by starting something he couldn't finish. He loved me too much to kiss me. We decided not to break each other's hearts.

The next day back at the PG, I stayed in bed reading, cozy and warm inside. I listened to the rain outside, wishing I had big windows to watch the storm; it felt like a lazy Sunday. My back had been hurting again. I drank hot tea and relaxed. Rakeesh texted me a poem:

> I'm sailing in the rain
> It's so insaaane
> But I can streak with the lightning
> And sculpt dreams from clouds
> What is crime and what is love?

I wanted some stimulating conversation and met up with my friend Vivek who organized raves. He was tall and thin, shaved his head, and had a goatee. He joked about looking like the Devil. He would blow his own mind with thoughts of real and imagined existence, of death, of what happens to the soul. He had seen evil beings inside people and other levels of reality. He was sensitive, intense, and sweet at the same time. He aspired to be a music producer; music filled him and took him to another place. Vivek's goal in life was to bring a feeling of freedom to others and to himself.

We had first met at Barista, a friend of a friend of a friend, at a table with a group of people. Barista was like that, you always saw someone you knew and they always introduced you to someone new. Over coffee, he asked to look at my fingertips. This was Vivek's thing. He explained there are four different spiral configurations and after inspecting mine he declared that I had all of them, which was unusual. Each spiral described an aspect of personality, having all of them meant I was in balance.

Vivek was always grasping for meaning and explanations for all his wild thoughts. He calmed the clamor of thought with dance and sometimes drugs, which usually expanded his mind and his confusion even further. We talked about the philosophy of yoga often, trying to find a method to his madness, trying to fit his ruminations into an existing construct.

We discussed God and the Devil, good and evil. What is the essence of good and evil outside of cultural constructs, societal rules, and religious allegories? Is there pure good? Pure evil? Or do they only exist as human manifestations? Mental creations?

"Sometimes on the dance floor I'll be so into the music, in my own world, and then I open my eyes and instead of people dancing around me, I see evil spirits. I see the evil inside people and it freaks me out," Vivek animatedly described, his eyes intense.

"Maybe it's just the drugs?" I wondered.

"I'm not on anything, no. I can just see inside people sometimes. I see the monsters."

"Do you think they'll hurt you?" I wondered.

"Yeah, sometimes I think they're going to surround me and I'll become like them."

"So you're afraid of the evil in you?"

He explained, "It's in all of us, right? We have both in us already, good and evil."

"In our minds or our souls?"

"If it's us, if it's 'me' then my soul, but it can be something more than that. Is it all in my head? Is it just my head messing with me? How could I actually see it then?"

"So then there is even more to think about if what is in us really isn't 'us' as well as the confusion of what is us. We have to purify on even more levels to get rid of the other elements as well as our own junk that we create."

Vivek sat forward. "That's why I'm interested in yoga. Tell me how to do that."

I sat back, chuckled, and slowly exhaled. "I know someone you should talk to. He's a healer and a yoga practitioner. He can talk to you about both. You need something way bigger and more profound than anything I could say."

"It's deep and I just get so tangled up in my ideas I can't see anymore."

Vivek's complex and hectic mind was full of too much potential in so many areas. He swam in chaos. The workings of the mind itself fascinated him. We went in circles about how the mind works but we never ended up anywhere. He had energies in him that flirted with the beyond but left him disturbed and vibrating in dissonance. His passionate striving for answers was inspiring.

I loved being challenged mentally. Which brought me back to my need to work. I wasn't finding anything. I had posted a resume on job search sites and spent hours weeding through odd jobs. The only thing I really had going for me was my education and fluency in English. I hoped someone would give me a chance.

Anil emailed that he would be in town on business the next day and wanted to meet up with me and Madalena. I emailed back a meeting place and called Madalena. We met near her flat in Frazer Town and decided to walk around. As we were walking and talking a downpour began. Madalena opened up her little umbrella and the three of us crammed under it laughing hysterically as everything but the tops of our heads got soaked.

Sherlock Holmes Pub played American rock music and poured draught beer. It wasn't too crowded on that rainy afternoon. Rakeesh met us there and we sat on the empty balcony, protected from the rain, and gossiped about the Institute. Madalena had become everyone's little sister there and they all wanted to know what was happening with her and she with them. We relaxed in our private little foursome, hidden by the sound of the pounding rain.

When the rain finally let up we went to dinner at an Italian restaurant and ate too much pasta. Madalena and I didn't want the evening to end. We felt fuller remembering our arrival in India and how much we had learned and experienced since then, and it was comfortable to be with old friends. As the evening wound down, Maheshwar called. We said our goodbyes and Madalena and I took an auto to the 13th Floor to meet him.

Upscale and swanky, the aptly-named bar was on the 13th floor of a building right on MG Road. It was nearly the tallest building in Bangalore with a beautiful view of the city. A miniature Empire State Building blinked in the distance and the lush palms and bamboo forest of Cubbon Park darkened in the distance at the end of the lights of downtown. The bar aired sport matches, mostly football or cricket, on flat screen TVs and served fusion cuisine appetizers and mixed drinks on glass tables and stone benches outside on the balcony. International workers and tourists crowded in with locals, vying over the limited seating. The air felt cleaner, the cool breeze calming above the chaotic noise of MG Road.

Mahesh brought some interesting friends and after having another drink and enjoying the view, we decided it was time for a midnight snack. Empire Hotel was the hot spot for post-clubbing food. It was the only place open, packed with noisy gangs of young people smoking and eating ravenously. The food came out fast, and was good.

We ran into Vivek there and he invited us to an after hours club. Madalena wanted to go but Mahesh refused to let her go without him. She was frustrated at his overprotectiveness and at the same time was trying to get back at him for not coming through for her when she needed help earlier in the day. I felt like a third wheel as they fought and made up. I ended up going alone with Vivek to Hideout.

Bangalore used to be known for its great nightlife but for political reasons a curfew was imposed and clubs started shutting down at 11:30pm. So some places, such as Hideout, sprang up outside the city limits. The club was a long dark room with a bar on one side, a DJ table in the middle on the other, and some makeshift strobe lighting at the end. It was barren but functional. Girls met boys for close dancing, touching and kissing in dark corners. I got into a groove and Vivek and I danced for hours in our own space.

We left around dawn and went to get coffee at the five star hotel Taj Residency. It felt surreal sitting at a table in a tourist hotel listening to the early morning conversations of Europeans on business trips, eating bacon and eggs and planning board meetings, while we had stayed up all night with house music, coffee and philosophical conversation.

I wanted to feel free and I felt exactly that.

Vivek drove me home in his car. A hot shower felt blissful. I ate breakfast and went to sleep. I wanted to continue my feeling of independence, being removed from my usual routine, the usual suspects and went to Koshy's. No one I knew would be there. Koshy's was a holdover from the British era. A large, open, high-ceilinged room with gently spinning wood fans instead of air conditioning where they served English food and beer. They also had addictively delicious South Indian coffee: rich, smooth, and strong without any bitterness. It was an intellectual hangout full of academics and artists smoking like it was going out of style and drinking warm beer all afternoon. I overheard conversations about independent film projects, post-modernism, communism, literary critiques, and political corruption. Deals were made, partnerships burgeoned, and ideas bloomed as tobacco smoke formed little clouds above everyone's heads, threatening to rain inspiration.

I wrote in my journal and came up with ideas for an article a DJ had asked me to write. He was starting a magazine and wanted a foreigner's perspective on Bangalore. I titled it "The City of Contradictions." I thought about everyone I had met—fashion designers, DJs, call center workers, yoga teachers, dancers, college students, IT professionals, school teachers, architects, international volunteers. I thought about all the social scenes, the professional opportunities and the growing divide between rich and poor. The juxtaposition of modern and traditional. The speed of development with an infrastructure struggling to keep up.

> Fast chaos, growth, energy, building
> Modernity, fashion, forward momentum, pollution
> Opportunity, oppression, status quo, change
> Poverty, begging, street sweepers, orphans
> Temples, offerings, smell of ghee, flower markets
> Haute cuisine, theater, avant-garde dance, Bharatnatyam
> Jeans, silk *sari* emporiums, Adidas, *bindis*
> Hamburgers, *thalis*, tea stalls, sushi
> Family, independence, paradox

I walked home in the orange afternoon light, beautiful and surreal.

That Saturday night Ajit, Madalena, myself, Mahesh, and three of his friends embarked on a fairly hilarious expedition, piled into one car with high hopes and a sense of adventure. We were going to Vivek's rave.

"Where's the party, *yaar*?"

Everyone seemed to know where we were going, Vivek's cryptic directions somehow crystal clear. We set off down Airport Road even though I was sure I was told Whitefield Road was the best way. They parallel for a while anyway. We headed east. We proceeded to drive in circles, arguing about what direction we were even facing after attempting to take a "shortcut" after the parallel was no longer parallel. "Where's the party, *yaar*?" We found ourselves down the same random deserted roads wondering why they looked familiar. We tried looking at maps.

We eventually began to notice the same few cars, blasting music, bumping and jumping, crammed with too many bodies, just as we were, taking the same circles we were. We were all lost. We'd pull up alongside each other, confer, and take off on the newly decided route. We'd lose each other. "Where's the party, *yaar*?" became our mantra.

Miraculously we finally found someone who knew the way and followed them down a dirt road canopied with large trees to an empty field. Empty except for a slew of cars, headlights winking at each other, music keeping bodies warm. Waiting and waiting. The equipment apparently also had trouble finding the spot. We blared music from the car, took turns warming up inside, and waited. We counted stars. We jumped up and down. We finally gave up around 4am and left, piling back in the car, sleeping on top of each other, until someone declared that we had made it home. Mahesh's friends dropped the four of us off together and we all crashed at Madalena's and slept until the afternoon.

The adventure was the journey not the destination. Our mantra sent us into giggling fits, which kept our spirits up when we wanted to abandon the effort. The goal wasn't what we had expected. We thought we were searching for an event but we laughed at the search and instead lived in the moment. We had reached our goal before we even embarked on the quest. It was us.

I dreamt I was sitting in a chair that could fly. I was at a house on the top of a hill with gorgeous gardens laid out before it, a forest and beautiful views surrounding it. So I flew around looking at it all. Then my Dad came and I didn't trust the chair anymore, I was afraid and suddenly grounded. I was afraid to try to fly again. I looked up at the dark night sky and a billion bright stars.

When we realized we were all awake someone made tea, someone else picked up some food, and we sat around exhausted but jovial. I longed to curl into Ajit's arms, cuddled together. Mahesh and Madalena slept with their arms around each other and it made me miss that companionship. I watched them, so peaceful and loving.

Ajit dropped me home. I read Tolstoy in bed, made tea and had a lazy Sunday at home. I felt another cold coming on. The pollution, smoke, and lack of fresh vegetables kept my immune system weak. The city seethed with this virus that attacked in a vicious circle. The whole city seemed sick. I longed for chicken soup and movies to watch in bed. I wanted my own home.

I felt my momentum, my focus, my purpose lagging. Why was I staying? I explored. I felt, I dreamt. I learned and expanded; I reached out and touched the unknown. I studied and processed and searched. But what had I done? I healed and focused; I lost focus. I distracted myself; I filled my mind and emptied it. I remembered and forgot. I let go and wanted to hold on.

From the inner perspective, the challenges I had faced fostered a greater understanding of my self. My self-awareness grew, as well as my awareness of how life challenges us and how our response effects every part of us. At times I could see the bigger picture, at times I could see my great limitations. I grew comfortable with those fluctuations. I could see outside of myself more clearly and look in as an observer. I could more easily flow into a soft sense of peace.

From an outer perspective, I was hyperaware of being caught in a spinning cycle of stagnation. I was falling back into my rut, unable to manifest my dreams and finally move in a new direction on a road that excited and inspired me. My obsession with "doing" was rooted in my incapacity to "do" what scared me, to fulfill my sense of who I am and why I am here. Exploring, learning, and absorbing are easy for me, manifesting my own understanding of the world through artistic expression is my challenge, my fear.

I was searching for a balance between my inner and outer and a connection between the two. I could see the dissonance more clearly in the extreme culture, both inner and outer were exaggerated. The inner was deeper, quieter, and more peaceful. The outer was emotional chaos, mentally noisy, and distracting.

If I left India, I felt I would lose the opportunity to fully explore finding this connection. Was I escaping reality or finally finding it on a different path?

18

Soul sister, balance, Bharat, spatiality, inner chaos

The healing center became my dream; I could teach there, live there, and continue my work in yoga and healing. Rashma knew a magnetic therapy doctor from Kerala who wanted to set up a clinic in Bangalore. The plan was to find a building where he could have one floor, and I another, and we could offer many types of therapies as well as bring in guests to give workshops. I would manage the center and teach and she would set up the non-profit and deal with the financial and legal side of things.

Her impetus was her son who had cerebral palsy and who had been helped by magnetic therapy. She wanted to provide hope and alternative therapies for other children and support for parents going through similar difficulties.

Rashma was my soul sister. Together we inspired each other to reach beyond, to attain our potential and find our paths to a deeper existence. We had the same dream, a dream rooted in our desire to give, to help, and to live our lives with purpose and from our hearts. I joyfully imagined a life of service. I imagined a way to practice balancing the different aspects of life, figuring out how to truly be a yogi. I wanted to reconcile the different aspects of myself, to practice understanding my desires and balancing my material and spiritual life.

Later that summer, Rashma introduced me to Bharat Thakur. She invited me to accompany her on a three-day meditation workshop.

Hundreds of people sat in anticipation on the floor of a large hall, eyes open, and searching in our hearts. A palpable force entered the room, his eyes deep in another world, but encased in the mundane energy of a sexually active, drinking, smoking man in his thirties. He had weight, heaviness, rootedness. His complexity and contradiction intrigued me. He spoke eloquently and with humor, unraveling complex philosophical ideas on the intricacies of the human soul. His website defines him in this way:

> Bharat has no philosophy. He has no interest in changing or replacing the ideas you have in your mind by another set of ideas. Bharat's only aim is to bring about a complete transformation, which can only happen when all the belief systems in your mind are destroyed. Meditation or enlightenment happens only when the mind is free from all beliefs. And Bharat's goal is freedom—complete and absolute freedom.[29]

So what does it all matter? Relinquish purity of body by smoking? Relinquish purity of mind by having love affairs? I think his argument is that you don't have to, if you are ultimately detached. Purity is in the mind. It's not what you do, but your belief about it. He didn't care what we believed about his lifestyle. If we judged him, then we were strengthening the existing belief systems in our own minds and we would find ourselves further from the goal of freedom. Encountering him was an exercise in non-judgment.

He provoked debate about hypocrisy, about expectations placed on spiritual guides, and simply about whether people thought he was truly enlightened or not. And I wondered, how important is that? That to me is a crucial point in the decision to completely surrender one's path to a guru as opposed to one's inner guru and the Divine. When people expect everything from one man or woman they feel betrayed when their expectations aren't met. They want someone else to do the work for them and just follow what they are told. If that person behaves in a way that challenges their mindlessness in the process, they blame the guru. He appeared to demonstrate the obstacles to the path he was describing.

I believed he had reason. That of course was my own perception.

Swami Satchidananda says, "If you know how to put your heart in God, you can rest there always and still play in the world."[30] When we realize our true Self we experience a level of detachment that allows for partaking in activities that may seem contrary to a healthy path, but without attachment to them they hold no power over the mind and remain benign. This level of detachment comes with full realization. In yoga this non-attachment is called *vairagya*.

As I haven't experienced full realization, my practice of *vairagya* is on a different level–I focus on the balance between the material and spiritual. I practice detachment and acceptance of my failures, I learn from my reactions and try to stay objective. I try to live without selfish motive, focusing on giving rather than getting. In order to increase my understanding of the power objects and desires have over me I cultivate awareness of my attachment to them. I try to find an awareness of what is truly me versus what is my ego-driven attachment. Swami Satchidananda affirms, "To really have this awareness, this isolation of perceiver and perceived, is Yoga."[31]

I feel the most free when I am wholly focused on the Divine, on my inner Self–there is no feeling of attachment there.

In a room of hundreds Bharat chose me to initiate. I could over-analyze that for hours. Then he initiated all of us in a *mantra*, which we were supposed to practice daily for hours. We were then told we would spend an hour in meditation together, either in the room or we could leave and find a more solitary spot. I went into the garden and began. It was sweet and easy.

I slowly came to realize everyone was milling around outside drinking tea. I didn't know how long I was there. I didn't know what had happened. We were supposed to sit for an hour–I couldn't imagine it had been that long. I saw myself getting up and joining the others. Then we resumed the workshop. I felt spatial, in two worlds at once. I saw myself there but my mind didn't seem to be. It was like I was walking through a movie where everyone was playing his or her part unaware of my presence because I wasn't a part of the movie; I was the audience but I was somehow watching from inside the screen.

Swami Bhoomananda explains the development of the mind in a way that struck a chord:

> I would like to say–the granite mind where the marks and impressions remain for centuries, will grow into a watery mind. Even as you draw a line in water, as you cut the water and then as you take the instrument away, the water heals itself becoming one homogeneous mass. The mind will behave in that manner with the external events. When the next development of the mind is attained, the mind becomes like air! In the air, even a mark or a line drawn will not be visible. I think you can still progress to the level of space–a spatial mind. My dear seekers, the spatial mind is the limit of attainment.[32]

The expanse of space. The expanse of letting go. The joy of emptiness. I never truly enjoyed meditation until I was given that *mantra*. Whether I chanted it or not, I was able to go deeper and feel joy, an addictive joy. I understood how someone could spend years lost in meditation and never want to leave it. Meditation is an experience that I think is impossible to truly explain. And the experience of it is fleeting and ever changing and deep and light and unfathomable. It is only method that can be taught and there is no guarantee a particular method will work for everyone.

Even with a method that begins to bring joy and spatiality, there are obstacles to meditation. Patanjali outlines these obstacles in Book 1 Sutra 30 as disease, dullness, doubt, carelessness, laziness, sensuality, false perception, failure to reach firm ground, and slipping from the ground gained.

Distraction seems so common and easy. So easy to slip into laziness and not take care of the body, not take care of the mind, not stay focused. It's so easy to let the mind run loose and imagine convolutions to disturb our evenness, our true perceiving, our detachment–thoughts that disturb the emotions, the heart, and our precarious energetic balance. We doubt rather than trust. We slip from the steep path, falling back to the bottom. We despair or lose interest and fall deeper into distractions. We lose sight of what is real. Focusing on what is not real creates a block to meditation, to clarity, to detachment.

By observing our own actions and thoughts as practices of these distractions we can identify the workings of the mind. More importantly, we can identify that our behavior is not motivated from our true Self but from illusion. From a detached perspective we can see the delusion we are placing ourselves under and by doing so, take the power away from those delusions. When the power of unreality is unplugged–only reality remains.

Ajit and I had gone dancing with the gang. As we left the club our hands touched, and our fingers entwined for a second. I felt like a plug connecting with a socket and the instant surge of energy shocked me. We let go before anyone noticed. Our eyes shined. I put my head on his shoulder on the way home; I needed to touch him. I avoided looking into his big beautiful eyes that made my emotions run wild.

We stayed up talking. He urged me to watch one of his favorite movies <u>Rang de Basanti</u>. The lead is an English woman rediscovering her family history in India and obsessing over an Indian revolutionary who her great grandfather had executed. She recruits a group of Indian students to act in her documentary about the Revolution. The project inspires them to get serious about their lives and what they believe in. The love interest tells her why he stays at university even after graduation a few years before. "In college we rule our destinies. But after college we have to dance to fate's tune."[33] Once you enter the world you become a nobody. Everything ends. Everyone goes their separate ways.

Ajit felt like that character. He knew what his fate would be; he wanted to delay losing himself in the void of a cancelled life. Of cancelled dreams. Dreaming meant loss. Loving meant loss. *Loss.*

The days went by. I missed having a schedule–teaching, dancing. No job. Visa renewal imminently necessary. I started to get restless without a purpose, the dance program had ended. The dance company had a break until June so my future at the studio, even if it was just to teach a community yoga class, was on hold. My room was stifling. While it was cool outside I couldn't manage to get that air inside. One window was a few feet away from the men's dorm so I had to keep the blinds pulled for privacy, no breeze, the other window pumped in smoke for some inexplicable reason. I couldn't create a draft.

I went out to get some actual air and do research online. I followed up on a few job listings. I emailed some contacts just to stay connected. I made a leap of faith, a no-thought decision, and bought a ticket to London. I felt more organized. Now I could put a timeline to working on the healing center.

I rewarded myself with a feast for lunch. Aromas of China was within walking distance from my PG. Cavernous and elegant, the restaurant was expensive in the evenings but had a great lunch special for a couple dollars. Soup, two dishes, rice, dessert, and tea. Broccoli, bok choy, carrots, cabbage, so many vegetables, so many choices. Lovely green tea and a dessert that quickly became my favorite: deep fried wonton wrappers drizzled in honey with vanilla ice cream.

Rashma and I began meeting more regularly to plan the healing center. She lived near Indira Nagar, a wealthier area of the city. A bit quieter with old trees still lining the streets and a large ex-pat community. The neighborhood was a relic, a reminder of the Bangalore of old, known for its many lakes, mild climate, and abundance of trees. I wasn't sure how many lakes remained as I never saw any. It seemed as if they had been filled in, and with so many trees cut down to make way for office buildings and roads, the climate was no longer moderated by the surrounding nature but by the overwhelming car exhaust, dry earth, and concrete. Once an idyllic refuge for those seeking recovery from an illness or the heat of summer, Bangalore was now a place of industry, technology specifically, and support for that industry by any means necessary.

I spent the day hanging out in Indira Nagar exploring where I would be living when we found a location for our center. There were modern clothing stores and restaurants and I found a Coffee Day on 100 Ft Road to wait for Rashma. We were supposed to meet, I called and called, she finally responded that she had been stuck in the office all day and couldn't get away. I was getting a headache from the incessant hammering on every corner, construction everywhere. I just missed the bus and waited ages for the next one. Back in my room I couldn't stand the smoke and decided to go out. I was grumpy.

I walked from my PG through the residential streets, through the little main street lined with giant trees, when a great clap of thunder sounded. A split second later the clouds gushed open. I dashed for a tree and achieved a minor amount of coverage. Across the street a man in a truck motioned for me to run over for shelter. I leapt into his passenger seat and waited for the rain to lessen. He sat smiling at me. It was a bit odd, and after a short while it started to feel even more odd, so I thanked him, jumped out and made my way from tree to tree, carport to carport and then gave up when I realized I had been soaked to the bone in the first few minutes anyway.

On the corner of the main road sat another Coffee Day, with deep leather chairs, walls of glass to watch the rain, and of course no hot drinks to warm up with because the power had gone out. I was stuck.

May 18 — Bad dreams last night. I don't remember too many details. I remember someone screaming and screaming. I remember being in the middle of a huge road with crazy traffic, trucks everywhere nearly killing me — I couldn't get out of the way, or across, or something. In another dream I was in an airport parking lot with Grandma and John and we had lost some luggage of someone else we were with. Again I was running around searching, confused.

Things just haven't been coming together over the past few weeks so I'm feeling uncertain. Living in an enclosed space with a curfew, spending more than I had expected, and being unable to make my own food is getting to me. Uncle and Auntie waiting up for me at 10pm, one day I'll remember what being 30 feels like. I need to get out of here. A little part of me is panicking about money. Bad mood. Need to take charge. But how? What's my direction? Days like this I want to leave.

I think there is some insecurity wrapped up in my mood. My need for attention and activity both being thwarted everyday.

I get lonely easily lately.

still raining .

I decided to leave the PG and stay with Ajit until I left for England. I wanted to save money, have some independence and a healthier environment. I managed to get an interview for an editing position at Macmillan Publishers. The initial interview was a five-hour marathon of written and oral exams, meeting with different editors, and waiting. They thanked me and I walked back to the bus station.

As I walked closer, I noticed masses of people, more than the usual masses, moving in groups here and there. I was told there was a demonstration, Shivaji Nagar had been barricaded and buses had been diverted.

Shivaji Nagar was one of the main bus terminals in Bangalore, a bustling open center with eight bus lanes and crowds of people. There was a huge map mounted on a wall with apparent bus routes but no indication as to which bus traveled along which route or what their final destination might be. The lanes were marked by bus number and end destination. The tricky part was knowing these two things, then going backwards, and finding the route.

Until I learned my routes, I would ask countless strangers and then yell up to the bus drivers my destination over and over until one would wave me in. This was a challenge as I wasn't the only one attempting this process; our little crowd at the bottom of the bus stairwell fought for attention, and sometimes the buses hardly stopped at all. People jumped off and on sometimes at a run. Other times a bus would sit indefinitely.

I did become somewhat of a master, much to the admiration of my local friends who never took the buses and were amazed at how adeptly I got around and covered so much of the city. At 5 or 10 rupees a ride I couldn't afford not to take the bus. No negotiating with disinterested auto drivers, no overcharging, no getting lost or purposely going the wrong way, or whimsically deciding they didn't want to go where you wanted to go.

I followed a line of walkers going in the general direction of my usual bus route and we all congregated on a street corner a half a mile away. Finally I saw my bus, jumped on, squeezed in, and made it home.

The next day I met up with Samir, a man I had met at Attakkalari. One day, while in college studying computer science, Samir decided he wanted to dance. He auditioned, was accepted, packed his bags, quit his degree, relocated to Bangalore, and has been dancing ever since. He had been a principal dancer in the company for years and had recently left to pursue a broader dance career. He felt limited by the Director's choreography and disinterest in the dancers' creative input. He studied through grants and scholarships at workshops in Europe.

He was passionate about movement.

Samir took me to OPUS, a dance studio owned by a friend he wanted to introduce me to in the hopes that I could teach yoga there. We had to wait around for the owner, so we decided to take a walk and have some tea. We went back and had a short meeting, an introduction really, but his friend thought we could possibly work something out. He said he would be in touch, we exchanged information and said goodbye. I invited Samir to lunch to thank him for the introduction.

We ate and talked for hours, then had three more cups of tea and talked for several hours more. Samir told me all about traveling in Europe dancing, all the amazing people he had met, and his dream of eventually having his own dance studio. I shared my travel stories and path to becoming a yoga teacher. He was sweet. We made plans to hang out again.

In the evening I met Rakeesh for dinner; he was leaving on a trip the next day. Rakeesh and I rarely had a light conversation. We were both a bit starved for intellectual stimulation and discussion of philosophies and the meaning of reality. We may have been contributing to each other's further dwelling in delusion but we needed each other to process that imbalance.

Driving to meet some friends he asked, "What about when you doubt God?"

"There are times you feel disconnected, you don't feel 'it' anymore," I responded. "I guess that's where faith comes in. God hasn't disappeared, just the thread we feel that connects us."

"But that's yoga, that's the practice. You should be able to feel it inside, know it's there no matter what's happening," he argued.

"Sure, you should, but it's not that easy, right?" I countered. "Unless you're a master, isn't that what *samadhi* is? You're beyond the influences of the material world; you exist in both worlds."

"Well there are different kinds of *samadhi*." Rakeesh was getting into his head.

"That always confused me. I guess I'm a little stuck in the Buddhist idea of enlightenment. I didn't think there were different kinds, you either experience it and are enlightened or you don't and aren't."

"No, there are different levels, there's a progress. If I didn't have certain experiences I wouldn't stay on this path. But I have moments of knowing. It just all seems for nothing. I've got to get back to the Himalayas. It makes sense there."

Rain splattered the windshield. I was again in a situation of not knowing what to say to someone who was depressed.

"Focus on those times when you felt inspired, when you felt connected. When you were focused on your yoga practice, you knew the truth," I offered.

"I know, I have to get back to it, it's hard though. I've been out of it."

"It's one of those things you have to force yourself to do at first and then you immediately remember why you do it and it gets easier and easier."

"Did I tell you about this new sequence Anil and I came up with? We were fooling around with inversions one day…" His eyes lit up as he described their joy and fun, when he was light and could play. *Play.*

We met up with a bunch of his friends at a bar and all toasted his safe travels. The next morning Rakeesh left for the Himalayas. He texted me a poem at 3am.

> I'm in the mountains.
> Where I belong.
> It's where I break into song.
> And feel my mother's encircling arms.
> Warm me with a nostalgic smile
> That awaited my imminent return.

He was home, with friends, climbing mountains again.

May 21 — Slept a few hours this afternoon. Did an hour of asanas. Juice. Ready for bed already.

Rashma can't meet me until I get back from UK. The healing center is still up in the air.

Too many men, running around, financial uncertainty, visa questions, uncle/auntie judgment, overspending, loneliness, homelessness, removed from yoga practice, health, losing my way? Maya. Exhaustion.

Monday I had my final interview at Macmillan and they offered me the editing position. I asked for a few days to consider. I went back and forth about it. Financially it would allow me to support myself in India but not cover my finanical responsibilities at home, namely my student loans and health insurance. I would also be committing to a 50-hour work week which would make starting the healing center almost impossible as I was to be managing it and teaching. It would also mean giving up any idea of continuing to dance. But it would be fulfilling in itself as a job I may enjoy, and I could live truly independently and comfortably in India.

I called my mother who told me I should grow up and do some real work instead of having fun. I broke down and cried for hours about my life choices and on giving up on my dreams as an artist through dance or writing. I had changed my life, found yoga and found myself, but couldn't support myself through teaching. It was heartbreaking.

I called my mother back and defended my current state as not just "having fun," I was trying to build something that came from my heart even if it was irrational or unlikely as a financial reality. I finally felt healthy after so many unhealthy years, years of sacrificing my dreams to take the responsible path. Where was I now? At least I wasn't depressed living a life not believing in myself. My mother said I had her support and gave me the assignment of looking in the mirror every day and greeting myself as an artist.

May 26 — It's time to get through my fears. To produce. To create. To take risks and at least know then that I tried. And that I was true to myself. This week I've really been confronted with my inner demons. It's been heavy.

I slept all day yesterday next to Ajit. I wish he could hold me.

I was losing myself here. Like a drug. I felt like I was in a world of escape — but I was escaping from the things that have made me healthier and stronger. So I've been getting weaker and more unfocused.

My decision this week has brought things back into focus: I'm here to get healthy.

That's why I came to India.

There is a wild energy here. That energy of change, of transformation that draws in so many people. So much passion. A land seething with revolutionary energy, you can feel the blood seeping up from under the red dust. Like living on a volcano.

Everything in India felt magnified, extreme, pushing me to my limits. India confronted me and made me confront myself. I didn't want to live in the past, I didn't want to live like the past, and I didn't want to drown in self-pity. My past made me who I am but I wanted to live in the present and work toward a future living true to myself.

I wanted some freshness. I asked Sameera who cut her hair and she offered to take me. She picked me up on her scooter and handed me a pink helmet; we drove to Jayanagar. She translated for me as I tried to explain what I wanted to the stylist. I was happy to just have done something new. We had a girly day of hair and shopping. I bought some shiny *bindis* to decorate my third eye and Sameera bought me a pair of silver earrings since I had complimented hers. She dropped me at Infinitea and went home to study.

It was a much needed break from the heavy week I was having emotionally. Madalena was busy. Rashma was swamped with a project at work. Rakeesh was out of town. Abhishek was studying. I was leaving soon, unsure of my future in India, risking stability, striving to live without fear, and hit by a deep loneliness amidst all this inner turmoil.

I let my imagination run with Ajit. I felt sick. I had lost control completely. I was madly in love. It was ridiculous; I thought I would see that clearly and could laugh at myself once I went to England and looked back with a different eye. At that moment I was deeply sad. My pride hurt, I was overemotional and convinced myself it was the loneliness.

I sat at Infinitea fueled by rich *masala chai* prepared to order with your choice of spices, mine were cardamom, ginger, and black pepper boiled down to a thick, rich, flavor exploding tea experience. Served in a pot for two or even three people, I usually managed to drink the whole thing by myself.

I was jittery from caffeine, spice and sugar, and vibrating with inner chaos.

May 26 — Too heavy. My whole self is imploding, emotionally overwhelmed. Muddled no, mired in maya. I'd love to go to an ashram right now. Have some space to get a different perspective, clarity. I sound like all those people I don't understand who run off to ashrams to run away from their own minds!

I bought a bottle of red wine on the way home and after dinner drank the whole thing. I finally felt relaxed. I needed the help–my body, my mind, and my heart were overwhelmed and constantly in a state of disturbance. I smiled. I listened to my new REM CD and felt a little bit like me again. Ajit sat next to me attempting to study but talked about music instead. He and Abhishek had been worried, they didn't know what to do with me. I had been so sad all week. I slept deeply.

The next morning I had the apartment to myself and practiced yoga for two hours, my mind focused and still. I meditated and felt my body change shapes. My torso stretched up, my legs and arms shrank. I was an orb shape, like an egg. Then I saw myself sitting on a giant lotus.

I stopped worrying. I made a decision to let go, to have faith again, to be present in the moment I was in and accept what was for what it was. Contentment comes from being okay with whatever happens. I committed myself to get back to my yoga practice, to read the *Sutras*, and meditate every day. I had a profound source of joy inside me that I had been losing sight of. I had hit some kind of bottom and instead of drowning I floated back up to the surface. I had lost sight of me and of my Self. But I had a vision now of that part of me and how it controlled the rest of me and decided to not continue to feed it.

There didn't need to be a struggle. I was creating it all in my own head. I was disturbing my own peace. I could stop reflecting the chaos around me in my self and instead see the world around me from my steady Self. A shift in perspective was what I needed, and a letting go. Peace was within me; I had to stop expecting the world to give it to me and stop blaming the world for taking it away from me.

I knew I was still attached but I thought maybe I just wouldn't hold on so tightly. I would start with trying to let go of the little things until I was steady enough to start letting go of the bigger things. It was all practice. I had been so caught up in experiencing life I had forgotten to continue the practice. *Practice.*

But the practice is everything. It is steadiness, it is contentment, it is peace. It is feeling Divine love. I had forgotten to worship above all else.

In meditation we practice concentration, and as the mind wanders we gently bring it back to a one-pointed focus. I decided to apply that idea to my mind in general–as it wandered into worry, stress, confusion, over-thinking I would gently bring it back to remembering those thoughts were all delusion and attachment. There is a better way to encounter the world; it just takes remembering to do it and allowing yourself to let go, and then working hard, being persistent, concentrating, and having courage.

I felt calmer and more centered. I rolled up my yoga mat and went to buy fresh vegetables at the local market. I made a salad and tea and turned my phone back on to re-encounter the world.

Madalena called; she had been in Sri Lanka for a few days to renew her visa. Being a young girl alone, she became a target and was manipulated into believing she had to pay a "fine" of $500 for her visa to get back to India. She was afraid of course that they wouldn't give it to her, as they knew she would be, so she paid. We talked about the future, staying in Bangalore, and planned to meet up when I got back from England.

Samir invited me out and being back in my focus on positive energy, I said yes. He picked me up in his car and said he wanted to surprise me. We drove to an old part of the city, Basavangudi, and walked under thick trees along shaded sidewalks. He led me through a park to the Nandi Temple, an ancient site of worship with a huge black bull covered in ghee. It was beautiful, serene, and sacred. We walked and talked through the park. It felt wonderful to be with a local, to see something historic and deep, to be accompanied as I explored the city.

I thought that was the surprise, but we got back in the car and drove to Jayanagar. Driving through this part of the city was a bit of a revelation. These were old neighborhoods with families who had lived in the same homes for generations, with established small businesses, as well as modern shops and restaurants. It felt grounded, as opposed to the transient feel of MG Road or Whitefield or the neighborhoods

I had lived in with students, international workers, or out of state visitors. It was local.

We parked in front of a shop called Corner House and to my great excitement, it was an ice cream parlor. I grinned; it was so old fashioned. I had a sundae with hot fudge and whipped cream and in that moment, I thought it was the most amazing thing I had ever tasted. We sat at a little table outside, the cool spoonfuls melting in the warm air, and let the sweetness pervade us.

Samir bravely let me drive his car on a dare, but after a few blocks, he insisted we pull over. I was laughing too much; it made him nervous. We stopped for coffee to calm his nerves.

After coffee, Samir enticed me back to his place with watching his box set of "Friends." He turned on the TV in his simple apartment, pushed the videocassette into the VCR, and sat next to me on his futon. He had a look in his eye; he reached over and kissed me. I was surprised, not only that he liked me, but that even if he did that he would kiss me. He was an exceptionally good kisser. We made out for hours with laughter in the background.

I did love to kiss and I had been denied for so long. I wouldn't say it was meaningless, it certainly wasn't, but it wasn't love. I liked Samir. I liked to be in his energy. I liked the attention and being with someone who wasn't bound by cultural mores, who was free in how he lived, who was fun. To be given what I had been longing for made me rebellious–rebellious against my own feelings, rebellious against my dreams. I convinced myself to live in the moment and be good to myself. To smile and be smiled at. To be light.

I was trying to let go of hope with Ajit. I was trying to let go of being hurt. I knew being with Ajit would only bring pain, disappointment, frustration, and loss. He had made it clear that his family would never accept me. We decided it was best to remain only as friends. But the mind and heart don't always agree. I tried denying the power of love. *Love.*

19

**Tarmac love, English tea, headstands in the garden,
"God has equal vision"**

I left India on May 30th after five full months of intensity. In the
end, it felt fairly sudden. I felt like I was leaving home to go
somewhere by force, not by choice–like a business trip I had to get
through and then return happily to my life. I packed my small carry-
on size suitcase and left all my other belongings at Ajit's house. He
always provided his home to me. He gave without condition, without
obligation, without expectation. He was my support, my security, my
comfort.

He came into my room as I packed and we just suddenly stopped
joking and flirting and were real.

"I'm going to miss you. Every day will be empty without you,"
he said.

"Me too."

"I always thought the best way to fall in love was to be friends first.
But then you risk losing that person to someone else."

We sat on my mattress; he gently rubbed his thumb on my lower
lip. He pulled me to him and kissed me.

"I can't imagine being apart from you," I said.

"Me too, sweetie."

We lay down together and held each other.

"You wouldn't even touch me before. Now you can hold me?"
I asked.

"Yes," he smiled. "I tried to not feel anything, to ignore how I felt. I know it doesn't make sense. But I don't care. You are my heartbeat. Without you, there is no meaning."

We hardly slept, Ajit wanted to keep talking; I wanted to stay awake, feeling him holding me. It felt like a closeness of beings, not bodies, like our souls were intertwined rather than our legs. Warmth of body and heart.

True love is Divine love, loving from the soul, not the body or the mind or the heart. True love is clarity, peace, and an overwhelming bliss. Romantic love can mirror this in the mind and heart. It can become addictive, increasing desire as it waxes and wanes, affecting the tides of emotion and stability. Seeking peace, we jump from boat to boat fooled by a mirage of promise—a promise that another person can bring us happiness, that the heart's tumult can be quelled, the storm of fears calmed, and peace attained under a romantic moon.

Ajit took me to the airport in an auto. We silently held hands; we had no more words. He waited until I was inside, and we smiled our good-byes. He waved until I disappeared through security.

Waiting at the terminal gate I shrank in my chair, in my own world, observing, as if I were invisible, these foreign bodies and voices around me—sunburned white skin, uniform of baggy khaki shorts and fitted Gap t-shirts or tank tops, sunglasses propped on top of the head, flip flops, and frequent visits to the enclosed glass smoking room. I was surrounded by loud laughs and English accents. I felt small and removed from these people who had always been so familiar.

I was in fact on my way home to my grandmother's house. Flying with my British passport, home to England, to my family, and I couldn't have felt more different from the people around me. I didn't grow up British but these were supposed to be my people. I certainly didn't feel Indian either. I felt Other.

Sitting on the plane, still on the tarmac, I felt as if a part of my physical body had been ripped off and was being left behind.

Ajit and I texted until I was forced to turn my phone off for take-off–holding onto connection. I was leaving home. I cried. Is this how my family felt? Going to the familiar, to family, but leaving home? Having a part of themselves torn out and left behind? Knowing that in time it would heal? At that moment, I didn't feel like I could heal.

How do I write my love story? From my heart only. From knowing what he was going to say before he said it, to drowning in his eyes; to skipping a breath when I got a message from him. I couldn't rest until he said goodnight. I felt the distance between us when I wasn't next to him. My heart stretched taut, linked to him. He was in every thought. He always made me smile, even when saying goodbye at the airport, the way he looked at me, through the pain I still smiled. Then my heart reminded me it was broken.

Love is feeling quiet when together and craving to be together when apart. Love is feeling the heart actually expanding, allowing us to love more. Love is not defining what we expect love to be but enjoying its manifestation.

I loved his quirks and silliness. He walked by me in a goofy way to make me smile. He reminded me of myself at 23-years-old–the me before depression, before I was drowning, and although I had changed so much since then, some things still hadn't quite dried out yet. I saw being with him as being with my younger self. I discovered that my lightness, silliness, and freeness that became weighed down were still there somewhere. I could still be cute and funny. Love can be rejuvenation or rediscovery or the safety to let the scared little part of yourself come back out into the sun.

> The crack of thunder roars deep into my heart
> My body shivers with rain energy
> Drops fat and full on red deep earth
> Sticky air cooling lungs, opening breath

Humid clinging of warm lips
Eyes pool love

Arriving at Heathrow, a world away from Bangalore Airport–clean, bright, organized, queues, colored lines on the floor to lead the way, efficient and shiny, I took a deep breath as I rolled out of customs to the awaiting masses. My grandmother waved vigorously and smiled; my step-grandfather John stood tall behind her, a beacon. So many questions. So little to say. We found our way through the lettered and numbered car park to John's new Jaguar with leather interior. The smell of dead cow was unwelcoming. We drove around countless roundabouts to the M25, circled London, and finally headed east to Essex.

Arriving at their house was arriving home for me. Soft carpet, clean, down comforter, western bath and shower, full refrigerator, European cheese, ice cream, velvet couch, cushions, television, soft and warm, flowered, quiet. So quiet. My familiar room with my grandmother's scent; she always offered an open door and welcoming smile. I unpacked and curled up with the sweater Ajit had leant me since I had no clothing to keep me warm in this climate. I inhaled his scent as if his arms were around me. I could feel his energy vibrating off the fabric.

The weather was warm enough to spend time in the garden. We drank Pimm's, munched on snacks, and I performed *asanas* for my 16-year-old cousin who wanted to be impressed. Headstands in the garden. She then performed her audition piece for me for The X Factor. She had passed the first round and was heading toward the second. We lunched outside at my aunt's house as well and had dinner in the garden at my uncle's. We sat on the patio with its green lawns and privacy, sipping wine, serenaded by the symphony of quiet. I wrapped myself in the warm blanket of family.

One afternoon, while I sat in the kitchen watching my grandmother prepare lunch, I asked her about her Indian heritage. My aunt's ears pricked up, she came over and began rolling her eyes expecting the usual brush off, which usually involved changing the subject. But with her eyes far away in a distant history, my grandmother talked for the first time of places she would like to revisit. The caves south of Delhi, towns I hadn't heard of, colorful markets, beauties she remembered reflected in her eyes. She told a story from her childhood and told us the things she missed–the scents, the sights, the flavors. My aunt's expression froze, speechless and a bit bewildered, afraid to interrupt.

My grandmother was admitting to her past, and with a fondness. She was claiming India as her own in her own way. That simple conversation was profound for me, for the family. I felt in my grandmother a complex and deep acceptance of the past, a truth, maybe a letting go of the burden of denial, a letting go of the fear. Maybe this freedom was momentary, but it was a seed. Either it would be watered or it wouldn't, but it had been planted.

Was that the answer to "Why India?" To reconnect a broken line? To heal a rift? To rejoin a gap in family history or the personal history of my grandparents? To weave back together a broken cloth providing the warp between England and India that could be woven with a weft of memories? Was I providing that reunion within myself as well, albeit so removed from my lived experience and my cultural background? Was this momentary smile in my grandmother's eyes the whole reason for going to India?

I didn't feel Indian in India. I didn't pick up Hindi as if it were my long lost mother tongue. But my ancestors are there, some molecular part of me, some part of the blood flowing through me is related to a past, not the present. Maybe I couldn't leave because of that deeper connection, not any cultural or even present day connection, but to something I wasn't aware of that wanted to be honored or to feel at home.

Sometimes inner work can be done without our awareness as long as we listen to what that voice is requesting. My body responded to those requests. Movement resonated with me; classical dance felt true for something inside me. That is where I felt my rhythm. My language. That was my connection to India; I connected on an ancient level. Choosing yoga as my path resonated with that ancient path.

Modern Indian culture was a challenge in dissonance for me. I saw peace and violence, freedom and bondage, movement and stagnation, lushness and barrenness. Paradox is not modern, but my place within that whirlwind of contradiction, chaos, and regulation was uncomfortable. I found friends from all walks of life, rebels and conformists, artists and dreamers, all my teachers in understanding this unfathomable complexity of cultures and how to weave ourselves into this wild fabric of contrasting textures and colors.

My heart grew and felt alive.

I couldn't wait to get back to India. I wanted to find my own home, start teaching yoga, open the healing center, take dance classes, and be with Ajit. I called him and he answered on the first ring. He had sensed I was going to call and was waiting. His voice was my home. He invited me to Gujarat to meet his mother. I was nervous but at the same time was sure it wouldn't actually happen. Reality was always different in the end.

I remembered the nights when I would talk to Ajit on the phone, sitting on the roof at the Catholic Center, looking up at the stars, feeling the cool breeze under my swaying palm trees. It seemed so far away. I felt like I had lived lifetimes.

London felt fairly surreal, walking through such order and cleanliness. The sidewalks sparkled, traffic stayed in clearly demarcated lanes, stopping and going according to the authoritative lights; queues formed with an understood organization, and I swam in all the empty space, the nearly empty streets, the wide paths. The heightened organization felt foreign, the buildings monolithic and staid. The old looked new as opposed to the new looking old.

I welcomed the peaceful pace, the space, the anonymity. At the same time, I felt isolated and non-existent. I felt out of place. Strangely invisible after months of acute visibility, I settled back into my body. My body as history, as an ancestral body. While this place was another part of my personal history, my culture, my created identity, I found it difficult to connect to these roots. I always imagined my family as 'other' here, as their own microcosm living within a greater strange society that I never understood. This strangeness was echoed in my mother's behavior whenever we came to visit. She would put back on her memory of an English accent, creating a dichotomy I couldn't reconcile. It was all put on out of a need to exist in an in-between place, neither home nor away, neither native nor foreign.

Getting my visa went smoothly, waiting on line to get a ticket, waiting in a room until called, waiting as a clerk read my paperwork, and then there was a hiccup. My mother was born in Pakistan. My paperwork was whisked away to an internal office. I was told to wait some more. I was allowed to explain why my mother was born in Pakistan and that she was a British citizen and I held my tongue about the racial profiling as they stamped my passport and allowed me to return to my life.

I spent the afternoon sitting on the grass in front of the Tate Modern on the South Bank watching the Thames flow by as lovers kissed and children played. I managed to get a tan somehow, I seemed to be immune to the sun in India but the English sun browned me. I walked for hours in warmth, freedom, solitude. I would miss that freedom in India.

I walked all the way back to Liverpool Street to catch the train back to my grandmother's house. I watched the busy commuters, their clickety clacking heels echoing around the cavernous space. I checked the huge board in the middle of the station that listed train platforms and times until mine appeared. I found an empty row and settled in, satisfied from the day. I always loved the train, the gentle chugging, the world flying past; it gave me time to think.

Two weeks flew by almost unnoticed, except for me gaining 10 pounds. My organs hurt; I felt sick; I didn't know how to say no to my well meaning grandmother. I ate, slept, and spent time with family. I laid on the couch and watched TV. I was constantly aware of the silence. I was in culture shock. I wanted to be alone as much as possible, a luxury I had missed while in India. The feeling that I missed home, while I was actually at home, confused me. Where did I belong now?

My internal clock never adjusted, I couldn't fall asleep before 2am and had to force my heavy eyelids open at 10am. I was nervous about how I would figure out staying in India. There were too many loose threads that could unravel at the slightest pull.

I talked to Ajit; he planned to pick me up from the airport the next day and take me home. We missed each other, we thought about each other constantly, and dreamt of kissing.

I listened to music at home alone and felt totally unattached to a reality. I felt echoes of how I felt in California before I left for India. Time and space were becoming blurred. Floating in a non-existent ether. Un-rooted. Unattached, impartial, content, placeless, Self without self, uninvolved in the world, in my place in any world. Floating bodiless in the ether.

Ether is an atmospheric medium, one of the elements, the space in between the earth and what is beyond, between the material and the ethereal. I felt I existed in that in-between space looking out at life manifestations, creations present around me, existing in a different space. What we see as reality is in our minds. The creation of "me" and how my life manifests is a function of my mind, my body and my senses. All these creations exist in the world while our beings float around each other in ether of which we are mostly unaware. Our beings are the same. We are one. We separate into manifested lives, material lives that exist from being embodied and walking the planet in that body.

The Dalai Lama explains reality:

> If we looked down at the world from space, we would
> not see any demarcations of national boundaries. We
> would simply see one small planet, just one. Once we
> draw a line in the sand, we develop the feeling of 'us'
> and 'them'. As this feeling grows, it becomes harder to
> see the reality of the situation.[34]

We create false definitions, cultural constructs, and illusions that
cloud our understanding of reality. The reality is of our oneness.
Oneness.

I wanted to exist with Ajit in a reality without separation, without politics, social mores, and cultural restrictions. We were connected on the
inside. Our hearts connected. Our energies sustained each other. We
felt an oneness with each other, a reflection of the oneness that is the
goal in spiritual practice. It was pure but all the complications of the
world muddled it.

I drew a parallel between having these moments of oneness in
my yogic path and losing them and having this experience of oneness
with another person, and losing it to the realities of outside influences.
Looking into Ajit's eyes removed the world, thoughts, time. It was a
practice in being fully present. It felt free. Then the thoughts would
creep back in and we would see our separation as two people with
many obstacles between us.

At the same time, my feeling of love had muddled my spiritual
path. It caused me great distraction and confusion. The communication between my connection to the Divine and my sense of self–my Self
and my self–was disjointed. I was striving for a balance.

I had moments of living with Ajit where I felt truly content, moments that felt balanced. A day when I would lay out my purple yoga
mat in the living room, practice *asana* and *pranayama*, sit in meditation, and then join Ajit on the balcony to eat fruit and talk about the

day. These moments were peaceful and filled with an equanimity and kind of timelessness. I felt my spiritual life and mundane life in harmony. It only existed in our own little cocoon.

Out in the world I felt lost.

Religion is an attempt at true communication between these points of intersection. The Mother describes how difficult this can be:

> For, in their spiritual ascent towards the Unknowable and Unthinkable, certain exceptional individuals have been able to transcend human nature and identify themselves with the object of their seeking in a sublime and, in a way, unformulable experience. But as soon as they sought to share the benefit of their discovery with others, they had to formulate it, and in order to be comprehensible their formula had, of necessity, to be human and symbolic.[35]

The human expression of the divine experience is necessarily human. This is the limitation of all this thinking. Thinking leads to more thinking. Thinking mires us back into *maya* where culture is created, divisions are defined, and inequalities are solidified. Interpretations abound to uphold desired power structures. The symbolism becomes too cryptic as traditions change and symbols are translated.

If all ancient religious and spiritual texts were written, created, told by men through the gauze of a culturally specific understanding to filter the divine truth, then the only "text" that one can trust as a woman, as anyone, is a personal communion with the Divine and an understanding of our own personal and cultural filters that may distort that pure knowledge. Both men and women must lift the gauze to reveal the human filters in order to go beyond human interpretation and experience knowledge beyond man and woman, beyond sexes, beyond discrimination and separation, beyond duality to oneness. Swami Satchidananda inspires us to "rise above":

> Babies do not make distinctions between rich and

poor, friend and enemy. You see such equal vision in
babies. That equal vision is what you call Yoga. Whoever lives with that kind of vision is called a divine person, a holy person. Because God has equal vision....
We should rise above these definitions. Whoever has
done that is called a refined person. That is the purpose of all the religions. All our practices, all our Yoga,
all our daily actions should help us in refining our
bodies and minds.[36]

Once we attain some level of refinement, clarity ensues, the fog of
confusion dissolves in the sun of daylight to reveal our true Self. We
see the rolling turmoil of the ocean, the trees rooted on the shore, and
hear the joyful singing of the birds flitting playfully on wind currents.
We feel the oneness of all that life within us, we feel the hearts of the
birds, hear the voice of the trees, and taste the vastness of life-giving
water. The impossible is possible when we remove the mind, when vision is from the third eye. This is true freedom.

Truth is inside us.

We practice going inward to find our true guru, to find the inner
guidance that is from the Divine. To shed all these layers is to remove
the obstacles that conceal the connection to our path. There are myriad paths to the truth. Listening deep inside can help direct us to our
destination along the path that works for us.

Yoga is universal and open in its guidance. It is a path that reso-
nates with my inner guidance. It may not resonate with yours. Listen
and sense what is deep inside you, learn to distinguish the noise of
distraction and *maya* from the peaceful silence of the truth.

Freedom.

Da da dã da tum, pound pound heel pound pound, cock head, eyes glance, shoulder sharp forward back, tã kha ta kee dum, arm follows the arc of the moon, sharp to the heart, reach, lean, down, up, tã kha ta kee tã, plie, knee down, eyes right left, hop up, balance on one foot.

Angles constructed and deconstructed, lips soft, fingers form and reform into distinct patterns, signals, circles of energy, gestures unfolding a story, breath moving body, inner beat moving the breath, heart resonating with a deeper rhythm.

Ta da dã...da dã tum...ta da dã da dã tum...tada dã dadã tumtadadã dadã tumtadadãdadãtum...The rhythm complicates, speed frenzies, down up, accent stop, eyes shift, hip out, arm reach, spin, spin, spin, slapping foot, arms open, palms up, spin, spin, spin...

The dancer separates herself from me, spinning out again into her own body. I see her in my mind. She leaves the dance in me and, unnoticed, slips back into the stone wall, taking her place among the pantheon of ancient dancers. She appears deceptively still when so much energy radiates from her form. My fingers caress the air thick like water, swirling above my head, entwined as I gaze upward. I gaze beyond, seeing through closed eyes.

Where it ended, where it began

I explored the eight-limbed path, the five energetic layers of the *koshas*, the duality of existence, and the oneness of all creation. I climbed and fell along the path. I spun in and out of awareness. I felt at times a greater understanding of humanity, spirituality, and myself. At other times I felt completely lost and confused. That is the nature of this life, this path.

There are many tools we can use to help us along this rocky terrain, to soften the impact. Yoga provides many in its open and accepting philosophy. At the root is compassion, at the canopy is the Divine. The eight limbs of Patanjali's Ashtanga Yoga are a comprehensive map of how and what to focus on in order to deepen spiritual awareness and live a peaceful life. Yoga unites the mind, body, and spirit, balancing our experience of each. It teaches ways to soften how we walk in this world, how we encounter the world walking on us, and how to keep alive the knowledge of what is beyond this world.

As a woman, I struggle with the imbalance I feel in this world and find yogic philosophy healing in its ability to calm my flames of anger, frustration, and sadness. Practicing detachment provides a level of peace and joy that goes far beyond the limitations of this existence. It is nearly impossible to change the world, but you can change yourself. The dream is for everyone to change themselves into compassionate, loving beings–then we can change the world. Fighting for this reality creates more fighting. Loving creates more love.

We come into the world with imprints from another world, another life lived by our soul, and spend our lifetimes adding more baggage, more impressions, more experiences to process. Life feels a little lighter when we actively encounter these experiences and focus on retaining a purity and sense of centeredness. Focus on different aspects of our self, heal any imbalances, create a divine resonance, and remain steady, centered, and whole. *Whole.*

Understanding the different energies of the *koshas* leads to an understanding of the layers of the self. What layers do we feed? What energies do we amplify? How do we stagnate ourselves within a certain life path by empowering one layer and disempowering the others? Are we progressing toward a deeper understanding and wisdom? Balancing these layers between the material and spiritual is a constant challenge for me. I feel as if I have one foot in and one foot out and am unable to choose where to step. The goal of yoga seems to be complete detachment from the material. I understand the possibility of this if I am alone, but I want to have a family, which is a material reality. I don't intend to detach from my children. My goals and the ultimate goal of yoga seem incongruous at this time of my life.

But the practice of yoga is so all encompassing and accepting that incongruity and paradox are not problems. Yoga can still lead me to a balance, support me in my struggles, and help soften the sharpness of life. It provides a map to follow on my journey within. All I can do is the best I can. And learn as I go, accepting mistakes as ways to improve myself, and hardships as ways to purify myself.

In June I left the comforts of my grandmother's house in England and excitedly flew home, back to India. Ajit picked me up and we were together. I was greeted by familiar smells and sounds and the thickness of the air. I was wrapped in the rich greenness and dense dark sky. I felt safe enveloped in Ajit's arms.

I found a school where I taught yoga classes, settled into my own little room in a quiet neighborhood, and began focusing on the dream of creating the healing center. Rashma and I gathered momentum and lost momentum, we found a building and lost it due to unforseen complications. We created advertising, found students and again lost the space. India seemed to be like that. Months passed by as we waxed and waned in progress.

I attended meditation workshops with Bharat Thakur and found a profundity to my meditation practice that I had never had before. I attended yoga classes of various styles and broadened my understanding of teaching. I visited several more ashrams.

I traveled north to the spiritual pilgrimage sites of Rishikesh and Haridwar. A friend from California was leading a yoga tour and Madalena and I joined in. We stayed at a large ashram which was popular with Indians and foreigners, and was crowded with both. The rooms were sparse, the meals basic and nutritious. It was also an orphanage and school and children would file past in the mornings on their way to class dressed in orange monk robes. Mataji, a woman in her fifties who had renounced worldly life to devote herself to the spiritual path taught us private workshops on Sanskrit chanting. She was a divinely blessed singer.

The ashram sat on the banks of the Ganges River. Marbled steps led down directly into the water. In the evenings they had an *aarti* ceremony where little lighted boats were sent into the river while a sea of orange clad devotees sang sacred songs.

One day we traveled by taxi a little farther north along a forested winding road to visit the sacred cave of the sage Vashistha. It was a small, dark, and damp cave where our little group sat for a while in meditation. Outside the cave, after rambling over a few rocks, lay a sandy beach. We all spread out to have our own private experience with the mighty river. I found a calm pool inlet and waded in fully clothed. The water was freezing but energetically powerful. I dunked myself in her and felt cleansed, centered, and fully alive.

Before returning to the South, I visited the Taj Mahal. A monumental representation of a place filled with the sacred but rounded in human feelings. The Taj Mahal appeared to float above the ground as if made of cloud, gleaming as if it were a jewel. The heaviness of the stone, the realness of the tangible structure seemed unreal in its ethereal essence. It existed across boundaries of spiritual and material. Sitting in the shade of a tree canopy on soft grass, watching this magnificent building float in a shifting shimmer, I was inspired on my own path.

When I finally left India nearly one year after my arrival, my heart hurt. It was so full. *Full.*

Language and Names

Over many years, India has changed the official names of many cities to their original, pre-British occupation names. The names used in this book were how I knew of a place through verbal introduction, my current guidebook, or official local usage. These names may not reflect the current name of a city or represent the current English commonly used spelling. I came across various spellings for most everywhere I went, due to how it was translated into English and the English alphabet. I chose one spelling to be consistent; that choice may not be the "correct" spelling or the currently used spelling.

I have changed the names of everyone I met to alleviate any insecurity, embarrassment, or family issues that may arise from invading their privacy. Many people did not care but I chose to change all names.

Indian English is different from American English. On top of learning the vastly different cultural vocabulary, I also had to learn the vastly different English vocabulary to be understood. I wish I had had a useful list of English to English translations before I went, to help me communicate more smoothly.

This is a small list of language nuances I learned along the way and their usage:

Hotel = Restaurant. "Did you go to a hotel for dinner?"
Cinema = Movie theater. "Let's see what's on at the cinema."

Paying Guest House (PG) = Motel, hotel, bed and breakfast. "I secured a room at a PG nearby."

Auto = Auto rickshaw. "It's raining, let's take an auto home."

Hall = Living room. "There's no space in the bedroom, I'll sleep in the hall."

Cousin brother = A male cousin.

Mobile = Cell phone.

Cell = Battery. "I need a new cell for my mobile."

STD = Pay phone.

Native = Hometown. "I'll be at my native next week."

Good name = Respectful way to ask your name. "What is your good name madam?"

Reduce = Lose weight. "If I practice yoga, will I reduce?"

Scary = Scared. "I was scary in the dark."

Only = A way to emphasize something. "The truth only is what I believe." Or similar to using the word "just." "I am just now eating." = "I am eating now only."

Too = So. "It was too much fun."

Too good = Cool.

Bad guy = A man who smokes, drinks, has sex before marriage, or who is a flirt. "Just forget about me, I'm a bad guy."

Flirt = Player. "Careful, they'll think you're a flirt."

Disc = Nightclub (discotheque). "Let's go to a disc tonight!"

Sponsor = Pay for. "Will you sponsor me for the disc?"

Hello = When answering a phone call: "What?" "I don't understand you." "Who do you want to speak with?" "I don't get what you're asking?" "Can you hear me?" Or various other possibilities that make little sense to a non-Indian English speaker.

Phone conversation:

R: "Hello?"

M: "Hi, it's Mitra."

R: "Hello?"

M: "Can you hear me?"

R: "Hello?"

M: "Is this Ravi's phone?"

R: "Hello?"

M: Silence.

R: "This is Ravi here."

M: "It's Mitra. Could you hear me?"

R: "Yes, hi Mitra. How are you?"

M: "Why did you just say hello?"

R: "Hello?"

M: "Are you still there?"

R: "Yes, I'm here. Where are you?"

Acknowledgements

Thank you to Integral Yoga for guiding me to this experience and providing my foundation in yoga. Thank you to Swami Ramananda for continually inspiring me along this path, always greeting me with an open heart and shining smile, and for agreeing to be a part of this project.

Thank you to the amazing women on my team: Sarah for unwavering patience and enthusiasm through the many, many re-writes and Amy for your perspicacious insights of a grammatical nature. I couldn't have done this without your support as professionals and as friends. You gave and you gave. Lindsey, you put beautiful images to my words and brought the world of this book to life. Thank you for your enthusiasm and talent.

I am grateful for my wonderful family with all their oddities and personalities, warmth and worldliness, strength and resilience–I appreciate every moment and wish there could be more.

And of course my Mom and Dad, thank you for making me who I am and giving me the wings to live a free life.

Mom, thank you for your unfathomable depths of support no matter what. You are my rock.

END NOTES

1. The Dalai Lama, *An Open Heart: Practicing Compassion in Everyday Life*, Little, Brown and Company, Boston, 2001, p29.

2. English interpretation from the Integral Yoga Institute.

3. Satchidananda, Swami, *The Yoga Sutras of Patanjali*, Integral Yoga Publications, Yogaville, 1978, p166.

4. Iyengar, BKS, *The Art of Yoga*, Harper Collins Publishers, New Delhi, 1993, p6.

5. Hanh, *Teachings on Love*, p5.

6. Rama, Swami, Ballentine MD, Rudolph, Hymes MD, Alan, *The Science of Breath*, The Himalayan Institute Press, Pennsylvania, 1979, p5.

7. The All Faiths Logo is a registered trademark/service mark of Satchidananda Ashram - Yogaville Inc. Used with permission. © 1986 Satchidananda Ashram - Yogaville Inc.

8. Hay, Louise L, *Heal Your Body*, Hay House, Inc, Carlsbad, 1984.

9. Tirtha, Swami Bhoomananda, *Prabhata-rasmih: Morning Rays*, Narayanashrama Tapovanam, Thrissur, 2000, piv.

10. The Mother, *Introduction to Auroville Pamphlet*, Auroville International USA, Sacramento, 2005.

11. The Mother, *The Sunlit Path: Passages from Conversations and Writings of The Mother*, Sri Aurobindo Ashram, Pondicherry, 1984, p22.

12. Satchidananda, *Yoga Sutras*, p48.

13. Hanh, Thich Nhat, *Teachings on Love*, Parallax Press, Berkeley, 1998, p3.

14. Satchidananda, *Yoga Sutras*, p54.

15. Lama, *An Open Heart*, p110-111.

16. Bhoomananda, *Morning Rays*, p6.

17. Bhoomananda, *Morning Rays*, p104.
18. Saraswati, Swami Ambikananda, translator, *Katha Upanishad*, Viking Studio, New York, 2001, p38.
19. Bhoomananda, *Morning Rays*, p97-98.
20. Hay, Louise L, *You Can Heal Your Life*, Hay House, Inc, Carlsbad, 1984, p145.
21. Satchidananda, Swami, "I am the Knower" in "Swami Satchidananda's Weekly Words of Wisdom", Integral Yoga Magazine, Satchidananda Ashram, Yogaville, 2007.
22. Saraswati, *Katha Upanishad*, p35.
23. The Mother, *Sunlit Path*, p194.
24. The Mother, *Sunlit Path*, p97.
25. Bhoomanada, *Morning Rays*, p92.
26. Sri Aurobindo and The Mother, *On Women*, Sri Aurobindo Society, Pondicherry, 1978, p67.
27. Aurobindo and The Mother, *On Women*, p6.
28. Bhoomananda, *Morning Rays*, p98.
29. "About the Master: Philosophy", BharatThakur.com, http://www.bharatthakur.com/Philosophy.html
30. Satchidananda, *Yoga Sutras*, p30.
31. Satchidananda, *Yoga Sutras*, p217.
32. Bhoomananda, *Morning Rays*, p103-104.
33. *Rang De Basanti*. Dir. Mehra, Rakeysh Omprakash. Perf. Aamir Khan, Atul Kulkarni, Kunal Kapoor, Sharman Joshi, Siddharth, Alice Patten, Soha Ali Khan. UTV Motion Pictures, 2006.
34. Lama, An Open Heart, p9.
35. Aurobindo and The Mother, *On Women*, p2-3.
36. Satchidananda, Swami, "Refine the Body and Mind" in "Swami Satchidananda's Weekly Words of Wisdom", Integral Yoga Magazine, Satchidananda Ashram, Yogaville, 2006.